GEORGE WASHINGTON *and* SLAVERY

GEORGE WASHINGTON
and SLAVERY

A DOCUMENTARY PORTRAYAL

FRITZ HIRSCHFELD

University of Missouri Press • COLUMBIA AND LONDON

Copyright © 1997 by
The Curators of the University of Missouri
University of Missouri Press, Columbia, Missouri 65201
Printed and bound in the United States of America
All rights reserved
5   4   3   2   01   00   99   98

Library of Congress Cataloging-in-Publication Data

Hirschfeld, Fritz, 1924–
    George Washington and slavery : a documentary portrayal / Fritz
Hirschfeld.
        p.   cm.
    Includes bibliographical references (p.   ) and index.
    ISBN 0-8262-1135-6 (alk. paper)
    1. Washington, George, 1732–1799—Views on slavery—Sources.
2. Slavery—United States—History—18th century—Sources.
I. Title.
E312.17.H648   1997
973.4'1'092—dc21   97-20590
                                                                          CIP

∞™ This paper meets the requirements of the
American National Standard for Permanence of Paper
for Printed Library Materials, Z39.48, 1984.

Designer: Mindy Shouse
Typesetter: BOOKCOMP
Printer and binder: Thomson-Shore, Inc.
Typeface: Minion

*To the memory of my father who found the
solution for racial harmony in his love of mankind*

CONTENTS

I NEVER MEAN (UNLESS SOME PARTICULAR CIRCUMSTANCES SHOULD COMPEL ME TO IT) TO POSSESS ANOTHER SLAVE BY PURCHASE; IT BEING AMONG MY FIRST WISHES TO SEE SOME PLAN ADOPTED, BY THE LEGISLATURE BY WHICH SLAVERY IN THIS COUNTRY MAY BE ABOLISHED BY SLOW, SURE, & IMPERCEPTABLE DEGREES.

—George Washington
September 9, 1786

PREFACE

N O H I S T O R Y of racism in America can be considered complete without taking into account the role that George Washington—the principal founding father—played in helping to mold the racist cast of the new nation. Because General Washington—the universally acknowledged hero of the Revolutionary War—in the postwar period uniquely combined the moral authority, personal prestige, and political clout to influence significantly the course and the outcome of the slavery debate, his attitudes and opinions on the subject—what he believed, what he said, and what he did—are of crucial importance to understanding how racism succeeded in becoming an integral and official part of our national fabric during its formative stages.

Many of the words in this book are Washington's quoted words—deliberately left undiluted and unedited. Stripped of the veneer of interpretation and paraphrasing, the original texts give vivid expression to Washington's innermost turmoils and contradictions. They reveal a hitherto relatively unknown side of his complex character and personality. His documented record on slavery is sketched out here for readers to evaluate and to judge as they see fit. Was Washington a diehard racist? Or was he the victim of the racist society in which he lived? Was he a man of principle and strong convictions? Or was he weak and vacillating in the face of the slavery challenge? Draw your own conclusions!

Another question needs to be addressed. Is it fair to Washington to judge him by the standards and values of the twentieth century? Slavery has long since been outlawed. The ideal of racial equality is a reality. Overt racism has become socially taboo. Is what Washington thought and said and did with regard to slavery more than two hundred years ago relevant? Perhaps it is best that this dark side of his life be quietly forgotten, and that only the patriotic and virtuous Washington be remembered and honored.

For the historian, it is not that easy. The legacy that Washington left to the nation—and that includes his slave legacy—lives on whether or not we approve of it and whether or not we choose to ignore it. It cannot be exorcised or eradicated. Nor can we forget or forgive the sufferings of the millions of African Americans who labored under the system of institutionalized slavery that Washington participated in, approved of, and actively promoted. Their descendants will carry the scars for generations to come. Washington's own dilemma with the issue of slavery is a legitimate piece in this mosaic. His story deserves to be told and to be incorporated as part of the historical record. And as this study makes very clear, Washington was neither immune nor insensitive to the crimes and evils committed in the name of human bondage. His conscience bore a heavy burden. That fact, too, deserves to be recognized and recorded.

ACKNOWLEDGMENTS

F IRST AND foremost I acknowledge a debt of gratitude to the documentary editors and scholars who assemble and collate the original papers that are the building blocks of any serious historical study. The primary material that they make available allows others to analyze, interpret, and draw valid conclusions about the personalities and events of the past.

Space does not allow me to list all of the individual editors whose work I have drawn on. However, one source in particular has been absolutely essential: the Washington Papers project at the Alderman Library of the University of Virginia in Charlottesville. Twenty years ago when I began my work, Donald Jackson was the editor of the papers and Dorothy Twohig his assistant. Don, unfortunately, has passed away, but Dorothy has taken his place. Both of these fine editors supported and encouraged me from the outset, and I now take this opportunity to register my obligation to them and to Dorothy especially, who remains a dear friend and colleague.

Also of importance is the library at George Washington's Mount Vernon estate. Numerous valuable documents relating to Washington's life and activities rest in those archives. Again, my two earliest contacts at Mount Vernon—dating back to 1976—are gone. John Castellani, the librarian and later director, died tragically in 1993; his assistant, Ellen McCallister, who succeeded him as librarian when he moved into the directorship, has retired. Both Castellani and McCallister were instrumental in guiding and assisting my preliminary research efforts. The present librarian, Barbara McMillan, and the historian, John Riley, have been equally generous in giving of their time and expertise.

Writing a manuscript is an arduous journey with an abundance of detours and bumps in the road. I was lucky. It seems that helping hands were always there at the critical junctures, including those of Franklin Bradley in Utica, N.Y.; Betty Dageforde in Denver; Ormonde deKay in New York City; Richard Maass in White Plains; Paul David Nelson in Berea, Ky.; Joan Seelaus in Washington, D.C.; Thad Tate and Michael McGiffert in Williamsburg; Richard Wentworth and Terry Sears in Champaign, Ill.; and Rike Wootten in Denver. And finally, Beverly Jarrett and her superefficient staff at the University of Missouri Press helped make this book a reality. Many, many thanks to one and all!

GEORGE WASHINGTON *and* SLAVERY

INTRODUCTION

T HE SUCCESSFUL conclusion of the War of Independence in 1783 brought George Washington face-to-face with a fundamental dilemma: how to reconcile the proclaimed ideals of the Revolution with the established institution of slavery. It was becoming increasingly and uncomfortably evident that, so long as black human beings in America could legally be considered the chattel property of their white masters, the rhetoric of equality and individual freedom was hollow.

Progressive voices urged immediate emancipation as the only avenue to resolve the contradiction; the Southern slave owners, of course, stood steadfast for the status quo. Washington was caught in the middle. As a Virginia plantation proprietor and a lifelong slaveholder, he had a substantial private stake in the economic slave system of the South. However, in his role as the acknowledged political leader of the country, his overriding concern was for the preservation of the Union. If Washington publicly supported emancipation, he would almost certainly have to set an example and take steps to dispose of his Mount Vernon slaves. If he spoke out on the side of slavery, how could he legitimately and conscientiously expect to uphold and defend the humanistic goals and moral imperatives of the new nation as expressed in the Declaration of Independence and embodied in the Constitution and the Bill of Rights? His was a balancing act that became more and more difficult to sustain with the passing years.

Until he left Mount Vernon in the spring of 1775, at the age of forty-three, to take command of the Continental army at Cambridge, Massachusetts, Washington had shown few visible qualms about the institution of slavery. Not only did he and his wife own numerous slaves, but he bought and sold them and conformed in most respects with the slaveholding practices of his period and region. He accepted slave labor as an economic necessity—particularly for the profitable operation of a large plantation, as was Mount Vernon—and seemed content to live within the traditional framework of a wealthy Virginia squire in the landed aristocracy.

In Cambridge, Washington was confronted with a novel and perplexing situation. Before his arrival, Massachusetts authorities had permitted the enlistment of black volunteers into the state militia. Now, the additional recruitment of African Americans—both free and slave—implied that the bondsmen among them would have to be given their freedom and that all African Americans, while serving in the military, would be eligible for rights and privileges equivalent to those enjoyed by whites. Washington was not prepared to grant these concessions to a race he had always deemed inferior. Indeed, he and his subordinate commanders, after duly debating the issue at a council of war in Cambridge on October 8, 1775, opted unanimously to keep the army white and to bar African Americans from being recruited or from volunteering. Only a surprise tactical move by the enemy forced Washington to reconsider this exclusionary policy.

Lord Dunmore, the last royal governor of Virginia, in an effort to bolster his Tory forces at the expense of the rebellious American slaveholders, announced in November 1775 that the British would free all slaves who were prepared to take up arms against their former masters. With approximately five hundred thousand slaves living within the borders of the thirteen colonies, the British offer of emancipation was something Washington could not afford to ignore. He promptly countered by reversing himself and rescinding most of his earlier discriminatory pronouncements. African Americans were now officially allowed to enroll in the Continental army.

With that historic decision, whether or not he realized at the time its far-reaching implications, and whatever face-saving rationalizations he put forward to justify his turnabout, Washington became directly responsible for setting in motion a momentous and irreversible progression of events. African American soldiers—carrying weapons, trained in the art of war, and seasoned in combat—would no longer be considered meek and submissive slaves; nor would they be satisfied to return to a condition of abject servitude after the war had ended. Military service was the first major step taken after almost 150 years of slavery to legitimatize the enslaved Americans' long march toward full equality with white Americans.

The victory at Yorktown in the fall of 1781 marked the climactic finale of the struggle for independence. After the signing of the peace treaty with England in 1783, Washington was able to resign his commission and return to his beloved Mount Vernon, universally admired and applauded as America's foremost citizen-soldier. Recalled to public service in 1787, he presided over the Constitutional Convention at Philadelphia. His subsequent unanimous election as the first president of the United States of America was a singular honor that acknowledged the immense respect and prestige he enjoyed among his fellow Americans. With the unique authority that he derived from his position as the nation's chosen leader in war and in peace, Washington carefully helped craft many of the precedents that, even today, continue to guide the country.

Yet Washington equivocated on the controversial issue of slavery. He refused to speak out publicly against the institution of involuntary bondage, although in the privacy of his home and in his personal correspondence he freely affirmed and reaffirmed his postwar commitment to a program of gradual abolition. Undoubtedly, one of the principal reasons Washington refrained from confronting the Southern proslavery faction—men who were firmly convinced that their economic survival depended on the plantation system, with its exploitation of cheap slave labor—was his belief that these same supporters of slavery had it within their power to tear the country apart, as they actually succeeded in doing in the next century. In keeping with his conservative nature and his proclivity for caution and moderation, Washington chose a path between the two extremes. He did what he felt was right and in harmony with his own deeply held personal convictions when he arranged in his will to free his slaves after his and his wife's deaths. But while he privately continued to give lip service to programs of emancipation, he consistently rejected all pleas to take a public, partisan stand on these volatile issues, which seemed even at that time to pose such a serious threat to the fabric of the nation.

Relying primarily on Washington's own words—his correspondence, diaries, and other written records—supplemented by the letters, comments, and eyewitness reports of family, friends, employees, aides, correspondents, colleagues, and visitors to Mount Vernon, together with contemporary newspaper clippings and official documents pertaining to his relationships with African Americans, I have traced his transition from a conventional slaveholder to a lukewarm abolitionist.

His conversion was neither easy nor complete. Washington could have done much more during his lifetime to bring about the emancipation of slaves, had he wanted to. If, for instance, he had harnessed the momentum of his immense popularity and great authority at the peak of his career to support actively the aggressive and well-organized late-eighteenth-century abolitionist movement, he might well have been instrumental in helping the abolitionists to prevail in the South. If so, the country might well have been spared the bitter agony of four years of civil war in 1861–1865.

Washington could just as readily have failed, however. His pressure and influence might have been stubbornly resisted by the obstinate slave owners of the South, and thereby the entire American experiment in democracy would have been placed in jeopardy. Everything that he had fought for, the innumerable sacrifices that had been endured, the risks that had been taken, the lives that had been lost, would have gone for naught if the nation were to be torn apart in an acrimonious dispute over slavery so soon after winning its freedom. Washington was determined to avoid at all costs this very real threat of dissolution. Whether right or wrong, his first priority was to establish and build the permanent political and economic union of the thirteen fledgling states.

In this objective he succeeded admirably. But the concessions on slavery that he accepted along the way were unsatisfactory and unworkable over the long term. By 1861 the nation was finally forced to confront squarely the issue of slavery. Further compromises with the Southern secessionists were no longer possible. President Lincoln, in order to persevere in his goal of maintaining the Union, had no realistic alternative but to engage the nation in the bloodiest civil war in modern history.

Washington could not have foreseen this disaster, but he did harbor some grave premonitions and disturbing concerns as to what might lie ahead. The record shows that he was upset, particularly in his later and more reflective years, by the nagging slavery question. He gloomily predicted, on at least several different occasions, that the ongoing and spreading bitter debates over the future of the institution of slavery would continue to be a source of growing unrest in the country unless the issue was quickly and conclusively resolved. Washington, however, did not have a viable format for emancipation to offer the nation other than the vague and pious hope for gradual abolition through the legislative process.

He himself experienced firsthand, on his estate at Mount Vernon, the painful difficulties and endless frustrations of trying to reconcile humanistic principles and well-meaning intentions with the established coercive slave practices. The one essential element that makes any slave system function efficiently is fear: the slaves' fear of punishment at the hands of their masters. So long as Washington was willing to impose harsh and strict disciplinary measures to drive his slaves into performing their daily allotted tasks, Mount Vernon flourished. Such were the circumstances that existed before the Revolution, when Washington felt no pressing need to worry about his public image outside Virginia. He could sell off his surplus slaves, or buy new ones, whenever it was economically prudent or socially expedient. He could hunt down runaways with impunity, whether they fled North or South. Infractions of the work rules on the Mount Vernon plantations were treated with appropriate severity. And in extreme disciplinary cases, the lash was not spared.

Washington's outlook changed dramatically when he stepped onto a world stage and into the limelight as commander in chief in the fight for independence.

His every decision, his every action became subject to intense scrutiny and partisan discussion and criticism. Furthermore, his elevated status as the de facto head of the nation brought him into intimate contact with many highly educated and sophisticated young men, most of whom were progressive, idealistic intellectuals and vociferous advocates of liberal reforms who regarded slavery as an abomination. Consequently, Washington's narrow parochial interests as a Virginia planter and slave owner had to be considerably modified and broadened to harmonize with his new personification as a leader with a national following and international responsibilities.

He reflected these civilizing influences to the extent that, upon his return to Mount Vernon after the war, he resolved (with certain reservations and exceptions) never again to be a party to transactions involving the purchase or the sale of slaves. Washington soon learned that there is little room in a slave order for an enlightened master. The moment he eased up and thus subdued the fear of chastisement, especially the dread anxiety of the slaves that they would be shipped out and sold, subtle changes began to occur. Washington could plainly see what was happening when he drew up the balance sheet for the Mount Vernon operations. Relaxed discipline had resulted in lower productivity; the slaves were consuming more than they were producing. Washington's self-imposed refusal to sell off excess slaves meant that there would be a growing number of hungry mouths to feed and bodies to clothe from the limited resources of his fields and pastures. The once prosperous Mount Vernon—one of the largest and best-managed plantations in Virginia—was operating at a loss; in fact, it was slowly but steadily sinking into bankruptcy.

Ironically, Washington's slaves had become a liability instead of an asset. He could have stopped the hemorrhaging and helped reverse the decline by simply selling off the unproductive and unnecessary slaves and once again strictly enforcing the old work rules. But it seems that he would not—or could not—bring himself to take these regressive steps, even though serious financial problems were staring him in the face.

To compound his troubles, the antislavery proponents, spearheaded by the Quakers, were busy encouraging wide-ranging efforts to free plantation slaves. Their propaganda, with its explicit promise of freedom, sanctuary, and a fresh start, caused mounting unrest among the Mount Vernon slaves. Some attempted to flee, and when Washington sought to have them returned forcibly to Mount Vernon, as he had in the past, he found that his hands were tied by the necessity to preserve his public image. He could no longer afford to antagonize abolitionist sensibilities in the North by blatant attempts (like advertising in northern newspapers) to retrieve his runaways. It is sad indeed to read of the clandestine and circumspect stratagems that Washington employed to try to retrieve these wayward slaves (and to keep those in his possession out of the clutches of the Quaker emancipationists) without stirring up a backlash of antislavery outrage in the states north of the Mason-Dixon Line.

The deteriorating situation at Mount Vernon and his precarious financial condition caused Washington, in his sunset years, to consider other ways of supporting his aristocratic lifestyle in which slave ownership was not a prerequisite. His reluctant endeavors to rent out most of the Mount Vernon plantations, keeping only the mansion house and the adjoining grounds for his private use, failed, partly because of the stringent terms regarding the treatment of the slaves that he insisted on imposing on any prospective tenants.

Only Washington's death in the winter of 1799 brought an end to the nagging headaches that his slaveholdings imposed on the tired and aging general. Whether the freeing of his family of Mount Vernon blacks by the provisions in his will was a sop to his conscience, a realization of the inevitable, or a final and genuine act of generosity will probably never be known. According to his own account, all three reasons apparently entered into his decision. His last legacy does serve to confirm to the world that George Washington stood squarely on the side of emancipation.

Washington was spared a public disclosure of this personal anguish. Almost from the moment that the issue of freedom for the slaves was put forward in the period following the Revolutionary War, Washington's stated position was clear and unequivocal. He said time and again that he favored, and would officially support, a program of gradual abolition if such were to be enacted by the legislative bodies at either the state or the federal level. In spite of the urgent pleadings of his friends and colleagues and of abolitionists, Washington refused to allow his personal views to go on public record or to be used in partisan debates. He knew very well that if he were to become an open advocate of emancipation without first having set free his own slaves, he would be vulnerable to the charge of hypocrisy. And since he obviously did not wish to free his slaves, or to have his integrity questioned or his reputation impugned, the safest course was to maintain a low profile while saying nothing in public that could be turned against him. Furthermore, Washington had no practical plan to advocate to the nation for abolishing slavery. His personal instincts were probably sound when he judged that most Americans, especially those in the South, were not prepared to accept former slaves as citizens with equal rights and privileges.

At the Constitutional Convention in Philadelphia in the summer of 1787, over which he presided as president, Washington continued to wear a cloak of benign neutrality. Officially, he took no active part in the formal discussions and proceedings, which at times inspired heated debates on slave matters. What he said confidentially, in conversations behind closed doors with the other delegates, has never been revealed. But it can be reasonably assumed that his personal views on slavery were either well known to his colleagues or communicated to them directly. His conservative opinions, it seems, were shared by a majority of the delegates. It comes as no surprise, therefore, that the end result of the Philadelphia convention, the Constitution of the United States, in its many delicately crafted compromises, gingerly tiptoed around the tough decisions concerning the future of slavery.

During Washington's tenure as president of the United States, none of his cabinet officers, including such trusted confidants and brilliant advisers as Thomas Jefferson and Alexander Hamilton, ever urged on him, according to the available records, any form of executive initiative dealing with abolition. It should also be noted that whenever antislavery proposals were actually brought before the U.S. House of Representatives by the Quakers, they failed to receive sufficient votes and were quietly shelved in committee. The Virginia General Assembly, too, did not see fit to vote out antislavery petitions that were introduced by its members. Thus, Washington, both as a public servant and as a citizen of the Commonwealth of Virginia, was never once called upon to declare publicly his personal convictions on the slavery issue.

Slave owners were shielded from the onslaughts of the emancipationists by a simple article of faith. They doggedly held that the slaves were a species of property and hence not subject to the laws governing the rest of the human race. Washington, especially in his younger years, may have drunk of this heady brew, but he was not addicted to it. Nor was he blind to the contradiction between the fundamental premise that the Southern slave owners had so stubbornly staked out for themselves and the philosophy encompassed in the Declaration of Independence: "that all Men are created equal, that they are endowed by their Creator with certain unalienable Rights, that among these are Life, Liberty, and the Pursuit of Happiness." It grew more and more obvious with each passing year that this dichotomy was not susceptible to a binding compromise and that no amount of sophistry could serve to bridge the widening gap between the pro- and antislavery forces.

Washington came to realize that slavery was permanently dividing the nation into two hostile camps, but by then he was an old man, his energies drained and his authority dissipated. It was beyond his power to affect significantly the ominous drift of events, even if he had wanted to. Within his immediate grasp lay only his final legacy to his country, eloquently expressed in the thoughtful and measured prose that constituted his will: the heritage of freedom belongs to all people—black as well as white.

Washington took a long time to make his decision—too long, many will say—and it came too late to have any meaningful impact on the course of the slavery debate. But for those who, like me, have become immersed in Washington's life; who have tracked his inner struggles; who have been alternately amused and appalled by his equivocations, callousness, rationalizations, pettiness, and obstinacy; yet who remain convinced that he was a man of pride and honor, of principle and of strong convictions, to whom change did not come easily, quickly, or painlessly—for us it is especially satisfying to conclude that in the end wisdom and compassion triumphed over self-interest and prejudice. George Washington rose to the full height of his character when he finally and irrevocably turned his back on slavery. One might hope, perhaps, that in a moment of quiet introspection he also came to grips with two universal truths: that the human race cannot be divided into inferior and superior beings and that every individual craves the dignity and respect that come with freedom and equality.

I. SLAVERY AT MOUNT VERNON

1

BUILDING AN ESTATE

WHEN HIS half-brother Lawrence died in 1752, George Washington came into possession of the family's 2,650-acre Mount Vernon estate.[1] Hand-in-hand with the acquisition of land came the acquisition of slaves, for the land by itself was useless as a means of generating regular income unless it could be made productive through the cultivation and harvesting of agricultural and animal commodities. Because the farm economy of the plantation South in eighteenth-century America was almost wholly dependent on slave labor, an increase in the amount of land to be farmed required a proportionate increase in the slave labor force needed to perform the essential farming chores.

In 1743, when his father, Augustine, died, eleven-year-old George Washington had inherited ten slaves. Then, when Lawrence Washington passed away in July 1752, George gained additional slaves through the terms of his half-brother's will. On December 10, 1754, he drew up a document, "Division of Slaves," apportioning Lawrence's slaves among the Washington heirs. On December 17 of the same year, he executed a lease agreement with Lawrence's widow, Ann, and her new husband, George Lee, which gave him official possession of the Mount Vernon estate and "the following Negroe slaves Viz: Nan. James Dula Grace Dublin Harry Roger Phillis Kate Ceasar Charles Farrow Doll Sue: George Lydia Murreah & Glasgow."[2]

The next major augmentation to Washington's slaveholdings resulted from his marriage on January 6, 1759, to the widow Martha Dandridge Custis. Legally,

---

1. "From 1757 to 1786 Washington added 5601 acres to his estate in seventeen separate purchases." One hundred and seventy-eight acres were transferred to Lund Washington. See Douglas S. Freeman, *George Washington: A Biography,* vol. 6, *Patriot and President,* 387, 392.

2. *The Papers of George Washington: Colonial Series,* ed. W. W. Abbot and Dorothy Twohig, 1:232.

the many African Americans that she owned were dower slaves and belonged to the Custis estate. However, throughout his lifetime Washington managed them as though they were his property. But he was always careful to list them separately as part of the Custis estate. Most of the dower slaves remained on the Custis plantations on the York River and elsewhere, although Martha Washington brought about a dozen of her personal servants with her when she removed to Mount Vernon in the spring of 1759. Washington almost certainly relocated some of the other dower slaves to the Mount Vernon farms whenever it suited his purposes, yet their exact number is unknown. What is methodically recorded are his periodic slave purchases as his landholdings grew steadily over the years:

> In 1754 he bought a "fellow" for £40.5, another named Jack for £52.5 and a woman called Clio for £50. Two years later he acquired two negro men and a woman for £86, and from Governor Dinwiddie a woman and child for £60. In 1758 he got Gregory for £60.9. . . . The year of his marriage he bought Will for £50, another fellow for £60, Hannah and child for £80 and nine others for £406. In 1762 he acquired two of Fielding Lewis for £115, seven of Lee Massey for £300, also one-handed Charles for £30. Two years later he bought two men and a woman of the estate of Francis Hobbs for £128.10, the woman being evidently of inferior quality, for she cost only £20. Another slave purchased that year from Sarah Alexander was more valuable, costing £76. Judy and child, obtained of Garvin Corbin, cost £63. Two mulattoes, Will and Frank, bought of Mary Lee in 1768, cost £61.15 and £50, and Will became famous as a body servant; Adam and Frank, bought of the same owner, cost £38. He bought five more slaves in 1772. Some writers say that this was his last purchase, but it is certain that thereafter he at least took a few in payment of debts.

The same source reports, "By 1760 he paid taxes on forty-nine slaves, in 1770 on eighty-seven and in 1774 on one hundred thirty-five."[3]

Washington never completely abandoned the practice of buying slaves. "Between 1770 and 1775 Washington's slave population more than doubled, principally the result of natural increase, for he purchased no additional slaves after 1772. By that time, however, he had spent well over £2000 on the procurement of captive labor."[4] As the years passed and the Mount Vernon slave population continued to expand, both by purchase and by natural increase, Washington expressed a growing reluctance and distaste toward the acquisition of more slaves. His reluctance was somewhat based on practical economic considerations; his distaste, it seems, was part of a newly acquired postwar morality. By 1786, the year in which he made the first known comprehensive inventory of his and

3. Paul L. Haworth, *George Washington: Country Gentleman,* 192.
4. John E. Ferling, *The First of Men: A Life of George Washington,* 68.

his wife's Mount Vernon slaveholdings, Washington was openly voicing these inhibitions. His outlook at the time on slave procurement can perhaps best be viewed through the negotiations he conducted with an old family friend, Col. John Francis Mercer:

> Mount Vernon 6th Novr 1786
>
> Dear Sir,
>
> . . . Altho' I have great repugnance to encreasing my Slaves by purchase, yet as it seems so inconvenient to you to make payment by other modes than those you have proposed, and so injurious as not to be accomplished at a less loss than 50 or more prCt; I will take Six or more Negroes of you, if you can spare such as will answer my purposes, upon the terms offered in your former letter. The Negroes I want are males. Three or four young fellows for Ditchers; and the like number of well grown lads for artificers. It is with you to determine, whether you can supply me with such Negroes. If you agree to do it, and will appoint a time, I would send for them; relying on your word that the whole are healthy, and none of them addicted to running away. The latter I abominate—and unhealthy negroes—women, or Children, would not suit my purposes on *any terms.*[5]

In his next letter to Mercer, Washington emphasized his unwillingness to be a party to any slave transactions that would result in the separation of families:

> Mount Vernon 24th Novr 1786
>
> Sir,
>
> . . . With respect to the negroes, I conclude it is not in my power to answer your wishes—because it is as much against my inclination as it can be against your's, to hurt the feelings of those unhappy people by a separation of man and wife, or of families; because no others than such as I enumerated in my last will answer my purposes, & because the price exceeds what I *supposed* Negroes would sell for in ready money; for, in this as with Certificates, having had no intention to buy, I have made no enquiry into the price they sold at; but conceived that for ready money the best labouring negroes (which are the kind I wanted) might have been had for £60—£70—or at most £75. Upon the whole then, for the balance, I must take payment in the manner formerly mentioned by you at this place—unless you should think that young Bob, (who has only a father without a wife) Tom the baker, Nessey & David, & James & Valentine (if of sufficient size to go to trades) could be separated without much uneasiness, & the prices of them, if not really the ready money prices, cou'd be abated.[6]

The two men continued to haggle, with Washington reiterating in a letter of December 5 his reluctance to proceed with the deal: "but as I have no desire of

5. *The Papers of George Washington: Confederation Series,* ed. W. W. Abbot and Dorothy Twohig, 4:336.

6. Ibid., 4:394.

adding to my present number by purchase, to accommodate you was the object I had principally in view."[7] In his communication of December 19, he laid down his final ultimatum to Mercer:

> Sir,
> . . . I will, in one word, fix my ultimatum with respect to the negroes proposed for sale. Which is to allow you three hundred pounds for young Bob (or an other fellow of his age & appearance), Tom the baker—Massey, David, James & Valentine; but this I do on the proviso that they answer your description in their ages, sizes & qualities; for unless the two last named boys are of sufficient size to be put to trades, they would not answer my purpose; because the persons with whom I should place them are Servants in this family whose terms will expire in less than three years.[8]

The deal with Mercer eventually fell through, and Washington wrote to him on February 1, 1787, "I am perfectly satisfied with your determination respecting the Negroes. The money will be infinitely more agreeable to me than property of that sort."[9] It is evident from this and similar correspondence that Washington's practice of buying slaves after the Revolutionary War—a practice that would continue sporadically until the end of his life—was governed chiefly by the immediate farm or household needs at Mount Vernon as well as by the opportunity to drive a good bargain. For example, in a letter to Col. Henry Lee of Leesylvania, Washington made the case for purchasing a bricklayer, but only under carefully prescribed conditions:

> Mount Vernon, February 4, 1787.
>
> My dear Sir:
> . . . It is not my wish to be your competitor in the purchase of any of Mr. Hunters tradesmen: especially as I am in a great degree principled against increasing my number of Slaves by purchase and suppose moreover that Negroes sold on credit will go high. yet if you are not disposed to buy the Bricklayer which is advertized for Sale, for your own use, find him in the vigour of life, from report a good workman and of tolerable character and his price does not exceed one hundred, or a few more pounds, I should be glad if you would buy him for me. I have much work in this way to do this Summer. If he has a family, with which he is to be sold; or from whom he would reluctantly part I decline the purchase, his feelings I would not be the means of hurting in the latter case, nor *at any* rate be incumbered with the former.[10]

7. Ibid., 4:442.
8. Ibid., 4:466.
9. John C. Fitzpatrick, ed., *The Writings of George Washington from the Original Manuscript Sources, 1745–1799*, 29:150.
10. Ibid., 29:154.

When his old and valued household cook, Hercules, ran away in Philadelphia in 1797, Washington wrote to his nephew George Lewis inquiring about the possibility of purchasing a replacement:

> Mount Vernon, November 13, 1797.
>
> Dear Sir:
>
> The running off of my Cook, has been a most inconvenient thing to this family; and what renders it more disagreeable, is, that I had resolved never to become the Master of another Slave by *purchase;* but this resolution I fear I must break.
>
> I have endeavoured to hire, black or white, but am not yet supplied. A few days ago, having occasion to write to Mr. Bushrod Washington on other matters, I asked if one could be had in Richmond; the following is his answer.
>
> "Mr. Brooke (late Governor) informs me that he had a very excellent Cook, with no other fault than a fondness for liquor (which a town afforded him too many opportunities of indulging) who is now in Fredericksburg, and is to be sold. I shall write to the Gentleman who has him, not to sell him till he hears from you. Should you, *under this character,* wish to buy, or hire him, please address a letter to Mr. George Murray of that place. He cooked for Mr. Brooke while he was in the Government."
>
> Let me ask you now, to see both Mr. Murray, and the man himself; and if upon conversing fully with the latter, you should be of opinion (from the account he gives of himself) that he is a good Cook, and would answer my purposes, then discover the *lowest terms* on which he could be had by purchase, or on hire; and inform me of the result by the first Post to wch. an answer shall be immediately given.
>
> I should like to know the age, and as far as you are enabled to ascertain it, the temper and looks of the man described. Whether he has a wife, and expects to have her along with him; and in that case, what children they have; with *her* age and occupation. By the time I can receive an answer from you, I expect Mrs. Forbes, who was Govr. Brooke's housekeeper, will be here as my housekeeper; and from her own knowledge of the person, and your account I shall be enabled to determine what answer to give.[11]

Washington eventually arranged to hire a white cook and therefore was not forced to break his resolve by purchasing Mr. Murray's slave.

This letter is the last recorded instance in which Washington considered a further slave acquisition. By contrast, his decision to no longer engage in the sale of slave property was unequivocal and had a far greater impact on both the personal lives of his slaves and the operations of his estate. The slaves undoubtedly felt more secure in the knowledge that they would not be sold or separated from their families and friends.

11. Ibid., 36:70–71.

It cannot precisely be determined when Washington made up his mind to discontinue selling slaves, but his decision likely was made during the Revolution while he was absent from Mount Vernon. The first indications of his unwillingness to sell his slaves appear in his correspondence with Lund Washington, his wartime estate manager, in 1778–1779. For example, on February 24, 1779, he wrote from Middle Brook, New Jersey, "My scruples arise from a reluctance in offering these people at public vendue." Such early, benevolent sentiments hardened over the years and were expressed periodically in his later correspondence, including a November 23, 1794, letter to his friend and neighbor Alexander Spotswood in which Washington emphatically declared, "I am principled agt. selling negros, as you would do cattle in the market."[12] From the known records, it seems that he was consistent in these convictions throughout the rest of his life.

Few of Washington's peers in Virginia shared his antipathy toward the accepted practice of marketing surplus slaves. Thomas Jefferson, for instance, who certainly shared Washington's philosophical views on the immorality of slave trading, nevertheless did not hesitate to sell his slaves whenever he needed the money or when it suited his farming requirements or social convenience. Washington's principles were not that elastic, however. Having once made up his mind, he resolutely stuck with his self-imposed obligation to support an excess slave population. To appreciate the nature of that burden, it is necessary to look closely at the composition and dynamics of the Mount Vernon slave community as set forth in the 1786 and 1799 inventories.

After nearly thirty years of building his estate through the acquisition of land and slaves, Washington decided in February 1786 to draw up a detailed and comprehensive accounting of his Mount Vernon slaveholdings. His diary entry for Saturday, February 18, 1786, duly noted: "Took a list to day of all my Negroes which are as follows at Mount Vernon and the plantations around it— viz.—"[13] He then proceeded to list the slaves by name, occupation and/or physical condition, and, whenever pertinent, marital status. The ages of the children were carefully observed, and in the right-hand column he kept a tally that was subtotaled and totaled. He also indicated by asterisks which slaves legally belonged to the Custis estate. Of the 216 slaves, 103 were Washington's property and 113 were the property of the Custis estate. Excluding the dead and incapacitated (6), there were 122 productive men and women in the Mount Vernon slave labor force and 88 children.

12. Ibid., 14:148, 34:47.
13. The complete February 1786 slave inventory can be found in *The Diaries of George Washington,* ed. Donald Jackson and Dorothy Twohig, 4:277–83.

The inventory began with the mansion personnel. Will, or Billy Lee, who was Washington's favorite huntsman before the Revolution and his body servant and close companion during the war, and who continued to serve his master in that capacity until he became a crippled alcoholic, headed the list with the imposing title "Val de Chambre." Frank and Austin were household waiters, and Hercules and Nathan were cooks. Giles, Joe, and Paris, a boy, were drivers and stable hands. Doll and Jenny were "almost past Service." Betty, Lame Alice, and Charlotte were seamstresses. Sall and Caroline were housemaids, and Sall Brass and Dolly were washerwomen. Al[i]ce, Myrtilla, Kitty, and Winny were spinners, although Winny was "old & almost blind." Schomberg was "past labour." Frank and Cook Jack were identified as "Stock keeper and old Jobber." Gunner, Boatswain, Sam, Anthony, Tom Davis, Will, and Joe were laborers. Jack was a "Waggonner," Simms was a "Carter," and Bristol was the gardener. Isaac, James, Sambo, and Tom Nokes were carpenters. Natt and George were blacksmiths, and Peter, who was lame, was a knitter. In addition, there were twenty-six children, ranging in age from three months to fourteen years, belonging to the female slaves attached to the mansion. Some of the women were very prolific: Little Alice had four offspring, Kitty had seven, and Myrtilla had five. None of the mothers, however, were listed as having husbands. Only four of the twenty-six children were older than twelve.

The inventory continued at the mill. Ben was the miller, and Jack, Tom, and Davy were coopers. On the River Farm, Davy was the black overseer and Molly was his wife. Ten laboring men and seventeen laboring women worked on that plantation. Twenty-three children, ranging in age from one month to thirteen years, belonged to the female slaves there: Daphne claimed four, Lidia, three, and Neck Doll, four. Only three of the youngsters were twelve or older. And again, the names of the fathers were not mentioned. At the Dogue Run Farm, Morris was the black overseer and Hannah was his wife. There were eight laboring men and ten laboring women. Brunswick, one of the laborers, was "Ruptured." Seventeen children belonged to the Dogue Run Farm women. Charity had four, Lucy had three, Sall had three, and Jones, who was stated to be dead, left behind three orphans. All of these boys and girls were nine years of age or younger. None of the fathers were named.

At the Ferry Farm there were five laboring men and ten laboring women. Fifteen children, ranging in age from six months to twelve years, belonged to the plantation women. Betty had six children, Doll had four, and Lucy had three. Again, the fathers were not identified. Finally, at the Muddy Hole Farm, Will was the black overseer. There were five laboring men and nine laboring women, as well as twelve children ranging in age from six months to fourteen years. Kate had four boys and girls. Fathers were not specified.

A number of conclusions can be drawn from this 1786 slave inventory. First, in a period of less than three decades, during which he was absent from home for nearly nine years while in command of the Continental army, Washington had succeeded in establishing a slave labor force that performed virtually all of the essential functions of the estate: from overseer to miller, from household cook to blacksmith. Second, the offspring of his female slaves assured him of a continuing supply of slaves to replace those who died or became incapacitated through age, illness, or accident. Third, the inventory confirms what Washington repeatedly stated in his postwar correspondence: he had no urgent need to purchase slaves (with only a few notable exceptions), since those he possessed, including their potential offspring, were adequate for his current as well as his foreseeable requirements. Fourth, if his slave population continued to increase over the years, as it undoubtedly would, given the proven fertility of the women, Washington had no viable alternative but to find an outlet for the surplus members of his slave family. And finally, the ratio of productive to nonproductive slaves, which in 1786 approached the 50:50 mark, represented a substantial, ongoing drain on his limited resources.

In the summer of 1799, when he instinctively felt that the end of his life was rapidly approaching, Washington drew up his second inventory of the Mount Vernon slave population. By now he had put aside as unworkable or impractical his previously proposed schemes for resettling the excess slaves on his outlying lands or on other plantations or for renting the Mount Vernon farms to tenant farmers. He had decided instead to proceed with the full emancipation of all his slaves after his and his wife's deaths. Thus, in preparing this final inventory, which would also serve to help expedite the terms of his will, he was motivated by different considerations than when he had made his 1786 accounting.

The 1799 inventory was headed "NEGROES Belonging to George Washington in his own right and by Marriage."[14] The slaves were again listed by name, but in two separate columns: the left-hand column was marked "G.W."; the right-hand column was marked "Dower," identifying the slaves who belonged to the Custis family. This inventory also provided more significant information about the individual slaves, particularly in terms of their marital relationships. It distinguished between those slaves who cultivated the soil and those who were engaged in the trades, and it made note of those who had "Passed labor or that do not Work." A recapitulation, which was not part of the 1786 inventory, effectively broke down and summarized the composition of the Mount Vernon slave community as of June 1799. Under the heading "Tradesmen and others, not employed on the

14. The complete June 1799 slave inventory can be found in Fitzpatrick, ed., *Writings*, 37:256–68.

Farms," were listed twenty-two men who belonged to Washington, thirteen dower male slaves, one woman who belonged to Washington, thirteen dower females, and two working boys who were dower slaves, for a total of fifty-one. Included in this category were "Smiths, Bricklayers, Carpenters, Coopers, Shoemaker, Cooks, Gardeners, Millers, House-Servants, Ditchers, Distillery, Postillions, Waggoners and Cartrs., Milk Maid, Spinners and Knitr."

All of the black laborers attached to the mansion were dower slaves: three men, nine women, three working boys, two working girls, and twenty-three children, for a total of forty. The laborers at Muddy Hole Farm who belonged to Washington consisted of three men, fourteen women, one working boy, and eighteen children, for a total of thirty-six. Only two men and two working girls at Muddy Hole were dower property. The laborers at the River Farm who belonged to Washington included three men, nine women, two working boys, two working girls, and ten children, for a total of twenty-six. The dower slave laborers at Muddy Hole consisted of six men, nine women, two working boys, one working girl, and ten children, for a total of twenty-eight. The laborers at the Dogue Run Farm who belonged to Washington included six men, seven women, one working girl, and ten children, for a total of twenty-four. The dower slave laborers at Dogue Run consisted of five women, one working boy, and eleven children, for a total of seventeen.

The laborers at the Union Farm (formerly the Ferry Farm) who belonged to Washington included two working men, one working woman, and two children, for a total of five. The dower slave laborers at the Union Farm consisted of four men, six women, three working boys, and fourteen children, for a total of twenty-seven. Nine of Washington's slaves and nine of the dower slaves were classified as unfit or unable to work. In the fall of 1786, well after the February inventory was completed, Washington finalized an agreement with Mrs. Penelope French and her executor for a lifetime rental of 552 acres of her land that adjoined his own estate. The terms of the contract included the hire of the slaves who were attached to Mrs. French's property.[15] At the time of the 1799 inventory, these slaves were itemized as follows in the "G.W." recapitulation column: nine men, nine women, two working boys, four working girls, and sixteen children, for a total of forty.

It is difficult to trace with any degree of accuracy the continuity of the individual Mount Vernon slaves from the initial 1786 inventory to the 1799 tabulation. Many slaves had the same names and can be identified only circumstantially through the meager mentions in Washington's diaries and correspondence and in the agricultural records and overseers' reports. However, one of the key personalities

15. Washington to William Triplet, Mount Vernon, September 25, 1786 (ibid., 29:16–21).

in the Mount Vernon slave hierarchy is readily spotted. Will, or Billy Lee, who was the proud "Val de Chambre" in 1786, has been downgraded, because of his afflictions, to shoemaker in 1799: "Will . . . Shoemr . . . Lame . . . no wife."

The interval between the February 1786 and the June 1799 inventories was marked by Washington's lengthy absences from Mount Vernon during the eight years he served the nation as its first president, residing in New York City and then in Philadelphia. During that period he had to entrust Mount Vernon to hired managers, who performed their assigned duties with varying degrees of competence. When Washington returned home permanently in late 1797, he immediately turned his attention to what had been neglected during this second protracted tour of public service. Probably the most crucial and explosive domestic problem he faced was the spiraling growth of the Mount Vernon slave population.

A comparison of the 1786 inventory with the one completed in 1799 shows the magnitude of his predicament: the 8,073-acre estate was now being worked by 201 productive slaves (a total of 317 slaves minus 116 nonproductive slaves, the latter being the 18 old or disabled slaves plus 98 slave children); in February 1786, the 7,365-acre estate had been adequately worked by only 122 productive slaves. Thus, the slave population had grown by 65 percent in little more than thirteen years, while the estate had expanded by less than 10 percent. If the trend were allowed to continue, Mount Vernon would slide into bankruptcy, as Washington himself bluntly predicted in a letter to Robert Lewis: "What then is to be done? Something must or I shall be ruined."[16] The multiplying slaves would eventually consume all of the estate's output.

There is no indication that Washington ever seriously entertained the idea of jettisoning his resolution to sell none of his slaves. Rather, he took the unusual step, for those times and circumstances and for a man of his class and stature as one of the largest plantation proprietors in Virginia, of arranging to emancipate all 124 of his Mount Vernon slaves. The beloved estate he had spent a lifetime building into a magnificent showplace and a profitable enterprise remained intact until the day of his death. Only after his passing did his heirs begin the task of dividing his estate; and only after Martha Washington's death did his slaves begin life as free men and women. This was a fitting conclusion for a slave plantation whose proprietor's personal conflict between principle and profit could no longer be practically reconciled—and whose ambitions and acquisitiveness for land and slaves had finally run their course.

16. Washington to Robert Lewis, Mount Vernon, August 18, 1799 (ibid., 37:338–39).

2

GONE TO WAR

GEORGE WASHINGTON was fortunate. While he was away at war, the operation and maintenance of the Mount Vernon estate rested in the trusted and competent hands of his cousin Lund Washington. As the general himself acknowledged when he returned home, he would have had an exceedingly difficult time remaining in the public service without Lund's reassuring presence to look after his business affairs:

> Mount Vernon 20th Novr 1785.
>
> Dear Lund,
> . . . I shall always retain a grateful sense of your endeavours to serve me; for as I have repeatedly intimated to you in my Letters from Camp, nothing but that entire confidence which I reposed, could have made me easy under an absence of almost nine years from my family & Estate; or could have enabled me, consequently, to have given not only my time, but my whole attention to the public concerns of this Country for that space.[1]

Lund Washington was well qualified to run Mount Vernon in the general's absence, having resided at the estate and served as Washington's assistant manager and business agent since October 1764.[2] Not only was he versed in the workings of the plantation, he was also a member of the Washington family circle. This long and close relationship between the two men greatly facilitated their ability to carry on the estate's farming activities by means of regular reports and correspondence. In addition to the usual concerns about the management of the plantations and worries about their finances during wartime, there was the fear that the

---

1. *Papers: Confederation Series,* ed. Abbot and Twohig, 3:373–74.
2. *Papers: Colonial Series,* ed. Abbot and Twohig, 7:320n.

British would target Mount Vernon and the Washington family for retaliation or
punishment. Washington first expressed this anxiety in a letter to Lund from the
camp at Cambridge on August 20, 1775: "I can hardly think that Lord Dunmore
[the Royal Governor of Virginia] can act so low, & unmanly a part, as to think
of siezing Mrs Washington by way of revenge upon me." Lund replied: "you may
depend I will be watchfull, & upon the least Alarm persuade her to move."[3] Several
weeks later, Lund mentioned his ideas for the defense of Mount Vernon in the
event that the enemy attacked.

> Mount Vernon Octbr 29th 1775
>
> Dr Sir
>
> . . . I think 50 men well Arm'd might prevent 200 from burng Mt Vernon
> Situated as it is, no way to get to it but up a Steep hill, and if I remember right
> General Gates told me it could not be done by the Shipg. I wish I had the
> musquets—I woud endeavour to find the men Black or White, that woud at
> least make them pay dear for the attempt.[4]

The threat to Mount Vernon appeared more menacing when Lord Dunmore
issued a royal proclamation in November 1775 formally announcing, among
other things, his offer of freedom to any slaves joining His Majesty's colors. Lund
promptly relayed the ominous news to Washington:

> Mount Vernon Dembr 3d 1775
>
> Dr Sir
>
> . . . Our Dunmore has at length Publishd his much dreaded proclamation—
> declareg Freedom to All Indented Servts & Slaves (the Property of Rebels) that
> will repair to his majestys Standard—being able to bear Arms—What effect it
> will have upon those sort of people I cannot tell—I think if there was no white
> Servts in this family I shoud be under no apprehension about the Slaves,
> however I am determined, that if any of them Create any confusition to make
> & [an] example of him, Sears who is at worck here says there is not a man of
> them, but woud leave us, if they believe'd they coud make there Escape—Tom
> Spears Excepted—& yet they have no fault to find[.] Liberty is sweet.[5]

Lord Dunmore's troops were subsequently defeated by the local militia, and
Dunmore was forced to leave Virginia. With his withdrawal, the immediate threat
to Mount Vernon evaporated. But six years later, in the spring of 1781, the British
returned to Virginia in strength and ravaged much of the countryside. As a part
of this planned invasion, His Majesty's sloop of war, the *Savage,* commanded by
Capt. Thomas Graves, together with an escorting flotilla, sailed up the Potomac,

---

3. *The Papers of George Washington: Revolutionary War Series,* ed. W. W. Abbot and Dorothy Twohig,
1:335; Lund Washington to George Washington, Mount Vernon, October 5, 1775 (ibid., 2:116).
   4. Ibid., 2:258.
   5. Ibid., 2:479–80.

burning and pillaging rebel (American) properties on both shores.[6] Pertinent extracts from Captain Graves's ship's log read as follows:

> Thursday [April] 12th Potowmack River Piscatway East off Shore 1/4 of a Mile. General Washington['s] House WSW.
> Friday [April] 13th In Potowmack River Piscatway East off Shore 1/4 of a Mile. General Washington['s] House WSW.
> Saturday [April] 14th Ditto.
> Sunday [April] 15th Sailing down the River Potowmack[7]

What actually happened during the three critical days that Mount Vernon lay under the guns of the British warships? John C. Fitzpatrick wrote:

> According to a copy found in the Toner Transcripts in the Library of Congress, taken from a manuscript memorandum made by Lund Washington in April, 1781, and inclosed in his letter of April 18, the loss suffered by Mount Vernon was principally in slaves. The British sloop of war *Savage,* commanded by Capt. Richard Graves, took "a very valuable Boat: 24 feet Keel," and the following slaves: "Peter, an old man. Lewis, an old man. Frank, an old man. Frederick, a man about 45 years old; an overseer and valuable. Gunner, a man about 45 years old; valuable, a Brick maker. Harry. a man about 40 years old, valuable, a Horseler. Tom, a man about 20 years old, stout and Healthy. Sambo, a man about 20 years old, stout and Healthy. Thomas, a lad about 17 years old, House servant. Peter, a lad about 15 years old, very likely. Stephen, a man about 20 years old, a cooper by trade. James, a man about 25 years old, stout and Healthy. Watty, a man about 20 years old, by trade a weaver. Daniel, a man about 19 years old, very likely. Lucy, a woman about 20 years old. Esther, a woman about 18 years old. Deborah, a woman about 16 years old."[8]

Lund Washington's letter of April 18, 1781, reporting on the presence of the British, has never been located. However, the Marquis de Chastellux, who was in Virginia at the time of this incident and who apparently had occasion to talk to Lund, set down in his memoirs a detailed account of what transpired between Capt. Thomas Graves and the estate manager:

> Mr. Lund Washington, a relation of the General's, and who managed all his affairs during his *nine years'* absence with the army, informed me that an English frigate having come up the Potomac, a party was landed who set fire to and destroyed some gentlemen's houses on the Maryland side in sight of Mount Vernon, the General's house; after which the Captain, (I think Captain [Thomas]

---

6. Fritz Hirschfeld, ed., " 'Burnt All Their Houses': The Log of HMS *Savage* during a Raid up the Potomac River, Spring 1781."

7. "A Journal of the proceedings of His Majesty's Sloop *Savage,* Thomas Graves Esqr. Commander Between the 15th March 1779 and the 20th May 1781. By Captn. Tho. Graves (signature)."

8. Fitzpatrick, ed., *Writings,* 22:14n. Fitzpatrick was mistaken in his reference to Richard Graves. The captain of the *Savage* was Thomas Graves, not his brother Richard, who was also a prominent British naval officer. See *The Naval Chronicle,* 359–60.

Graves of the Actaeon [*Savage*]) sent a boat on shore to the General's, demanding a large supply of provisions, etc. with a menace of burning it likewise in case of a refusal. To this message Mr. Lund Washington replied, "that when the General engaged in the contest he had put all to stake, and was well aware of the exposed situation of his house and property, in consequence of which he had given him orders by no means to comply with any such demands, for that he would make no unworthy compromise with the enemy, and was ready to meet the fate of his neighbors." The Captain was highly incensed on receiving this answer, and removed his frigate to the Virginia shore; but before he commenced his operations, he sent another message to the same purport, offering likewise a passport to Mr. Washington to come on board: he returned accordingly in the boat, carrying with him a small present of poultry, of which he begged the Captain's acceptance. His presence produced the best effect, he was hospitably received notwithstanding he repeated the same sentiments with the same firmness. The Captain expressed his personal respect for the character of the General, commending the conduct of Mr. Lund Washington, and assured him nothing but his having misconceived the terms of the first answer could have induced him for a moment to entertain the idea of taking the smallest measure offensive to so illustrious a character as the General, explaining at the same time the real or supposed provocations which had compelled his severity on the other side of the river. Mr. Washington, after spending some time in perfect harmony on board, returned, and instantly despatched sheep, hogs, and an abundant supply of other articles as a present to the English frigate.[9]

The Marquis de Chastellux diplomatically omitted from his memoirs the fact that the true purpose of Lund Washington's friendly negotiations with the British captain was to try to secure the return of the slaves who had fled Mount Vernon with the enemy raiding parties. The Marquis de Lafayette, in command of the Continental troops in Virginia, did comment frankly on this matter in a confidential letter to General Washington sent from Alexandria on April 23, 1781:

When the ennemy came to your house many Negroes deserted to them. This piece of news did not affect me much as I little value those concerns but you cannot conceive how unhappy I have been to hear that Mr. Lund Washington went on board the ennemy's vessels and consented to give them provisions. This being done by the gentleman who in some measure represents you at your house will certainly have a bad effect, and contrasts with spirited answers from some neighbours that had their houses burnt accordingly. You will do what you think proper about it, my dear General, but, as your friend, it was my duty *confidentially* to mention the circumstances.[10]

The actions of Lund Washington placed the general in an awkward position. On the one hand, he was undoubtedly relieved to learn that his house and property

9. Marquis de Chastellux, *Travels in North America in the Years 1780, 1781 and 1782*, 2:597.
10. Louis Gottschalk, ed., *The Letters of Lafayette to Washington, 1777–1799*, 187.

had been saved. On the other hand, he felt the sting of Lafayette's reprimand. Lund took the heat:

New Windsor, April 30, 1781.

Dear Lund:

Your letter of the 18th came to me by the last Post. I am very sorry to hear of your loss; I am a little sorry to hear of my own; but that which gives me most concern, is, that you should go on board the enemys Vessels, and furnish them with refreshments. It would have been a less painful circumstance to me, to have heard, that in consequence of your non-compliance with their request, they had burnt my House, and laid the Plantation in ruins. You ought to have considered yourself as my representative, and should have reflected on the bad example of communicating with the enemy, and making a voluntary offer of refreshments to them with a view to prevent a conflagration.

It was not in your power, I acknowledge, to prevent them from sending a flag on shore, and you did right to meet it; but you should, in the same instant that the business of it was unfolded, have declared, explicitly, that it was improper for you to yield to the request; after which, if they had proceeded to help themselves, *by force,* you could but have submitted . . . this was to be preferred to a feeble opposition which only serves as a pretext to burn and destroy.

I am thoroughly perswaded that you acted from your best judgment; and believe, that your desire to preserve my property, and rescue the buildings from impending danger, were your governing motives. But to go on board their Vessels; carry them refreshments; commune with a parcel of plundering Scoundrels, and request a favor by asking the surrender of my Negroes, was exceedingly ill-judged, and 'tis to be feared, will be unhappy in its consequences, as it will be a precedent for others, and may become a subject of animadversion.[11]

To the Marquis de Lafayette, Washington offered this apologetic explanation:

New Windsor, May 4, 1781.

My dear Marquis:

The freedom of your communications is an evidence to me of the sincerety of your attachment; and every fresh instance of this gives pleasure and adds strength to the band which unite us in friendship. In this light I view the intimation contained in your letter of the 23d. Ulto., from Alexandria, respecting the conduct of Mr. Lund Washington.

Some days previous to the receipt of your letter, which only came to my hands yesterday; I received an acct. of this transaction from the Gentn. himself, and immediately wrote, and forwarded, the answer of which the inclosed is a copy. this Letter, which was written in the moment of my obtaining the first intimation of the matter may be considered as a testimony of my disapprobatn. of his conduct; and the transmission of it to you as a proof of my friendship;

11. Fitzpatrick, ed., *Writings,* 22:14–15.

because I wish you to be assured that no man can condemn the measure more sincerely than I do.

A false idea, arising from the consideration of his being my Steward and in that character was more than the trustee and guardian of my property than the representative of my honor has misled his judgment and plunged him into error (upon the appearance of desertion in my Negros, and danger to my buildings) for sure I am, that no man is more firmly opposed to the enemy than he. From a thorough conviction of this, and of his integrity I entrusted every species of my property to his care; without reservation, or fear of his abusing it.

The last paragraph of my letter to him was occasioned by an expression of his fear, that all the Estates convenient to the river would be stripped of their Negros and moveable property.

I am very happy to find that desertion had ceased.[12]

Regarding the loss of his runaway slaves, Washington could console himself with a bit of good news, as indicated in a later notation by Lund: "Frederick, Frank, Gunner, Sambo, Thomas recovered in Philadelphia. Lucy, Esther were recovered after the siege of York [Yorktown]. The Genl. pd. salvage on Tom, in Philadelphia but I cannot tell what it was. I pd. 12 Dollars expence on him from Philadelphia here."[13] Washington did not abandon his attempts to recover the other Mount Vernon slaves who had chosen to depart with Captain Graves's raiding expedition, as a letter to Daniel Parker indicates:

> Head Quarters, April 28, 1783.
> Sir:
> Being informed by Colo Humphrey as well as by your Letter to me, that you have been induced to accept, for the present, the superintendence of the Embarkation from N York of the Tories and Refugees who are leaving the Country, and to prevent if possible, their carrying off any Negroes or other property of the Inhabitants of the United States; [and having seen Sir Guy Carleton Orders on this Head] I take the Liberty of inclosing to you a List and description of Negroes which has been sent me by Govr. Harrison of Virginia, and to beg that you will improve the Opportunity you will have, of obtaining and securing them agreeable to the Govr's Request, if they are to be found in the City. Your Endeavours will not only be very obliging to the Governor, but will be thankfully acknowledged by me.
>
> Some of my own slaves, [and those of Mr. Lund Washington who lives at my Ho] may probably be in N York but I am unable to give you their Descriptions; their Names being so easily changed, will be fruitless to give you. If by Chance you should come at the knowledge of any of them, I will be much obliged by your securing them, so that I may obtain them again. . . .

12. Ibid., 22:31–32.
13. Ibid., 22:14n.

[PS Since writing the above I have received a Letter from Mr. Lund Washington respecting *some* of his Negroes, a list of which with my own is herewith inclosed.][14]

Certainly, Washington wanted his slave property returned. But for what purpose? Three years earlier, he had shown the first signs of ambiguity with respect to his long-established practice of buying and selling slaves. Lund Washington's growing impatience with the general's lack of specific instructions is obvious in this letter:

Mount Vernon April 8th, 1778

Dr Sir,

Yours of March 29th by Genrl Woodford was deliver'd me on monday with regard to sellg the Negroes Mention'd you have put it out of my power, by saying you woud not sell them without their Consent—I was very near Sellg Bett, indeed I had sold her for 200£ to a man Liveg in Bottetourt Cty, But her Mother appeard to be so uneasy about it, and Bett herself made such promises of amendment, that I coud not Force her to go with the Man, to another Man at the same time I offord Phillis for £200, but she was so alarmed at the thoughts of being sold that the man cou'd not get her to utter a Word of English, therefore he believed she cou'd not speak—the man was to come two days after—when he came she was Sick & has been ever Since, so that I sold neither of them—those Negroes that come from Crawfords are now in the small Pox by Enoculation [Orford] got Frost Bit in comeg down, and it is not yet Well—so that unless I was to make a Publick Sale of those Negroes & pay no regard to their being Willing or not, I see no probability of sellg them—but this is a matter that may be fixd upon you.[15]

By September, Lund's irritation had reached the point that he virtually demanded a definitive answer from the proprietor:

Mount Vernon Septmbr 2d 1778

Dr Sir

. . . you again say you wish to get quit of negroes, before the rect [receipt] of this you will find that in a former Letter I have desired that you will tell me in plain terms, whether I shall sell your negroes at Publick sale or not, & how many of them & indeed who.[16]

While Lund Washington was pressing for answers, George Washington was equivocating. In a lengthy letter of August 15, 1778, which obviously crossed with Lund's of September 2, Washington again stated and restated his desire to be rid

14. Ibid., 26:364–65.
15. Letters of Lund Washington, Mount Vernon Library.
16. Ibid.

of slaves, but he did not spell out for his estate manager a detailed plan for the divestment of his slave property:

> I have premised these things to shew my inability, not my unwillingness, to purchase the Lands in my own Neck at (almost) any price, and this I am yet very desirous of doing if it could be accomplished by any means in my power, in the way of Barter for other Land; for Negroes (of whom I every day long more and more to get clear of). . . . If Negroes could be given in Exchange for this Land of Marshall's, or Sold at a proportionable price, I should prefer it. . . . For this Land also I had rather give Negroes, if Negroes would do, for to be plain I wish to get quit of Negroes.[17]

In a letter of February 24, 1779, Washington further refined his thinking, but he still left in abeyance any final decision on the eventual disposition of the Mount Vernon slaves:

> Middle Brook, February 24[–26], 1779.
>
> Dear Lund:
>
> I wrote to you by the last post, but in so hasty a manner as not to be so full and clear as the importance of the subject might require. In truth, I find myself at a loss to do it to my own satisfaction [even?] in this hour of more leisure and thought, because it is a matter of much importance and requires a good deal of judgment and foresight to time things in such a way as to answer the purposes I have in view.
>
> The advantages resulting from the sale of my negroes, I have very little doubt of; because, as I observed in my last, if we should ultimately prove unsuccessful . . . it would be a matter of very little consequence to me, whether my property is in Negroes, or loan office Certificates. . . . the only points therefore for me to consider, are, first, whether it would be most to my interest, in case of a fortunate determination of the present contest, to have negroes, and the Crops they will make; or the sum they will now fetch and the interest of the money. And, secondly, the critical moment to make this sale.
>
> With respect to the first point (if a negro man will sell at, or near one thousand pounds, and woman and children in proportion) I have not the smallest doubt on which side the balance, placed in the scale of interest, will preponderate: My scruples arise from a reluctance in offering these people at public vendue, and on account of the uncertainty of timeing the sale well. In the first case, if these poor wretches are to be held in a state of slavery, I do not see that a change of masters will render it more irksome, provided husband and wife, and Parents and children are not separated from each other, which is not my intentions to do. And with respect to the second, the judgment founded in a knowledge of circumstances, is the only criterion for determining when the tide of depreciation is at an end; . . . To hit this critical moment then, is the point; and a point of so much nicety, that the longer I reflect upon the subject, the more embarrassed I am in my opinion; for if a

---

17. Fitzpatrick, ed., *Writings,* 12:326–28.

sale takes place while the money is in a depreciating state, that is, before it has arrived at the lowest ebb of depreciation; I shall lose the difference, and if it is delayed, 'till some great and important event shall give a decisive turn in favor of our affairs, it may be too late. Notwithstanding, upon a full consideration of the whole matter; if you have done nothing in consequence of my last letter, I wou'd have you wait 'till you hear further from me on this subject. I will, in the meanwhile, revolve the matter in my mind more fully, and may possibly be better able to draw some more precise conclusions than at present, while you may be employed in endeavouring to ascertain the highest prices Negroes sell at, in different parts of the Country, where, and in what manner it would be best to sell them, when such a measure is adopted, (which I think will very likely happen in the course of a few months.)[18]

Whatever else George and Lund Washington may have written on the subject of the Mount Vernon slaves is unknown, for the surviving correspondence is incomplete. What is known is that when the general returned to Mount Vernon in 1783 and resumed control over his estate, he held fast, with only a few exceptions, to his oft-professed intention, which first found consistent expression in his wartime letters to Lund, to refuse to engage in further slave-trading activities. Although Washington was unwilling to take any meaningful steps to divest himself of his slave property, it may be fairly concluded that the seed of emancipation was initially planted in the turmoil of the war years.

18. Ibid., 14:147–49.

3

WASHINGTON AS SLAVE MANAGER

T HE WORK ethic reigned supreme at Mount Vernon, while humanity ran a distant second. On January 1, 1789, Washington wrote a lengthy set of instructions—titled "A View of the work at the several Plantations in the year 1789. and general directions for the Execution of it"—to John Fairfax, one of his overseers for the Mount Vernon farms: "To request that my people may be at their work as soon as it is light—work 'till it is dark—and be diligent while they are at it can hardly be necessary, because the propriety of it must strike every manager who attends to my interest, or regards his own Character—and who on reflection, must be convinced that lost labour can never be regained—the presumption being, that, every labourer (male or female) does as much in the 24 hours as their strength, without endangering their health, or constitution, will allow of."[1]

Washington set the example he expected others to follow. He was usually up and about before dawn: riding over his estate; planning, supervising, and directing the daily activities of his work crews; giving orders to his overseers and to his male and female laborers in their respective tasks; occasionally dismounting and personally lending a hand when necessary. In his own words: "I begin my diurnal course with the Sun; that if my hirelings are not in their places at that time I send them messages expressive of my sorrow for their indisposition; then having put these wheels in motion, I examine the state of things further . . . by the time I have accomplished these matters, breakfast (a little after seven Oclock . . .) is ready. This over, I mount my horse and ride round my farms, which employs me until it is time to dress for

---

1. *The Papers of George Washington: Presidential Series,* ed. W. W. Abbot and Dorothy Twohig, 1:223.

dinner."[2] His constant presence among his "people" was the essential ingredient of his success as a plantation manager. It seems that nothing of importance escaped his attention. Discipline and order prevailed, and his industry and acumen as an agriculturist and a businessman were generously rewarded. Mount Vernon grew into one of the largest and best-managed plantations in the Commonwealth of Virginia, and George Washington became a wealthy man, his status as a successful landed proprietor assured.

The Potomac river served as the lifeblood of the Mount Vernon estate. Up and down its slow-moving current traveled the sailing ships that linked Mount Vernon with the rest of the world. They carried tobacco and other farm products to ports as far away as England and as near as the Chesapeake Bay. On their return voyages, they brought the necessities and the luxuries that allowed the Washingtons to maintain their standard of living. In addition, the Potomac's bountiful supply of herring provided the Mount Vernon slaves with one of the main staples of their daily diet. Finally, the mansion that stood on the crest of a hill overlooking the broad river was laid out to take full advantage of the spectacular vistas as well as the refreshing cool breezes that blew in from the waterway during the hot steamy summer months. (*View of Mount Vernon*, woodcut by J. Weld, published December 18, 1798, by L. Stockdale, Piccadilly, England, courtesy of the Library of Congress, Washington, D.C.)

2. Washington to James McHenry, Mount Vernon, May 29, 1797 (Fitzpatrick, ed., *Writings*, 35:455).

A profitable and efficient plantation operation may have been Washington's top priority, but a close second was his ambition to achieve aesthetic perfection. Jean B. Lee points out,

> Washington set out to organize, harmonize, perfect, and beautify everything in sight. Ground for new fields had to be cleared, broken, and tilled; old fields needed improvement. No field was to present "a grievous eye-sore." "Let the hands at the Mansion House Grub well, and perfectly prepare the old clover lot," he ordered.
>
> "When I say grub well I mean that everything wch. is not to remain as trees should be taken up by the roots; so . . . that the Plow may meet with no interruption, and the field lye perfectly smooth for the Scythe. . . . I had rather have one Acre cleared in this manner, than four in the common mode."[3]

The white estate managers and overseers who helped Washington achieve these goals were also well taken care of. Most received free housing, subsistence, a guaranteed annual cash stipend, and a share of the crops or proceeds. These inducements were carefully spelled out in legally binding contracts. Other white artisans and trained professionals were paid according to the demand for their individual skills and were usually given similar written agreements. White indentured servants could look forward to their freedom at the end of specified periods of service.

With the exception of the black overseers and certain selected individuals, the slaves, who constituted the backbone of the labor force at Mount Vernon and who performed virtually all of the hard and menial chores as well as many of the semiskilled functions, were entitled to nothing more than food and a roof over their heads. A minimal clothes ration and a modicum of medical care for the seriously ill were the major fringe benefits. These African Americans thus had some semblance of cradle-to-grave security, but with one vital and significant exception: the proprietor had the sole and undisputed right to sell off his chattel property whenever it suited his purposes. Therefore, from the slave's point of view, the master's commitment was neither secure nor comforting. In fact, the implied or covert threat of being sold, particularly of being sent to the West Indies, was a very effective means for maintaining discipline among the slave population.

As a military man wedded to military systems and by nature a strict disciplinarian, Washington appreciated the necessity of keeping his slave labor force under tight control. The rigid protocol that distinguished the farming operations at Mount Vernon was the subject of a slightly whimsical commentary by Sen. William MacLay of Pennsylvania in a diary entry of May 1, 1799:

---

3. Jean B. Lee, "Laboring Hands and the Transformation of Mount Vernon Plantation, 1783–1799."

"The more I am acquainted with agricultural affairs the better I am pleased with them. Insomuch that I can find no where so great satisfaction, as in those innocent and useful pursuits" (Washington to Arthur Young, December 4, 1788). (Etching by Louis Conrad Rosenberg, copyright 1932 by the George Washington Memorial Association, Inc.)

It is under different overseers. Who may be stiled Generals—under Whom are Grades of Subordinate Appointments descending down thro Whites Mulattoes Negroes Horses Cows Sheep Hogs &ca. it was hinted that all were named. The Crops to be put into the different fields &ca. and the hands Horses Cattle &c. to be Used in Tillage pasturage &ca. are arranged in a Roster calculated for 10 Years. the Friday of every Week is appointed for the Overseers, or we will say Brigadier Generals to make up their returns. not a days Work, but is noted What, by Whom, and Where done, not a Cow calves or Ewe drops her lamb, but is registered. deaths &ca. Whether accidental or by the hands of the Butcher, all minuted. Thus the etiquette and arrangement of an army is preserved on his farm.[4]

Furthermore, Washington imparted this typically stern advice and warning to his Mount Vernon overseers:

4. Kenneth R. Bowling and Helen E. Veit, eds., *The Diary of William MacLay and Other Notes on Senate Debates*, 9:258.

Philadelphia, July 14, 1793

. . . Tho' last mentioned, it is not of the least importance; because the peace and good government of the negroes depend upon it, and not less so my interest and your own reputation. I do therefore in explicit terms enjoin it upon you to remain constantly at home (unless called off by unavoidable business or to attend Divine Worship) and to be constantly with your people when there. There is no other sure way of getting work well done and quietly by negroes; for when an Overlooker's back is turned the most of them will slight their work, or be idle altogether. In which case correction cannot retrieve either, but often produces evils which are worse than the disease. Nor is there any other mode but this to prevent thieving and other disorders, the consequence of opportunities.[5]

Washington was decidedly opinionated when writing about his slaves. The thousands of pages of his diaries, correspondence, and agricultural records include a seemingly unending litany of complaints, accusations, sarcastic remarks, and cynical observations with reference to his slave laborers. Betty Davis, who according to the 1799 inventory worked in the mansion, was a periodic target for abuse: "If pretended ailments, without apparent causes, or visible effects, will screen her from work, I shall get no service at all from her; for a more lazy, deceitful and impudent huzzy, is not to be found in the United States than she is." Of his carpenters he wrote: "if I have not formed a very erroneous, and unjust opinion of the conduct of my Negro Carpenters, there is not to be found so idle a set of Rascals. In short it appears to me, that to make even a chicken coob, would employ all of them a week; buildings that are run up here in two or three days (with not more hands) employ them a month, or more."[6]

A common subterfuge of the Mount Vernon slaves was to feign illness. Washington warned his manager William Pearce, in a letter dated January 12, 1794, not to be taken in by a notorious offender named Sam: "A fellow . . . who under pretense (for I believe this is the greatest part of his complaint) of an Asthmatical complaint never could be got to work more than half his time, has not done a days work since I left Mount Vernon in October. examine his case also, but not by the Doctor, for he has had Doctors enough already, of all colours and sexes, and to no effect. Laziness Is I believe his principal ailment."[7] Then there were those, like Peter, who took advantage of the master by riding his horses for their own pleasure and amusement. Washington expressed his annoyance at these antics in instructions to another estate manager, Anthony Whiting: "I have long suspected

---

5. "To the Overseers at Mount Vernon" (Fitzpatrick, ed., *Writings*, 33:11–12).

6. Washington to William Pearce, Philadelphia, March 8, 1795, February 22, 1794 (ibid., 34:135, 33:275).

7. Washington to Pearce, Philadelphia, January 12, 1794 (ibid., 33:242).

that Peter, under pretence of riding about the Plantations to look after the Mares, Mules, &ca:, is in pursuit of other objects; either of traffic or amusement, more advancive of his own pleasures than my benefit."[8]

Laziness, idleness, and malingering were only part of the problem; the other part was theft. Stealing was a major and enduring aggravation for Washington. By his own account, the thieving was a highly organized activity involving slaves, white servants, and even fences in Alexandria to handle the stolen goods, "for to be plain, Alexandria is such a recepticle for every thing that can be filched from the right owners, by either blacks or whites; and I have such an opinion of my Negros (two or three only excepted): and not much better of some of the Whites, that I am perfectly sure not a single thing that can be disposed of *at any price*, at that place, that will not, and is not, stolen, where it is possible; and carried thither to some of the underling shop keepers, who support themselves by this kind of traffick."[9]

It may fairly be concluded that nothing was sacred at Mount Vernon. Anything that could be sold or eaten was vulnerable. A primary target was the meat house, the contents of which were obviously too tempting to be left unprotected or unguarded: "I wish you could find out the thief who robbed the Meat house at Mount Vernon, and bring him to punishment. And at the sametime secure the house against future attempts. . . . Nathan has been suspected, if not detected, in an attempt of this sort formerly; and is as likely as any one to be guilty of it now. Postilion Joe has been caught in similar practices; and Sam, I am sure would not be restrain[ed] by any qualms of conscience, if he saw an opening to do the like." Equally tempting was an occasional glass or two of wine imbibed discreetly by the household help, who claimed that visitors drank it all, though the master suspected otherwise.[10]

The carpenters were not above suspicion of engaging in petty larceny, either. In a letter to Whiting on February 3, 1793, Washington told his manager to keep track of the twelve-penny nails: "I cannot conceive how it is possible that 6000 twelve penny nails could be used in the Corn house at River Plantn. but of one thing I have no great doubt and that is, if they can be applied to other uses, or converted into cash, rum, or other things, there will be no scruple in doing it." Whiting was also warned about Caroline, another of Washington's problem slaves: "It would, I conceive, have been better to have entrusted the cutting out of the Linnen to the Gardeners wife than to Caroline; who, was never celebrated for her honesty; and

8. Washington to Anthony Whiting, Philadelphia, December 30, 1792 (ibid., 32:279).
9. Washington to Pearce, Philadelphia, June 1, 1794 (ibid., 33:394–95).
10. Washington to Pearce, Philadelphia, June 7, 1795, and November 23, 1794 (ibid., 34:212, 42).

who, it is believed, would not be restrained by scruples of conscience, from taking a large toll, if she thought it could be done with impunity." And he was likewise cautioned to guard against theft by those who sheared the sheep.[11]

How to motivate people to work is a riddle as old as civilization. Motivating slaves is even more challenging. One solution depends on fear and an escalating system of punishments; another is based on a program of rewards and incentives. Washington relied on both techniques. Compulsion was exerted in the form of a series of steps, beginning with the gentle and leading to the drastic, that were to be applied in maintaining discipline and productivity. Although Washington much preferred an early and timely warning—"that they be prevented, as far as vigilance can accomplish it, all irregularities and improper conduct. And this oftentimes is easier to effect by watchfulness and admonition, than by severity; and certainly must be more agreeable to every feeling mind in the practice of them"—he was determined that "if the Negroes will not do their duty by fair means, they must be compelled to do it."[12]

When, for example, Muclus proved obstinate and immune to verbal prodding, Washington suggested that he be threatened with demotion to a less desirable job: "I wish you to tell Muclus, as from me, that if his pride is not a sufficient stimulus to excite him to industry, and admonition has no effect upon him, that I have directed you to have him severely punished and placed under one of the Overseers as a common hoe negro." When Charlotte misbehaved, Washington approved of Whiting's administration of some unspecified "correction" as suitable punishment: "Your treatment of Charlotte was very proper, and if She, or any other of the Servants will not do their duty by fair means, or are impertinent, correction (as the only alternative) must be administered."[13]

The word *correction* carried several different connotations in Washington's lexicon. It could mean demotion, as in the case of Muclus. It could also mean corporal punishment. In principle, Washington was opposed to the use of the lash. It was cruel and might result in permanent physical injury to a valuable slave. But occasionally, and generally only as a last resort, he relied on the whip as a necessary evil. There are a number of direct references to whipping in Washington's correspondence with his managers. For instance, he gave Pearce the following specific instructions: "I think Mr. [William] Stuart [the overseer at River Farm]

11. Washington to Whiting, Philadelphia, February 13, February 17, and June 2, 1793 (ibid., 34:327, 348, 483).

12. Washington to Whiting, Philadelphia, May 5, 1793 (ibid., 34:442–43); Washington to James Anderson, Philadelphia, February 20, 1797, Mount Vernon Library.

13. Washington to Whiting, Philadelphia, May 19 and January 20, 1793 (Fitzpatrick, ed., *Writings*, 32:463, 307).

ought to be informed if ever Folwers [Fowlers?] Ben comes on the Farm you are to give him a good whipping, and forbid his ever returning."[14]

Although Washington did not actively encourage whipping, he certainly countenanced it. At the same time, he recognized that certain overseers had to be watched carefully lest they resort too readily to flogging. In a letter to Pearce, Washington observed that Hyland Crow "is an active man, and not deficient in judgment. If kept strictly to his duty [he] would, in many respects, make a good Overseer. But I am much mistaken in his character, if he is not fond of visiting, and receiving visits. This, of course, withdraws his attention from his business, and leaves his people too much to themselves which produces idleness, or slight work on one side and flogging on the other; the last of which besides the dissatisfaction which it creates, has, in one or two instances been productive of serious consequences." Crow apparently had a mean and sadistic streak that Washington recognized. Indeed, in writing to Pearce about a runaway named Abram, he warned against leaving the slave's forthcoming punishment to Crow: "Let Abram get his deserts when taken, by way of example; but do not trust to Crow to give it [to] him; for I have reason to believe he is swayed more by passion than judgment in all his corrections."[15]

For the incorrigible offender there was reserved the ultimate fate, as outlined in a letter to Whiting:

> I am very sorry to hear that so likely a young fellow as Matildas Ben should addict himself to such courses as he is pursuing. If he should be guilty of any atrocious crime, that would affect his life he might be given up to the Civil authority for trial; but for such offences as most of his colour are guilty of, you had better try further correction; accompanied with admonition and advice. The two latter sometimes succeed when the first has failed. He, his father and mother (who I dare say are his receivers) may be told in explicit language that if a stop is not put to his rogueries, and other villainies by fair means and shortly; that I will ship him off (as I did Waggoner Jack) for the West Indias, where he will have no opportunity of playing such pranks as he is at present engaged in.[16]

From the beginning of the building of his Mount Vernon estate, Washington had in mind the upgrading of his slave labor force. As early as 1759, he included a clause in an agreement with John Askew, a white carpenter he had hired, obligating the artisan to "use his best endeavour's to instruct in the art of his trade any Negro

14. Washington to Pearce, Philadelphia, March 1, 1795 (ibid., 34:128).
15. Washington to Pearce, Philadelphia, December 18, 1793, and March 30, 1794 (ibid., 33:193, 309).
16. Washington to Whiting, Philadelphia, March 3, 1793 (ibid., 32:366).

or Negroes which the said George Washington shall cause to work with him during the twelve month." More often, skills were imparted by one slave to another, often at the master's insistence. For example, Washington instructed Whiting that "Doll at the Ferry must be taught to Knit, and *made* to do a sufficient days work of it. . . . Lame Peter if no body else will, must teach her, and she must be brought to the house for that purpose."[17]

In searching for a suitable young black to fill an opening as gardener, Washington reviewed for Pearce the qualifications of various prospective candidates for the position:

> Let Sam supply the place of Bristol, until I come home; unless (which does not occur to me at present) a likely and well disposed young fellow of mans growth, or near it, should be found on my estate fit to make a Gardener of. If one, not among the Dower Negros, could be selected, it would be preferred. Honesty, with some degree of acuteness, are desirable; but in whom amg. my people these are to be found, I know not. Sam has sense enough, and has had a little experience, but he wants honesty, and every other requisite; particularly industry. . . . The children of Daphne at the river farm are among the best disposed negros I have, but I do not recollect whether there be any of a fit size.[18]

He also took an interest in the selection of a competent and experienced midwife to look after the pregnant female slaves and their anticipated offspring:

> When I was at home, an application was made to me by Kate at Muddy hole (through her husband Will) to lay the Negro Women (as a Grany) on my estate; intimating that she was full as well qualified for this purpose as those into whose hands it was entrusted and to whom I was paying twelve or £15 a year; and why she should not be so I know not; but wish you to cause some enquiry to be made into this matter, and commit this business to her, if thereupon you shall be satisfied of her qualifications. This service, formerly, was always performed by a Negro woman belonging to the estate, but latterly, until now, none seemed disposed to undertake it.[19]

The most skilled jobs on the Mount Vernon plantation were ordinarily reserved for white men, but the next levels were almost always occupied by slaves. When he sought a "*first rate Miller*" for his flour mill, Washington specified in his correspondence with Oliver Evans, "There is moreover a smart young negro man who acts as an Assistant in the mill, in which business he has been employed for several years and of course may be calculated upon as understanding the common

---

17. "Indenture with John Askew," September 1, 1759 (*Papers: Colonial Series*, ed. Abbot and Twohig, 6:340); Washington to Whiting, Philadelphia, November 4, 1792 (Fitzpatrick, ed., *Writings*, 32:205).

18. Washington to Pearce, Philadelphia, March 15, 1795 (ibid., 34:145).

19. Washington to Pearce, Germantown, Pa., August 17, 1794 (ibid., 33:469).

and ordinary business of a mill."[20] The position of overseer was the highest post at Mount Vernon to which a slave could aspire. By the time of the February 1786 slave inventory, three of the five farms had slave overseers. According to Washington, Davy, the black overseer at Muddy Hole Farm, was equal in most respects to any of the white overseers: "Davy . . . carries on his business as well as the white Overseers, and with more quietness than any of them. With proper directions he will do very well and probably give you less trouble than any of them except in attending to his care of the stock of which I fear he is negligent as there are deaths too frequent among them." A diary entry for December 19, 1785, reveals that "Davy a Mulatto Man who has for many years looked after my Muddy hole Plantation, went into the Neck to take cha[rge] of the River Plantation in the room of Jno. Alton deceased. And Will (Son of Doll) was sent to Muddy hole as an Overseer in his place."[21]

In recognition of their deserving conduct, Washington's slave overseers received substantial quantities of pork. In December 1787, he noted in his diary:

> Killed the following Hogs to day.
>
> | | | | |
> |---|---|---|---|
> | From the Neck | 18 | weight | 1650 |
> | Ferry | 4 | Do. | 335 |
> | | | | *1985* |
>
> Disposed of them as follow
>
> | | |
> |---|---|
> | Thos. Bishop & T. Green | 800 |
> | Richd. B. Walker | 152 |
> | Overseer Morris | 300 |
> | Ditto at Frenchs | 300 |
> | Ditto Muddy hole | 228 |
> | Carpenter Isaac | 202 |
>
> 1982
>
> Overseer Da[v]y retained 3 of his Hogs agreeably to order.

The year before, Washington had recorded giving Morris, the overseer at Dogue Run, 45 pounds of pork; Davy, the overseer at River Farm, 55 pounds; Will, the overseer at Muddy Hole, 157 pounds; and Isaac, the overseer of the carpenters, 116 pounds. In addition to these extra rations, some of the slave overseers lived comfortably with their wives and children in small houses on their respective

---

20. Washington to Evans, Philadelphia, January 25, 1792 (ibid., 31:465). Evans (1755–1819) was an inventor and builder of mechanical machinery, including flour mills of advanced design. See *Dictionary of American Biography*, 5:208–9.

21. Washington to Pearce, Philadelphia, December 18, 1793 (ibid., 33:194); *Diaries*, ed. Jackson and Twohig, 4:252.

farms. Even though they were still legally Washington's chattel property and sub-ject to all of the constraints and restrictions of the slave system, they enjoyed other privileges and benefits. On special occasions, like horse races, when Washington felt particularly generous, he "Allowed all my People to go to the races in Alexandria on one of three days as best comported with their respective businesses—leaving careful persons on the Plantations."[22]

Irrespective of his personal opinion of his slaves, one thing was certain: if they were to be productive and hardworking, they had to be kept healthy and be rea-sonably well fed. These two overriding concerns absorbed much of Washington's time and energy and were crucial to his balance sheet, because they constituted by far the greatest portion of the expenses of supporting his slave population. Every week, without fail, whether he was in residence at Mount Vernon or away on business or pleasure, Washington received from each of his farm overseers a detailed report covering all aspects of their activities. The single most significant item in these reports was a breakdown of the tasks on which the male and female laborers were being used and exactly how much time had been committed to each job. In addition, Washington wanted to know who was sick or injured and therefore unable to work. Entries such as "Sambo sick with pain in his back 3,"[23] meaning that Sambo, because of his backache, had been unable to work for three days, appeared with monotonous regularity, varying only by name and symptoms.

While the weekly sickness and absenteeism reports often led to emotional outbursts in which Washington denounced the slaves for their idleness, laziness, malingering, deceit, and so on, a substantial number of the reported aches and pains were real and were serious enough to justify medical treatment. The record indicates that whenever he was convinced of the authenticity of symptoms, Washington tried to ensure that proper care was promptly forthcoming. He gave these specific instructions to Whiting:

> Although it is last mentioned, it is foremost in my thoughts, to desire [that] you will be particularly attentive to my Negros in their sickness; and to order every Overseer *positively* to be so likewise; for I am sorry to observe that the generality of them, view these poor creatures in scarcely any other light than they do a draught horse or Ox; neglecting them as much when they are unable to work; instead of comforting and nursing them when they lye on a sick bed. I lost more Negros last winter, than I had done in 12 or 15 years before, put them altogether. If their disorders are not common, and the mode of treating them plain, simple and well understood, send for Doctr. Craik in time. In the

22. *Diaries*, ed. Jackson and Twohig, 5:49, 86, 233.
23. Washington's farm ledger, September 22, 1798, Washington Papers, Alderman Library, Uni-versity of Virginia.

last stage of the complaint it is unavailing to do it. It is incurring an expence for nothing.

Washington later wrote further on the matter, offering Whiting the benefit of his insights along with some of his favorite nostrums:

> When I recommended care of and attention to, my Negros in sickness, it was that the first stage of, and the whole progress through the disorders with which they might be seized (if more than a slight indisposition) should be closely watched, and timely applications, and remedies be administered; especially in Pleurisies, and all inflammatory fevers accompanied with pain when a few days neglect, or want of bleeding, might render the ailment incurable. In such cases sweeten'd Teas, broths, and, (according to the nature of the complaint, and the Doctrs. prescription) sometimes a little Wine may be necessary to nourish and restore the patient; and these I am perfectly willing to allow when it is really requisite. My fear is, as I expressed to you in a former letter, that the under overseers are so unfeeling, in short viewing the Negros in no other light than as a better kind of Cattle, the moment they cease to work, they cease their care of them.[24]

Washington's diary entries from late January and early February 1760 illustrate his personal solicitude for the health of his slaves:

Monday Jany. 28th.

Found the new Negroe Cupid ill of a pleurisy at Dogue Run Quarter & had him brot. home in a Cart for better care of him.

Wednesday Jany. 30th.

Cupid was extreame Ill all this day and at Night when I went to Bed I thought him within a few hours of breathing his last.

Thursday Jany. 31st.

He was somewhat better. . . .

Sunday, Feby. 3d.

Breechy was laid up this Morning with pains in his breast & head attended with a fever.

Monday Feby. 4th.

Breechy's pains Increasd and he appeard extreamely ill all the day. In Suspense whither to send for Doctr. Laurie or not.

Visited my Plantations and found two Negroes sick at Williamson's Quarter viz. Greg and Lucy—ordered them to be Blooded.

Tuesday Feby. 5th.

Breechy's pains Increasg. & he appearing worse in other Respects inducd me to send for Dr. Laurie. . . .

Friday Feby. 8th. 1760.

Rode to my Plantatns. and ordered Lucy down to H[ome] House to be Physickd.[25]

24. Washington to Whiting, Philadelphia, October 24 and 28, 1792 (Fitzpatrick, ed., *Writings*, 32:184, 197).

25. *Diaries*, ed. Jackson and Twohig, 1:229–32, 235.

Smallpox was one of the dread diseases of the eighteenth century. It was highly infectious and often fatal. Washington himself had survived an attack of smallpox while in his teens that had the fortunate effect of giving him lifelong immunity. His own experiences had made him a fervent advocate of inoculation, and he saw to it that all of his people, including his slaves, were adequately protected. In a letter to John Augustine Washington dated June 1, 1777, he wrote: "I firmly believe, and my own People (not less I suppose than between two and three hundred) getting happily through it by following these directions is no inconsiderable proof of it. Surely that Impolitic Act, restraining Inoculation in Virginia, can never be continued. If I was a Member of that Assembly, I would rather move for a Law to compell the Masters of Families to inoculate every Childborn within a certain limited time under severe Penalties."[26] Smallpox was obviously a serious threat, for it could, if unchecked, wipe out overnight his entire slaveholdings. Before the procedure of inoculation had been fully brought into practice, Washington had had a taste of the disease's devastating effects:

> Sunday May 4th.
>   . . . Set out for Frederick to see my Negroes that lay Ill of the Small Pox. . . .
> Monday May 5th.
>   Reach'd Mr. Stephenson in Frederick abt. 4 Oclock just time enough to see Richd. Mounts Interrd. Here I was informd that Harry & Kit, the two first of my Negroes that took the Small Pox were Dead and Roger & Phillis the only two down with it were recovering from it.
> Thursday May 8th.
>   Got Blankets and every other requisite from Winchester & settld things upon the best footing I coud to prevt. the Small Pox from Spreading—and in case of its spreading for the care of the Negroes. Mr. Vale Crawford agreeing in case any more of the People at the lower Quarter getting it to take them home to his House—& if any of those at the upper Quarter gets it to have them removd into my Room and the Nurse sent for.[27]

Washington's genuine concern for the health of his slave "family" is frequently reflected in his correspondence. For example: "If proper care and attention has been paid to Cilla's child, it is all that humanity requires, whatever may be the consequences; these I would have bestowed on all." When tragic deaths did occur, Washington emphasized that the welfare of the slaves was the estate manager's responsibility and could not be left entirely in the hands of brutal overseers: "I am sorry to find by your last reports that there has been two deaths in the family since I left Mount Vernon; and one of them a young fellow. I hope every necessary

---

26. Washington to John Augustine Washington, Middle Brook, N.J., June 1, 1777 (Fitzpatrick, ed., *Writings,* 8:158).
27. *Diaries,* ed. Jackson and Twohig, 1:276–77.

care and attention was afforded him. I expect little of this from McKoy [Henry McKoy, overseer], or indeed from most of his class; for they seem to consider a Negro much in the same light as they do the brute beasts, on the farms; and often times treat them as inhumanly."[28]

The battle of wits between master and slave took place in several arenas. But the one where the slave stood the best chance of shirking his or her work was in playing sick. During his lifetime, Washington accumulated a large body of wisdom relating to the art of detecting phony illness claims. He advised Pearce: "I never wish my people to work when they are really sick, or unfit for it; on the contrary, that all necessary care should be taken of them when they are so; but if you do not examine into their complaints, they will lay by when no more ails them, than ails those, who stick to their business, and are not complaining, from the fatigue and drowsiness which they feel as the effect of night walking, and other practices which unfit them for the duties of the day."[29] Washington wrote more on the same subject in a later letter to Pearce:

> I observe what you say of Betcy Davis &ca. but I never found so much difficulty as you seem to apprehend, in distinguishing between *real* and *feigned* sickness; or when a person is *much* afflicted with pain. Nobody can be very sick without having a fever, nor will a fever or any other disorder continue long upon any one without reducing them: Pain also, if it be such as to yield entirely to its force, week after week, will appear by its effects; but my people (many of them) will lay up a month, at the end of which no visible change in their countenance, nor the loss of an oz of flesh, is discoverable; and their allowance of provision is going on as if nothing ailed them. There cannot, surely, be any *real* sickness under such circumstances as I have described; nor ought such people to be improperly endulged. It should be made one of the *primary* duties of every Overseer to attend closely, and particularly to those under his care who really are, or pretend to be, sick; to see that the first receive aid and comfort in time, and before it is too late to apply them; and that the others do not impose upon him.[30]

Time and again Washington warned his managers that the slaves would take advantage of them if they relaxed their guard. He urged them to be both skeptical and vigilant of any pretensions or excuses that were likely to be put forward: "Is there anything peculiar in the cases of Ruth, Hannah, and Pegg, that they have been returned sick for several weeks together? Ruth I know is extremely deceitful; she has been aiming for some time past to get into the house, exempt from work;

---

28. Washington to Whiting, Philadelphia, December 16, 1792; Washington to Pearce, Philadelphia, May 10, 1795 (Fitzpatrick, ed., *Writings*, 32:266, 34:193).
29. Washington to Pearce, Philadelphia, May 18, 1794 (ibid., 33:369).
30. Washington to Pearce, Philadelphia, March 22, 1795 (ibid., 34:153–54).

but if they are not made to do what their age and strength will enable them, it will be a very bad example to others, none of whom would work if by pretexts they can avoid it."[31]

There was one legitimate and credible complaint from his slaves that Washington tended to listen to and to act upon. That complaint concerned the quality and quantity of their food rations. Washington prided himself on being a competent and fair master. Providing his slaves with an adequate diet was an obligation he felt bound to honor. It was also, of course, in his own self-interest to do so. But just how much food was enough and what kind of food could be considered nourishing and acceptable were gray areas that could never be clearly defined to everyone's satisfaction. Washington outlined the pros and cons of this sensitive issue in a memorandum to Whiting:

> It is not my wish, or desire, that my Negros should have an oz of meal more, nor less, than is sufficient to feed them plentifully. This is what I have repeated to you over and over again; and if I am not much mistaken, requested you to consult the Overseers on this head, that enough, and no more than enough, might be allowed. . . . Formerly, every Working Negro used to receive a heaping and squeezed peck at top of unsifted meal; and all others (except sucking Children) had half a Peck, like measure, given to them; with which I presume they were satisfied, inasmuch as I never heard any complaint of their wanting more. Since the meal has been given to them sifted, and a struck peck only, of it, there has been eternal complaints; which I have suspected arose as much from the want of the husks to feed their fowls, as from any other cause, 'till Davy assured me that what his people received was not sufficient, and that to his certain knowledge several of them would often be without a mouthful for a day, and (if they did not eke it out) sometimes two days, before they were served again; whilst they (the negros) on the other hand assured me, most positively, that what I suspected, namely feeding their fowls with it, or sharing it with strange Negros, was not founded. Like complaints were made by the People at Dogue run and at Union farm; which altogether hurt my feelings too much to suffer this matter to go on without a remedy. Or at least a thorough investigation into the cause, and justice of their complaints; for to delay justice is to deny it. It became necessary therefore to examine into the foundation of the complaints, *at once,* and not to wait until a pretext should offer to increase the allowance. Justice wanted no pretext, nor would admit of delay. If the application for more was unjust no alteration *at all,* ought to have been made; for, as I at first observed, I am no more disposed to squander, than to stint; but surely the case is not so difficult but that the true and just quantity may be ascertained; which is all they have a right to ask, or I will allow them.[32]

31. Washington to Pearce, Philadelphia, July 27, 1794 (ibid., 33:447).
32. Washington to Whiting, Philadelphia, May 26, 1793 (ibid., 32:474–75).

Whatever the outcome of the bickering over quantities and quality, there never seemed to be any doubt in Washington's mind that his slaves deserved to be well fed:

> In looking over the last weekly report that has been forwarded to me, I perceive the allowance of Meal to Muddy hole is increased one peck; Union Farm, and River farm two pecks each, and Dogue Run Farm three Pecks: Whether this addition, with what goes to their absent hands is sufficient, I will not undertake to decide; but in most explicit language I desire they may have plenty; for I will not have my feelings again hurt with Complaints of this sort, nor lye under the imputation of starving my negros and thereby driving them to the necessity of thieving to supply the deficiency. . . . for if, instead of a peck they could eat a bushel of Meal a week fairly, and required it, I would not withhold or begrudge it [to] them.[33]

Washington's style of management changed relatively little over the approximately four decades he presided at Mount Vernon. As he gradually expanded his estate through the acquisition of land and slaves, he structured his holdings into five separate farm establishments. Each farm was a complete entity with its own overseer and work crews. The weekly farm reports from the overseers furnished him with the input he needed to manage his operations. By comparing the activities of the farms over a given time, Washington could, for example, judge their efficiency and productivity. He could also readily identify trouble spots and take prompt corrective action. He knew at a glance the exact status of his crops and livestock, and he was able to plan in advance the allocation of his laborers to meet his future consumption and marketing requirements. Washington has frequently been characterized as a scientific farmer. He deserves that reputation not only because of his prolific knowledge of crops, livestock, and land, but also because of the effective system of management that he successfully instituted at Mount Vernon.

As Stephen Innes has pointed out, Washington was a "true agricultural innovator." He had early on "abandoned tobacco culture and was growing corn, wheat, oats, and rye. He had also completed the transition to a much more mechanized agriculture. On the Mount Vernon complex, there were sufficient meadowland, straw, fodder, and other forage crops to feed as many draft animals as could be utilized. . . . Washington seldom used fewer than nine and, at peak periods, could keep as many as twenty-seven plows going simultaneously as well as several harrows, carts, and wagons." Innes has methodically analyzed the division of labor on the Mount Vernon estate.

33. Washington to Whiting, Philadelphia, April 28, 1793 (ibid., 32:437–38).

A list of slaves, which includes their occupation and residence in 1786, further clarifies the reasons for a particular division of labor in the fields. Washington kept twenty-eight of his adult male slaves at the home house, where most of them performed craftwork and domestic service. The males included waiting men, cooks, stablemen, stockkeepers, carpenters, smiths, a gardener, a carter, and a wagoner. In addition, a male miller and three coopers occupied and ran a nearby gristmill. There were only thirteen adult women at the home house, who were assigned to washing, spinning, sewing, and house service. On the four outlying quarters, all adults were agricultural laborers, except for three male overseers. (The wives of two of the three foremen were apparently exempted from field labor.) On each farm, women outnumbered men. A total of thirty-one male slaves worked the outlying farms, but forty-six "laboring women" carried out a substantial proportion of the agricultural tasks.[34]

The following tabulation given by Innes provides a detailed breakdown by gender, skills, and seasons of the year of the tasks performed by the slave laborers at Mount Vernon during 1786–1787:

MEN

Skills

overseer	shoemaker
sawyer	house servant
carpenter	ferryman
miller	carter/wagoner
cooper	brickmaker/bricklayer
blacksmith	gardener

Winter

work on millrace	work in new ground
dig ditches	frame barn
plow	make fagots
cut rails, posts, and timber	shell corn
cut firewood	cut straw
haul timber and grain	thresh wheat and rye
kill hogs	strip tobacco
help fill icehouse	make baskets and horse collars
maul rails	beat out hominy
make fences and livestock pens	tend stable
saw timber	tan leather
build roads	do odd jobs

Spring/Summer

plow	cradle at harvest of wheat and rye
harrow	roll grain fields

34. Stephen Innes, ed., *Work and Labor in Early America,* 178–79.

seine fish

sow carrots, cabbage, flax, barley,
  oats, wheat, and clover

weed peas

cut straw

cut brush and burn logs

tie and heap hemp

thresh wheat and clover seed

plant potatoes and jerusalem
  artichokes

make corn hills and weed corn

plant corn, pumpkins, and
  peas and replant these

bind at harvest

shock wheat and oats

gather basket splits and tan bark

cut and maul fence rails and posts

clean swamp

fill gullies

grub fields

dig ditches

make baskets and horse collars

cut hay and clover

cut corn stalks

cut firewood

shell corn

Fall

harvest corn and peas

plow

sow winter grain

harrow

thresh peas

make livestock pens and feed
  racks

WOMEN
Skills

milking

spinning

weaving

washing

ironing

cooking

doing scullery

being house servant

Winter

help at icehouse

cut and gather cornstalks

beat out hominy

hoe new ground

thin trees in swamp

clean out stable

heap dung

carry fence rails

grub swamp, woods, and
  meadow

husk and shell corn

burn brush

fill gullies

plow

kill and salt hogs

thresh wheat, rye, and clover
  seed

strip tobacco

pack fish

strip basket splits

make baskets

Spring/Summer

dig post holes

make fences

heap and burn trash

chop plowed ground

harrow

plow

prepare meadow for oats and
  timothy

make hills for sweet potatoes
  and plant them

weed pumpkins (old women
  and those with young children)

grub meadow
clear new grounds
load dung in carts
gather and spread fish offal
make holes for corn
make pumpkin hills
plant and replant melons
sow carrots
hoe corn ground
bind oats at harvest
stack wheat and rye at harvest
thresh wheat and clover seed
cut sprouts from tree stumps
    in fields
pile grass tussocks hoed
    out of weedy ground
hoe rough or wet ground plows
    can't touch

care for cattle
pick up apples
level ditches
chop after harrows
grub after plows
clean hedgerows
clean fields
fill gullies in fields
spread dung
hill for peas
plant corn
weed peas
plant cabbages
cut up cornstalks
shell corn

Fall

break and swingle flax
chop in flax
make livestock pens
cut down cornstalks
harvest corn

thresh rye, clover seed, peas,
    wheat, oats
dig carrots
clean oat and wheat seed
pile cornstalks

BOYS

weed peas
clear trash from fields
carry wheat at harvest
thresh wheat
assist tanners
help in stable
fence (with women's gang)
grub meadow (with women's
    gang)
fill gullies (with women's gang)

hoe around stumps
burn brush
help with carting
work on road
gather cornstalks
do odd jobs
make corn hills (with women's
    gang)
plant corn (with women's gang)

GIRLS

make hay
beat out hominy
burn brush
help with carting
make fences
bake bread
plow (age 14)
shell corn

secure grain at harvest
    (ages 16, 13, and 12)
thresh wheat
work on road
help in stable
get water for washing
tend sick children

CHILDREN

gather at harvest that   carry at harvest
    included children not taken
    out before[35]

Slaves in the feudal plantation system of eighteenth-century Virginia were relegated to the status of serfs, and there is no evidence that Washington ever regarded them as anything else. In virtually all of his extensive agricultural records, the Mount Vernon slaves appear as little more than economic units. Because a slave was looked upon as a valuable asset, and because Washington was a competent and conscientious bookkeeper, a great deal is known of the business transactions involving them: their market value; the cost of their upkeep; their diet and food requirements; their health and medical problems; their productivity; their supervision and discipline; their clothing allotments; their training and skills; their marital relationships; their births and deaths; and similar relevant data. Of their human side, however, next to nothing is known. Washington was only marginally interested in this aspect of slave life, and the Mount Vernon slaves themselves, being mostly illiterate, left no known written accounts of their individual identities, feelings, ambitions, and experiences. From their master's point of view (the only one available to the historian) their sole useful function was to work hard cultivating his plantation in order to generate a return on his investment. The female slaves, in addition to laboring alongside the men, were encouraged to procreate, thereby increasing the proprietor's slaveholdings. In his exploitation of slave labor, Washington was no different from his peers of the Southern slave-owning aristocracy.

Washington had few illusions about slave labor. While it was cheap and expendable, it was also inefficient and unreliable. He gave to a friend and correspondent in England, Arthur Young, this frank appraisal of the economics of the slave system as he knew it in 1792 and practiced it in Virginia:

> high wages is not the worst evil attending the hire of white men in this Country, for being accustomed to better fare than I believe the labourers of almost any other Country, adds considerably to the expence of employing them; whilst blacks, on the contrary, are cheaper; the common food of them (even when well treated) being bread, made of the Indian Corn, Butter milk, Fish (pickled herrings) frequently, and meat now and then; with a blanket for bedding: In addition to these, ground is often allowed them for gardening, and priviledge given them to raise dung-hill fowls for their own use. With the farmer who

35. Lois G. Carr and Lorena S. Walsh, "Economic Diversification and Labor Organization in the Chesapeake, 1650–1820," in ibid. 185–88. From *Diaries*, ed. Jackson and Twohig, 5:1–259; Journal of Work on Plantations, [1786]–1787, Washington Papers, Library of Congress.

has not more than two or three Negros, little difference is made in the manner of living between the master and the man; but far otherwise is the case with those who are owned in great numbers by the wealthy; who are not always as kind, and as attentive to their wants and usage as they ought to be; for by these, they are fed upon bread alone, which does not, on an average, cost more than seven dollars a head pr. Ann [annum] (about 32/. Sterling). . . . the cost of labour . . . may be said to vibrate with white men, between ten and fifteen pounds, and for black men between Eight and twelve pounds sterling pr. Ann, besides their board. . . . Blacks are capable of much labour, but having (I am speaking generally) no ambition to establish a *good* name, they are too regardless of a *bad* one; and of course, require more of the masters eye than the former.[36]

From the spring of 1759, when he brought his bride, Martha, to Mount Vernon, until the spring of 1775, when he left home to take command of the Continental army, Washington was his own estate manager and personally supervised and directed his labor force. Drawing on the information available in the weekly overseers' reports, Washington's agricultural records and account books, the tax lists, his diaries, and his correspondence, plus some interpretation and deductive reasoning, it can be reasonably concluded that Washington was successful in making slave labor work to his advantage and profit by: (1) requiring long, hard working hours; (2) maintaining close and constant personal supervision; (3) keeping overhead down by providing his slaves with the bare necessities for their health and welfare; (4) installing a system of punishments, ranging from verbal scolding to physical whipping, as a negative incentive; (5) instituting the program of weekly farm reports by his overseers that enabled him to effectively control and plan the farm chores assigned to the slaves; (6) purchasing slaves who possessed the specific skills needed on the estate; (7) ridding himself of the troublemakers, the laggards, and the surplus slaves by selling them on the market; (8) using the threat of being sold or shipped to the West Indies as an effective means of maintaining discipline and ensuring good behavior; (9) training and promoting those slaves who showed promise and ability as artisans and semiskilled laborers; and (10) recovering runaways and making examples of them in order to discourage others from attempting to flee.

The Revolutionary War kept Washington away from Mount Vernon for about nine years. In his absence, Lund Washington carried on the farming and business operations of the estate with a high degree of competence. The Revolution gave Washington his first taste of supervising Mount Vernon by mail and through a surrogate manager, and the arrangement worked well primarily because Lund

36. Washington to Arthur Young, Philadelphia, June 18, 1792 (Fitzpatrick, ed., *Writings*, 32:65–66).

was experienced and capable. The Revolution also introduced a new factor into Washington's life: he had, as a result of his successful military leadership, become a public figure sensitive to public opinion. This new influence manifested itself in his growing reluctance to sell any of his slaves and even perhaps his willingness to divest himself of his slave property. Upon his return to Mount Vernon in December 1783, Washington resumed his role as estate manager, but with one significant difference: he now had made a firm resolve never to sell another slave and a somewhat looser resolve not to purchase any more.

Washington barely had time to catch his breath before he was called to national duty for a second time. The eight presidential years brought more lengthy absences from Mount Vernon. This time Washington had to rely on a number of different estate managers to look after his affairs by proxy; once again he relied on the mails for communicating his orders and instructions. Washington's young nephew George Augustine Washington, whose health failed, had to be replaced as manager in the winter of 1791–1792. Anthony Whiting, his successor, "drank freely—kept bad company at my house and in Alexandria—and was a very debauched person";[37] he died in July 1793. Howell Lewis, also a relative, was in charge for several months until the arrival of William Pearce, who remained at Mount Vernon for three years and was succeeded in Washington's final years by James Anderson. The latter two managers proved eminently satisfactory to Washington, but the absence of his own strong hand and the frequent change of managers led to a degree of confusion among the Mount Vernon slave population. Their unrest was fueled as well by the abolitionist movement in the northern states, which spilled over into Virginia, and by the presence of Quaker agitators. There was also the awareness by the slaves that their master was no longer willing to place them on the auction block or to forcibly separate families. What had undoubtedly been intended by Washington as a kind and thoughtful gesture had the unforeseen consequence of making the slaves less amenable to discipline and disciplinary measures.

In his last two years in residence at Mount Vernon, from 1797 to 1799, it is clear that Washington had lost heart for the management of his estate. He was old and he was tired. He went through the motions but without his usual vigor and enthusiasm. He now wanted desperately to be rid of the burden of his slaves and live out his remaining years in relative ease and contentment. The challenges and pressures of supervising a large plantation with more than three hundred slave laborers held no further charms for him. The growing number of surplus and unproductive slaves, which he could not dispose of due to his self-imposed

37. Paul Wilstach, *Mount Vernon: Washington's Home and the Nation's Shrine,* 194.

restriction, raised the specter of bankruptcy. His faith in the future of the plantation slave system in the South had been deeply shaken by the rhetoric of freedom and his own reluctant acceptance of the principle of gradual emancipation. But it was not easy to shrug off the habits of a lifetime. Almost to the very end Washington was occupied with chasing runaways; denouncing the idleness, laziness, and deceit of his slaves; continually reviewing the weekly overseers' farm reports and noting his approval with an "Exd. GW" at the end of each summary; optimistically preparing a detailed and comprehensive program for the next year's crop plantings; and, of course, riding in his usual manner the well-worn circuit of his farms. Above all, even in old age, Washington had not lost his perfectionist vision of beauty, harmony, and order, as he had stated in a letter to Pearce in 1793: "I shall begrudge no reasonable expence that will contribute to the improvement and neatness of my Farms; for nothing pleases me better than to see them in good order, and every thing trim, handsome, and thriving about them; nor nothing hurts me more than to find them otherwise."[38]

The question is often asked, "What kind of a slavemaster was George Washington?" As is shown by the instructions he sent to his new estate managers on managing a slave labor force—describing techniques that he had developed and refined over a period of nearly four decades and that had proved to be both efficient and effective—Washington treated his slaves as well as was necessary in order to keep them disciplined and productive, but he was not concerned with their personal happiness. Even though he euphemistically referred to them as "my people" and "my family," the truth is that Washington had installed a patriarchal order at Mount Vernon in which his "people" were dutiful and deferential workers who had few privileges and no rights. Tobias Lear, his faithful secretary and confidant, who, as a well-educated and liberal-minded New Englander, never felt comfortable with slavery, put the best face on it when he wrote, "The negroes are not treated as blacks in general are in this Country, they are clothed and fed as well as any labouring people whatever and they are not subject to the lash of a domineering Overseer—*but still they are slaves.*"[39]

---

38. Washington to Pearce, Mount Vernon, October 6, 1793 (Fitzpatrick, ed., *Writings*, 33:111).
39. Stephen Decatur Jr., *Private Affairs of George Washington: From the Records and Accounts of Tobias Lear, Esquire, His Secretary,* 315.

4

Through the Eyes of Foreign Visitors

S OME OF the most interesting and informative descriptions of slave life at Mount Vernon are to be found in the diaries and memoirs of the foreigners who visited Washington's estate in the years following the Revolutionary War. Because there was no European equivalent of the plantation slave system as it existed in the American South in the eighteenth century, the institution tended to draw the particular attention of the curious travelers who had the privilege of staying at Mount Vernon as the guests of the Washingtons. The visitors were usually prominent men who carried letters of introduction from individuals who had known or had been associated with the general during the Revolution. Therefore, when they arrived at Mount Vernon, these visitors were not only assured of a warm welcome but had the unique opportunity of acquainting themselves with the wide scope of activities at the estate, with their proud and genial host as their personal guide. They also had the chance to engage in frank and open conversations with Washington on many subjects, ranging from politics to slavery.

One of the most noteworthy accounts is that of a Polish traveler invited by Washington to stay at Mount Vernon in the summer of 1798. Julian Ursyn Niemcewicz, who was descended from a long line of Polish nobility, had lived in America as an exile for about ten years. His public service career in Poland as a soldier, politician, educator, poet, pamphleteer, and statesman had been a distinguished one. He was also an intimate friend of Gen. Tadeusz Kósciuszko, a brilliant commander of artillery who had served with distinction under Washington. The impressions that Niemcewicz gathered during his ten-day sojourn at Mount Vernon were duly recorded in his diary. His perceptive observations about the Mount Vernon slaves are especially instructive:

Not counting women and children the Gl. has 300 Negroes of whom a large number belong to Mrs. Washington. Mr. Anderson [James Anderson, Washington's estate manager at the time] told me that there are only a hundred who work in the fields. They work all week, not having a single day for themselves except for holidays. One sees by that that the condition of our peasants is infinitely happier.

Blacks. We entered one of the huts of the Blacks, for one can not call them by the name of houses. They are more miserable than the most miserable of the cottages of our [Polish] peasants. The husband and wife sleep on a mean pallet, the children on the ground; a very bad fireplace, some utensils for cooking, but in the middle of this poverty some cups and a teapot. A boy of 15 was lying on the ground, sick, and in terrible convulsions. The Gl. had sent to Alexandria to fetch a doctor. A very small garden planted with vegetables was close by, with 5 or 6 hens, each one leading ten to fifteen chickens. It is the only comfort that is permitted them; for they may not keep either ducks, geese, or pigs. They sell the poultry in Alexandria and procure for themselves a few amenities. They allot them each *one pack* [peck], one gallon [*sic*] of maize per week; this makes one quart a day, and half as much for the children, with 20 herrings each per month. At harvest time those who work in the fields have salt meat; in addition, a jacket and a pair of homespun breeches per year. . . . Gl. Washington treats his slaves far more humanely than do his fellow citizens of Virginia. Most of these gentlemen give to their Blacks only bread, water and blows.

Either from habit, or from natural humor disposed to gaiety, I have never seen the Blacks sad. Last Sunday there were about thirty divided into two groups and playing at prisoner's base. There were jumps and gambols as if they had rested all week.[1]

Another guest at Mount Vernon was Count Luigi Castiglioni. The count, who had been born in Milan to an old and prominent Italian family, was devoted to the natural sciences, particularly botany. He arrived in America in the spring of 1785 and spent approximately two years touring the thirteen states and sections of Canada, making numerous scientific observations of the flora and fauna in the regions he traversed. He was also curious about the political and social institutions of the newborn republic. When the count returned to Milan, he transcribed his journal in the form of a running commentary entitled *Viaggio negli Stati Uniti* (Travels through the United States). Of his stay at Mount Vernon he wrote: "He [Washington] devoted much time to agriculture, employing a large number of Negroes who, under his supervision, scarcely knew that they were slaves. Washington had thus been able to cultivate his fields and to bring them to a flourishing state."[2]

1. Julian Ursyn Niemcewicz, *Under Their Vine and Fig Tree: Travels through America in 1797–1799, 1805 with Some Further Account of Life in New Jersey,* 101–2.

2. Taken from a translation of the original manuscript. See Howard R. Marraro, "Count Luigi Castiglioni: An Early Italian Traveller in Virginia, 1785–1786," 484.

Count Castiglioni also made note of the Virginia plantation system, referring to a piece in the March 1787 issue of *American Museum,* a magazine published in Philadelphia. The unsigned article attacked the lifestyle of the planter class, accusing many planters of being indolent and brutal while their slaves were treated worse than common beasts: "The author [Count Castiglioni] deplored the fact that this was partly true but he pointed out that there were planters like Washington, Jefferson and Madison who were very interested in the development of agriculture and in the welfare of the Negro."[3]

Another foreign traveler stopping over at Mount Vernon was Jacques Pierre Brissot de Warville, a French journalist, publisher, and politician. He was more blunt and outspoken in his opinions. Although he was inclined to agree with Castiglioni's overall conclusion that Washington was a kindhearted and benevolent slave owner, he had few illusions regarding the injustices inherent in the slave system. Brissot spent three full days at Mount Vernon as Washington's guest in November 1788. He incorporated his discussions with his host into a book, *Nouveau. Voyages dans les Etats-Unis* (New travels in the United States), which was first released in his native country in 1791. His portrayal of the Mount Vernon slaves and their master is colorful, flattering, and without doubt exaggerated:

> There are slaves in Virginia only because it is believed that they are necessary for raising tobacco. But this crop is decreasing every day in this state and will continue to decrease. The tobacco grown near the Ohio and Mississippi is infinitely more plentiful, of better quality, and requires less labor. When it finds an outlet to the European market, Virginians will be forced to abandon this crop and raise instead wheat, potatoes, and cattle. Intelligent Virginians are anticipating this change, and are beginning to grow wheat.
>
> Chief among them must be listed that astonishing man who, though a beloved general, had the courage to be a sincere republican and who is the only one not to remember his own glory, a hero whose unique destiny it will be to serve his country twice and to open for it the road to prosperity after having set it on the road to liberty.
>
> Now *wholly* occupied with improving his land, developing new crops, and building roads, he is giving to his fellow citizens a useful example which will no doubt be followed. Nevertheless, he does own, I am forced to say, large numbers of Negro slaves. They are, however, most humanely treated. Well fed, well clothed, and required to do only a moderate amount of work, they continually bless the master God gave them.[4]

Conditions had changed materially by April 1797, when Washington played host to three royal adventurers from France. Based on what they saw and heard, these young Frenchmen were not so sanguine as Brissot de Warville about the

---

3. Ibid., 490–91.
4. Jacques Pierre Brissot de Warville, *New Travels in the United States of America, 1788,* 237–38.

happiness of the Mount Vernon slaves. Louis-Philippe, the Duc d'Orléans and a future king of France (1830–1848), was twenty-four years old when he came to America, accompanied by his two younger brothers, the Duc de Montpensier and the Comte Beaujolais, and their manservant, Beaudoin. After their father fell victim to the revolutionaries in Paris and was summarily guillotined by the radical mob, it was discreetly arranged for the three sons to take a long trip away from their strife-torn country until the turmoil of the French Revolution had subsided and order had been restored. America was their chosen destination and Mount Vernon one of their first stops during a two-year exile that included an extensive tour of the North American continent and parts of the Caribbean.

Louis-Philippe kept a log of his experiences and reflections. Judging by the relatively lengthy entries on the subject, Washington's slaves were a prime topic of interest during the five-day stopover at Mount Vernon. In one entry, the inquisitive Frenchman thoughtfully analyzed the future of the institution of slavery in the United States:

> The general owns ten thousand acres of land around Mount Vernon. Hardly half of it is under cultivation. There are about 400 blacks scattered among the different farms. These unfortunates reproduce freely and their number is increasing. I have been thinking that to accomplish their emancipation gradually and without upheaval it might be possible to grant them first a status in mortmain by depriving their owners of the right to sell them. Virginia law imposes the same punishment on a master who kills a slave as on any other murderer, but the law is very rarely applied; as slaves are denied by statute the right to bear witness, the charge is never proved. General Washington has forbidden the use of the whip on his blacks, but unfortunately his example has been little emulated. Here Negroes are not considered human beings. When they meet a white man, they greet him from a distance and with a low bow, and they often seem amazed that we return their greeting, for no one here does so. All agricultural labor in Virginia is performed by blacks, who on the various farms are housed in wretched wooden shacks here called *quarters.* Usually these shacks swarm with pickaninnies in rags that our own beggars would scorn to wear. So why should we be surprised if the blacks are lazy, when their labor never profits them? On the contrary, it profits those whom they must naturally hate.
>
> The last census in Virginia showed 770,000 inhabitants. It is estimated that some three-fourths of them are blacks. This ratio is terrifying, and will sooner or later prove deadly to the southern states. Ideas of freedom have already made headway among them; apparently Quakers, Anabaptists, and Methodists circulate the doctrine. The general's blacks told Beaudoin that they had clubs in Alexandria and Georgetown, that Quakers came to visit, and that they hoped they would no longer be slaves in ten years. . . . The general's house servants are mulattoes, some of whom have kinky hair still but skin as light as ours. I noticed one small boy whose hair and skin were

so like our own that if I had not been told, I should never have suspected his ancestry. He is nevertheless a slave for the rest of his life.[5]

Richard Parkinson, a middle-aged English farmer from Lincolnshire who decided to discover the rewards that the New World might offer to an enterprising man of the soil, landed at Norfolk, Virginia, in November 1798 fortified with hard cash, an assortment of valuable breeding stock, and credentials, including published books, as an agricultural expert. His original intention had been to enter into an agreement to lease one of Washington's Mount Vernon farms. Parkinson had already corresponded with Washington on this proposed arrangement, and though his scheduled arrival was surrounded by a degree of confusion, he was, in due course, warmly welcomed at Mount Vernon by the general.

To the surprise of almost everyone, however, Parkinson did not like what he saw, and he minced no words in saying so. The land was poor and worn out; the crops were meager; the animals were substandard; and so on. An astonished Washington was given an earful by this uninhibited and opinionated Englishman. Yet there was probably more truth in Parkinson's blunt appraisal of Washington's farming operations than the general may have cared to admit. Washington was now an old man with less than a year to live, and Mount Vernon reflected his declining vigor. Furthermore, the cumulative effects of his long absences in the public service, the growing restlessness among the slave population, and the difficulty in finding competent help had all taken their toll on the productivity of the Mount Vernon farms. Still, few men had dared to be as bold and as forthright as Parkinson was in criticizing to his face the sensitive general's beloved estate.

Parkinson did not go through with the deal to lease Washington's land. Instead, he moved on and for a year or so farmed rented acreage near Baltimore. But he remained on good terms with Washington and would occasionally call on him at Mount Vernon. He later wrote, "His behaviour to me was such, that I shall ever revere his name." When Parkinson returned to England at the turn of the century, disappointed and disillusioned with his exposure to the American culture and way of life, he set down in a two-volume book, *A Tour in America in 1798, 1799, and 1800,* his detailed notes describing his experiences. Parkinson's conclusions were devastatingly critical of American farming methods and practices. Furthermore, he expressed an intense dislike of the United States and its people.

The irascible Englishman did not approve of slavery, but neither did he have any use for African Americans: "They are so lazy by nature." This mind-set clearly influenced his assessment of the strict disciplinary measures Washington

5. Louis-Philippe, *Diary of My Travels in America, Louis-Philippe, King of France, 1830–1848,* 31–35.

exercised over his slaves: "The management of negroes was a great obstacle: for, notwithstanding the great inhumanity so generally spoken of by those who are not acquainted with them, they will not do without harsh treatment. Only take General Washington for an example: I have not the least reason to think it was his desire, but the necessity of the case: but it was the sense of all his neighbours that he treated them with more severity than any other man." Parkinson was puzzled by, and had no plausible explanation for, the tough language and the scolding tone he said Washington employed when giving orders to his slave laborers: "The first time I walked with General Washington among his negroes, when he spoke to them, he amazed me by the utterance of his words. He spoke as differently as if he had been quite another man, or had been in anger."[6]

The reasons Mount Vernon had been for so many years such a well-managed plantation did not escape Parkinson's shrewd and practiced eye: "I think a large number of negroes to require as severe discipline as a company of soldiers: and that may be one and the great cause why General Washington managed his negroes better than any other man, he being brought up to the army, and by nature industrious beyond any description, and in regularity the same." Another point in Washington's favor was that he was a very careful and prudent manager, especially as it concerned the feeding and clothing of his slaves: "He regularly delivered weekly to every working negro two or three pounds of pork, and some salt herrings, often badly cured, and a small portion of Indian corn." "General Washington weighed the food for all his negroes young and old; and as he was a man of minute calculation, he probably knew what they cost, to a fraction. It is said that he never clothed them until they were of a certain age."[7]

Nevertheless, the system of Virginia slave labor that Parkinson saw functioning at Mount Vernon during Washington's final year did not make economic sense to him. He had difficulty comprehending how Washington's inefficient farms were adequate to support and maintain his large and chiefly unproductive slave establishment:

> It is a paradox to me to conceive how they can be profitable to the owner. Observe, General Washington's number at Mount Vernon was four hundred—men, women, and children; and out of that number only seventy were able to work. And although the General was said both to feed and clothe them in a more scanty manner than any other man, I do not know how it was effected in that poor barren soil; nor could it be done at all but from the herring fishery adjoining to his estate in the Potowmac, which is the greatest part of their

6. Richard Parkinson, *A Tour in America in 1798, 1799, and 1800,* 2:440, 418–20.
7. Ibid., 436, 419, 454.

food, with bread of Indian corn, of which they are the best of cultivators, as it requires the use of the hoe.[8]

If Parkinson had met Washington and seen Mount Vernon at an earlier and brighter period, before the inevitable aging process and the demands and responsibilities of further years of public service had taken their considerable toll, he would undoubtedly have told a different story. Robert Hunter Jr., an English merchant, stopped overnight at Mount Vernon in November 1785, almost thirteen years prior to Parkinson's arrival in America, and recorded in his journal this glowing picture of vitality and enterprise:

> *Mount Vernon*, Thursday, November 17
> I rose early and took a walk about the General's grounds, which are really beautifully laid out. He has about 4,000 acres, well cultivated, and superintends the whole himself. Indeed, his greatest pride now is to be thought the first farmer in America. He is quite a Cincinnatus, and often works with his men himself: strips off his coat and labors like a common man.
> The General has a great turn for mechanics. It's astonishing with what niceness he directs everything in the building way, condescending even to measure the things himself, that all may be perfectly uniform. . . .
> He is one of the most regular men in the world. When no particular company is at his house, he goes to bed always at nine, and gets up with the sun. . . .
> [William] Shaw [his secretary] tells me he keeps as regular books as any merchant whatever—and a daily journal of all his transactions. . . .
> It's astonishing what a number of small houses the General has upon his estate for his different workmen and Negroes to live in. He has everything within himself—carpenters, bricklayers, brewers, blacksmiths, bakers, etc. etc.—and even has a well-assorted store for the use of his family and servants. . . .
> The General has some hundreds of Negroes on his plantations. He chiefly grows Indian corn, wheat, and tobacco. . . .
> I fancy he is worth £100,000 sterling, and lives at the rate of three or four thousand a year—always keeping a genteel table for strangers that almost daily visit him, as a thing of course.[9]

These six contemporary eyewitness accounts of Mount Vernon that mention slaves and slavery, written at different times by men from different walks of life with different temperaments, values, and prejudices, constitute the only available body of writings from which to try to build an accurate outsider's portrait of slavery at Mount Vernon. There are, of course, other contemporary eyewitness accounts by visitors to Mount Vernon, but none are so explicit or so informative on the subject of slaves as the ones quoted above. Despite their sketchy, fragmented,

8. Ibid., 447–48.
9. Quoted in Mount Vernon Ladies' Association of the Union, *Annual Report*, 21–26.

and often contradictory nature, as a whole they leave the distinct impression that George Washington was a very hard taskmaster and that the living conditions and the daily routine of the average Mount Vernon slave can at best be described as a borderline existence.

5

MISTRESS OF THE MANSION

THE MANSION was virtually the exclusive domain of Martha Washington. From the day she arrived at Mount Vernon in the summer of 1759, she took charge of the household and the domestic affairs of the Washington estate. It was one of the blessings of the Washingtons' marriage that she was an excellent manager who kept the complex and varied activities of the mansion functioning in a smooth and orderly fashion. Susan G. Detweiler notes in *George Washington's Chinaware*, "Mrs. Washington's knowledge of the domestic arts was learned at the home of her parents in New Kent County, Virginia. She was the eldest of eight children and doubtless shared some responsibility for the care of younger siblings in a household which was only moderately affluent. When she married Daniel Parke Custis at the age of eighteen, she became the mistress of a home that reflected her husband's position as a member of a prosperous and influential Virginia family." Slaves were a natural part of her life and surroundings, and she relied upon them to perform under her supervision the myriad household chores: "As part of her dower she had brought one hundred and fifty slaves. These, with those already on the estate, came under her particular care. Those not destined to become field hands had to be taught to spin and weave, to knit and sew, to cook and serve. All this the lady of Mount Vernon supervised and directed."[1]

Detweiler offers a more precise description of the composition of the household staff in her prologue:

1. Susan G. Detweiler, *George Washington's Chinaware*, 13; Marie Kimball, *The Martha Washington Cook Book*, 17.

When George Washington brought his bride to Mount Vernon in the spring of 1759, one of their first joint tasks was to arrange for Martha's household help. They chose eleven slaves to take care of her domestic chores and look after her two small children. Martha was apparently as well organized as her husband and handled her staff with skill and efficiency. From all accounts, she was a kind and thoughtful mistress who treated her slaves humanely. However, when they showed signs of laziness, produced slovenly work, stole, or otherwise misbehaved, she called on her husband to enforce discipline. (Courtesy of the Mount Vernon Library)

Martha ran her large and busy household with about a dozen servants who came with her at the time of her marriage and later intermarried with the slave population at Mount Vernon. In 1759, her household staff numbered eleven: one full-time and one part-time waiter; two women in the kitchen who served as cook and scullion; two women who did the washing and ironing; and one seamstress who worked on the sewing and mending. Mrs. Washington and her two children had personal servants and her husband a body servant. Twenty-seven years later, she continued to manage with the same number; however, by 1786 men had taken on the cooking. On the shoulders of the temperamental Hercules and his assistant Nathan fell the responsibility of preparing the food; Frank and Austin were full-time waiters; three women were now required to do the sewing; two housemaids and two washers completed the list.[2]

Martha Washington, by all accounts, was a gentle, refined, and considerate person. She deferred to her husband on matters of discipline, where harsh words and threatening gestures were at times thought necessary. For instance, in a letter from Philadelphia dated December 23, 1792, Washington took up with his estate manager, Whiting, this complaint about the laxness of the sewers: "It is observed, by the Weekly reports, that the Sewers make only Six shirts a week, and the last

2. Detweiler, *Chinaware*, 13–14.

week Caroline (without being sick) made only five; Mrs. Washington says their usual task was to make nine with Shoulder straps, and good sewing; tell them therefore from me, that what *has* been done, *shall* be done by fair or foul means; and they had better make choice of the first, for their own reputation, and for the sake of peace and quietness. otherwise they will be sent to the several Plantations, and be placed as common laborers under the Overseers thereat."[3]

As in all forms of organized society, the Mount Vernon slaves had established their own hierarchy. At the top of the order stood the household servants, most of whom, by design or otherwise, were mulattoes. They were the ones who were daily in close physical proximity to the center of power, and they enjoyed the many prerogatives that flowed from this association. They wore fine clothes; partook of the best food and drink; worked amid luxurious surroundings; occasionally were chosen to accompany the master and/or mistress on their travels; rubbed shoulders with the elite company that came to visit the general and his family, from whom they frequently received generous tips; shared in the prestige that radiated from Washington's military and political accomplishments; and were treated with far greater consideration and respect than the ordinary field hands.

Much of the activity in the mansion of course revolved around the diminutive figure of Martha Washington.

> Washington Custis remembered his grandmother's "admirable manage-ment of her servants and household, going through every department before or immediately after breakfast. . . . her young female servants were gathered in her apartment to sew under her own supervision and they became beautiful seamstresses. . . . bad bread was a thing entirely unknown at Mount Vernon; that too was mixed every night under the eyes of the mistress. Immediately after breakfast Mrs. Washington gave orders for dinner appointing certain provisions, a pr of ducks, a goose or a turkey to be laid by, to be put down in case of the arrival of company; a very necessary provision in that hospitable mansion."[4]

Another picture of Martha Washington at home is presented in a letter written around the turn of the century by Mrs. Edward Carrington to her sister: "Let us repair to the old Lady's room, . . . which is precisely in the style of our good old Aunts—that is to say, nicely fixed for all sorts of work. On one side sits the chambermaid with her knitting; on the other a little colored pet learning to sew. An old decent woman is there with her table and shears cutting out the negroes' winter clothes, while the good old lady directs them all, incessantly knitting herself."[5]

3. Fitzpatrick, ed., *Writings*, 32:277.
4. Detweiler, *Chinaware*, 14.
5. Benson J. Lossing, *Mary and Martha: The Mother and the Wife of George Washington*, 314.

The image of an idyllic family existence unfortunately had a darker side. Two of the most prized of the mansion personnel, Hercules, the chief cook, and Oney Judge, a bright young seamstress, ran away to freedom when they had the opportunity. Martha Washington wrote to her sister, Elizabeth Dandridge Henley, on August 20, 1797, venting her frustrations: "am obliged to be my one [own] Housekeeper which takes up the greatest part of my time,—our cook Hercules went away so that I am as much at a loss for a cook as for a house keeper.— altogether I am sadly plaiged." And Washington had this to say about Oney Judge: "She has been the particular attendant on Mrs. Washington since she was ten years old; and was handy and useful to her being perfect Mistress of her needle. . . . the ingratitude of the girl, who was brought up and treated more like a child than a Servant (and Mrs. Washington's desire to recover her) ought not to escape with impunity."[6]

Regrettably for the historical record, Martha Washington chose to destroy virtually all of her personal correspondence with her husband before her death,[7] leaving a large void, particularly in the area of domestic affairs. Only her extensive correspondence with relatives and friends remains for posterity, and much of that is concerned solely with mundane family matters. However, in a surviving note to Elizabeth Powel describing some of the household duties and responsibilities of the mansion personnel, Martha identifies closely with her husband's views on the deficiencies and generally negative qualities of the Mount Vernon slaves.

Mount Vernon 20th May 1797

My Dear Madam

Your polite and affectionate letter of the 9th instant I have been duly honoured with, and thank you sincerely for the assurances you have given me of continuing your enquiries for such a servant as you conceive will answer my purposes.—

The qualities you enumerate and describe, are exactly such as would answer these purposes; and fortunate indeed should I think myself if they could be obtained—

Drudgery duties either in the Kitchen or house would not be required of him—To superintend boath and make others perform the duties allotted them is all that would be asked of him unless *unusual* occations should call for particular exertions (which is not likely to happen)—

6. Joseph E. Fields, comp., *"Worthy Partner": The Papers of Martha Washington,* 307; George Washington to Oliver Wolcott Jr., Philadelphia, September 1, 1796 (Fitzpatrick, ed., *Writings,* 35: 201–2).

7. "Destruction and dispersal of the papers began very early when Mrs. Washington reportedly burned all the correspondence she had exchanged with Washington during his lifetime—overlooking only two letters, we believe" (*Diaries,* ed. Jackson and Twohig, 1:xlii).

There are always two persons, a man and woman, in the Kitchen; and servants enough in the house for all needful purposes—These require Instructions in some cases, and looking after in all—To be trust worthy—careful of what is committed to him—sober and attentive, are essential requisits in any large family, but more so among blacks—many of whom will impose when they can do it.[8]

Martha Washington, it seems, also shared her husband's deep-seated racial prejudices. Writing to her niece Fanny Bassett Washington from Philadelphia on May 24, 1795, she observed, "Black children are liable to so many accidents and complaints that one is heardly sure of keeping them I hope you will not find in him much loss the Blacks are so bad in thair nature that they have not the least gratatude for the kindness that may be shewed to them."[9]

Martha Washington's lifelong interests centered on her husband and on her immediate family. Domestic tranquillity was her foremost concern. Slaves had always been an integral part of her household, and she expected everyone there to be obedient and diligent in the performance of their chores. In return for their loyal services, they were reasonably well treated and looked after. But this tightly knit, inward-looking world of the mansion over which Martha Washington presided would fall apart in the end. When Oney Judge ran off to marry her lover in New Hampshire, and Hercules absconded to find happiness with his convivial companions in Philadelphia, these were harbingers of what lay ahead. Once Washington had passed from the scene in December 1799 and his firm and authoritative hand was no longer present to enforce the discipline so essential in managing a slave plantation, the effects of his absence quickly became apparent.

Not only did the Mount Vernon slaves grow increasingly restless and difficult to manage—particularly those who had belonged to the proprietor and knew that by the terms of his will they would gain their full freedom upon the death of his aging widow—other factors as well were beyond her control. James Anderson— the estate manager hired by the general in October 1796—resigned. He cited these reasons for leaving in his letter to Martha Washington dated July 21, 1800.

Madam
    Ever since I had a Management of this Estate (I am sorry to say) it has been very unproductive.
    This spring past, the prospect was a little flattering. But from the attacks of the Fly, and Rust, the crop of wheat will be very poor, and that crop is all the Dependence. . . .

8. Fields, comp., *"Worthy Partner,"* 302.
9. Ibid., 287.

> And being fully convinced that the sales (after rendering to the House at
> Mount Vernon the articles wanted for consumption there) will not nearly
> Ballance the expence that I must confess I feel hurt. And think it my Duty to
> resign. And do hereby beg leave to inform that on the last of December next,
> I shall retire from the management of this Estate of Mount Vernon.[10]

In spite of the many vicissitudes, Martha Washington—until her closing days—continued to be deeply involved and emotionally committed to the welfare of her Mount Vernon family—black and white. For example, she wrote to Mary Stillson Lear on November 11, 1800: "we have had an uncommon sickly autumn; all my family whites, and Blacks, have been very sick, many of ill—thank god they have all recovered again and I was so fortunate as not to loose any of them."[11]

Martha Washington soon joined her husband and was laid peacefully to rest alongside him in their common burial vault. Today, the mansion stands as an honored monument to its illustrious owners. But the picture of the master and mistress presiding over the ancestral home is not complete without taking into account the role of the slaves. These humble servants have long since been buried and forgotten. However, their essential contributions in providing physical comforts and thus helping make possible the luxury, elegance, style, charm, and hospitality that were the pride of the Washington household deserve at least a nod of recognition and certainly a place in the history of Mount Vernon.

10. Ibid., 391.
11. Ibid., 394.

6

S L A V E   V I G N E T T E S

T H E   M O S T   distressing accounts of slavery at Mount Vernon are the early ones that depict Washington as a callous buyer and seller of slave property. A cover letter that he wrote to Capt. Joseph Thompson of the schooner *Swift*, dispatching a rebellious and unruly field hand to the West Indies—a common practice of the time since the West Indies sugar plantations, mainly run by the British and the French, were notorious for their harsh discipline of nonconforming and troublesome blacks—portrays a man singularly preoccupied with efficiency and sharp trading and wholly indifferent to any human sentiments.

> Sir,   Mount Vernon July 2d 1766.
> With this Letter comes a Negro (Tom) which I beg the favour of you to sell, in any of the Islands you may go to, for whatever he will fetch, & bring me in return for him
> One Hhd of best Molasses
> One Ditto of best Rum
> One Barrl of Lymes—if good & Cheap
> One Pot of Tamarinds—contg about 10 lbs.
> Two small Do of mixed Sweetmeats—abt 5 lb. each
> And the residue, much or little, in good old Spirits
> That this Fellow is both a Rogue & Runaway (tho. he was by no means remarkable for the former, and never practised the latter till of late) I shall not pretend to deny—But that he is exceeding healthy, strong, and good at the Hoe, the whole neighbourhood can testifie & particularly Mr Johnson and his Son, who have both had him under them as foreman of the gang; which gives me reason to hope he may, with your good management, sell well, if kept clean & trim'd up a little when offerd to Sale.
> I shall very chearfully allow you the customary Commissions on this affair, and must beg the favour of you (least he shoud attempt his escape) to keep

A strict code of discipline governed the lives of the Mount Vernon slaves. The harshest measure—and the one most dreaded by the blacks—was to be sold or traded to the West Indies. Few slaves survived for very long the tropical climate, the endemic diseases, and the cruel and inhumane treatment that they received at the hands of the overseers on the sugar plantations. All of this was of little concern to George Washington in 1766 when he decided to ship off Tom, who was apparently a notorious and incorrigible troublemaker. Washington was clearly relieved to be rid of him while at the same time gaining some tasty delicacies for his dinner table. Furthermore, he felt it was in his best interests to make an example of Tom. By instilling among his laborers the fear of this severe punishment, he helped to maintain the demanding work routine that was always his first priority. (Courtesy Library of Congress, Washington, D.C.)

him handcuffd till you get to Sea—or in the Bay—after which I doubt not but you may make him very useful to you.

I wish you a pleasant and prosperous Passage, and a safe & speedy return, being Sir, Yr Very Hble Servt

Go: Washington[1]

Washington's slave-trading activities continued uninterrupted almost to the outbreak of the Revolutionary War. Two further vignettes from his correspondence illustrate his apparent indifference to the human degradation and suffering caused by such cruel bargaining in the marketplace for men, women, and children. The first example comes in a letter addressed to Daniel Jenifer Adams:

1. *Papers: Colonial Series,* ed. Abbot and Twohig, 7:453–54.

Mount Vernon July 20th 1772

Sir,

The Money arising from the Sales [of flour in the West Indies] I would have laid out in Negroes, if choice ones can be had [for] under Forty pounds Sterl; . . .

If the Return's are in Slaves let there be two thirds of them Males, the other third Females—The former not exceeding (at any rate) 20 yrs of age—the latter 16—All of them to be strait Limb'd, & in every respect strong & likely, with good Teeth & good Countenances—to be sufficiently provided with Cloaths.[2]

The second appears in a letter to Gilbert Simpson dated February 23, 1773: "I also send you a fine, healthy, likely young Girl which in a year or two more will be fit for any business—her principal employment hitherto has been House Work but [she] is able, or soon will be to do any thing else."[3]

Washington was regarded by his contemporaries, as well as by historians and biographers of later generations, as a pillar of moral rectitude and integrity. These respected virtues were evident in both his public and his private life. The highest of standards also applied to those who moved within his immediate vicinity, and certainly to the invited guests who partook of his hospitality at Mount Vernon. Indeed, one visitor, in a sarcastic and titillating aside to a fellow New Yorker and former Revolutionary War comrade, revealed his impatience with the conventional hospitality being offered by his Mount Vernon host: "Here we are, three meals a day and a quadrille at night—The Great Man retiring to his study after breakfast, and we to our room. Will you believe it, I have not humped a single mullato since I am here, O tempora Moses!"[4]

There arise periodically suggestions to the effect that Washington was a lecher who carried on with his female slaves and clandestinely fathered illegitimate children by them. These slanders can be traced back to attempts by the British during the Revolution to discredit Washington. The accusations were ignored at the time because no credible proof was ever offered to substantiate them. Nevertheless—more than two centuries later—after these alleged indiscretions have been minutely and methodically examined by generations of historians and Washington biographers and have been found to be baseless—they still continue to be bandied about. George Washington certainly had moral shortcomings, but licentious behavior was not one of them.

2. Ibid., 9:70.
3. Ibid., 9:185.
4. Lt. Col. William North to Lt. Col. Benjamin Walker, Mount Vernon, March 9, 1784. Quoted from a copy in the Mount Vernon Papers, Mount Vernon Library. The original is at the Historical Society of Pennsylvania, Philadelphia.

A man who valued (perhaps inordinately) his slave property, Washington was known for his relentless pursuit of runaways. The loss of Hercules, the valued chef of the Washington household, was considered a minor disaster by the Washington family. The general was determined to track down this prize possession and return Hercules to his rightful place in the Mount Vernon kitchen. Tobias Lear, Washington's longtime personal secretary, recounted in his memoirs the celebrated disappearance of Uncle Harkless, as he was affectionately called:

> It is sad to relate that Uncle Harkless was so captivated with the delights of Philadelphia that in 1797, on the day Washington left the city to retire to private life at the end of his second term, he ran away rather than return to Mount Vernon. Although diligent inquiries were made for him, he was never apprehended. All through that spring and summer Mrs. Washington was without a satisfactory cook, and finally, almost, it would seem, in despair, Washington wrote Major George Lewis, one of his nephews, about buying a slave in Fredericksburg who was reputed an excellent chef, "with no other fault than a fondness for liquor." The letter, dated November 13, 1797, starts with a paragraph very illustrative of the President's attitude toward slavery, as it reads:
>
> "The running off of my cook has been a most inconvenient thing to this family, and what renders it more disagreeable, is, that I had resolved never to become the master of another slave by *purchase,* but this resolution I fear I must break."[5]

While Washington sought a replacement for his chef, he did not relax his tenacious pursuit of the fugitive Hercules. On March 10, 1797, he sent Lear the following instructions: "I pray you to desire Mr. Kitt to make all the enquiry he can after Hercules, and send him round in the Vessel if he can be discovered and apprehended."[6] Later, an impatient Washington took matters into his own hands and directly importuned Frederick Kitt, his former household steward in Philadelphia, to intensify the search.

> Mount Vernon, January 10, 1798.
>
> Mr. Kitt:
>
> We have never heard of Hercules our Cook since he left this [place]; but little doubt remains in my mind of his having gone to Philadelphia, and may yet be found there, if proper measures were employed to discover (unsuspectedly, so as not to alarm him) where his haunts are.
>
> If you could accomplish this for me, it would render me an acceptable service as I neither have, nor can get a good Cook to hire, and am disinclined to hold another slave by purchase.

5. Decatur, *Private Affairs of George Washington,* 296–97.
6. Fitzpatrick, ed., *Writings,* 37:578.

If by indirect enquiries of those who know Herculas, you should learn that he is in the City, inform Colo. Clemt. Biddle thereof, and he will, I hope, take proper measures to have him apprehended at the moment one of the Packets for Alexandria is about to Sale, and put him therein, to be conveyed hither; and will pay any expence which may be incurred in the execution of this business; which must be managed with address to give it a chance of Success; for if Herculas was to get the least hint of the design he would elude all your vigilance.[7]

Some weeks later, Washington again urged Kitt to press the hunt for the elusive Hercules: "Continue your enquiries, I pray you, after Herculas; and if you should find it necessary, hire some one who is most likely to be acquainted with his haunts, to trace them out; and if you should learn of him, advise with Colo. Biddle on the most effectual mode of securing him until he can be put on board one of the Packets for Alexandria with a strict charge to the Master not to give him an opportunity of escaping. Whatever cost shall attend this business Colo. Biddle will pay."[8]

When Hercules made good his escape to freedom in Philadelphia, he left behind at Mount Vernon a young daughter. The child was gently interrogated by Beaudoin, the manservant of the French nobleman Louis-Philippe, who, with his brothers, was visiting with Washington at the time of this incident. Louis-Philippe noted a fragment of their conversation in his diary: "The general's cook ran away, being now in Philadelphia, and left a little daughter of six at Mount Vernon. Beaudoin ventured that the little girl must be deeply upset that she would never see her father again; she answered, *Oh! sir, I am very glad, because he is free now.*"[9]

Washington, from time to time, singled out promising young Mount Vernon slaves to be encouraged and groomed for promotion to more desirable positions. The name of Cyrus appears initially in a letter Washington wrote to his manager William Pearce on March 15, 1795: "Cyrus, besides being a Dower slave, is strongly suspected of roguery and drinking; otherwise he would do very well, as he is likely, young, and smart enough." The young slave seems to have mended his ways, for his name turns up again in a letter to Pearce dated December 13, 1795. Cyrus is now a serious contender for the relatively important rank of personal servant to the master, but before being selected, he must meet Washington's exacting specifications: "If Cyrus continues to give evidence of such qualities as would fit him for a waiting man, encourage him to persevere in them; and if they should appear to be sincere and permanent, I will receive him in that character when I retire from public life, if not sooner. To be sober, attentive to his duty, honest,

---

7. Ibid., 36:123–24.
8. Washington to Kitt, Mount Vernon, January 29, 1798 (ibid., 36:148).
9. Louis-Philippe, *Diary of My Travels in America*, 32.

obliging and cleanly, are the qualifications necessary to fit him for my purposes. If he possesses these, or can aquire them, he might become useful to me, at the same time that he would exalt, and benefit himself."[10]

It seems that Cyrus was successful in his endeavors, prompting Washington to remind Pearce of the fastidious grooming he felt was necessary to make the slave presentable for his new status in the mansion:

> Philadelphia, May 1, 1796.
>
> Mr. Pearce:
>   I would have you again stir up the pride of Cyrus; that he may be the fitter for my purposes against [the time when] I come home; sometime before which (that is as soon as I shall be able to fix on the time) I will direct him to be taken into the house, and clothes to be made for him. In the meanwhile, get him a strong horn comb and direct him to keep his head well combed, that the hair, or wool may grow long.[11]

Despite his often harsh treatment of them and his seeming indifference to their personal welfare, Washington appears to have been held in high regard by his slaves. In fact, James T. Flexner claims, "Eyewitness accounts exist of blacks weeping when Martha departed, rejoicing when George Washington returned." One eyewitness account of a Washington homecoming (on which Flexner partially based his own observation) was incorporated into these two lines of verse by Washington's longtime military aide and close personal friend and admirer Col. David Humphreys: "Return'd from war, I saw them round him press, / And all their speechless glee by artless signs express."[12]

A vignette based on a private conversation Washington is said to have held in the summer of 1798 with a sophisticated and worldly visitor to Mount Vernon is particularly appropriate because it encompasses Washington's vision of the future of slavery in the United States. John Bernard, a highly regarded comic actor and impresario who began his career in his native England, had migrated to the United States at the end of the eighteenth century and quickly won a prominent place for himself in the budding American theater. According to his memoirs, *Retrospections of America, 1797–1811,* he met General Washington by chance on the road between Alexandria and Mount Vernon—the two men converged to help a distressed couple whose carriage had overturned—and was later invited by Washington to accept his hospitality. Bernard recorded his version of the ensuing dialogue:

---

10. Fitzpatrick, ed., *Writings,* 34:145, 393–94.

11. Ibid., 35:34.

12. James T. Flexner, *George Washington: Anguish and Farewell, 1793–1799,* 443; David Humphreys, "A Poem on the Death of General Washington," in *The Miscellaneous Works of David Humphreys,* 180.

In our hour and a half's conversation he touched on every topic that I brought before him with an even current of good sense, if he embellished it with a little wit or verbal eloquence. He . . . regarded the happiness of America but as the first link in a series of universal victories; for his full faith in the power of those results of civil liberty which he saw all around him led him to foresee that it would, ere long, prevail in other countries, and that the social millenium of Europe would usher in the political. . . .

A black coming in at this moment, with a jug of spring water, I could not repress a smile, which the general at once interpreted. "This may seem a contradiction," he continued, "but I think you must perceive that it is neither a crime nor an absurdity. When we profess, as our fundamental principle, that liberty is the inalienable right of every man, we do not include madmen or idiots; liberty in their hands would become a scourge. Till the mind of the slave has been educated to perceive what are the obligations of a state of freedom, and not confound a man's with a brute's, the gift would insure its abuse. We might as well be asked to pull down our old warehouses before trade has increased to demand enlarged new ones. Both houses and slaves were bequeathed to us by Europeans, and time alone can change them; an event, sir, which, you may believe me, no man desires more heartily than I do. Not only do I pray for it, on the score of human dignity, but I can clearly foresee that nothing but the rooting out of slavery can perpetuate the existence of our union, by consolidating it in a common bond of principle."[13]

13. John Bernard, *Retrospections of America, 1797–1811*, 90–91.

7

THE SUNSET YEARS

I N T H E summer of 1799, Washington made his second and final inventory of the Mount Vernon slave population. Of the 317 slaves counted, 78 were adult males, 86 were adult females, 114 were children, and 29 were classified as working boys and girls; about half of the slaves (49 percent) were considered either too young or too old to work.[1] Washington, who was fully cognizant of the burden of a mostly nonproductive labor force, complained of his dilemma to his nephew Robert Lewis:

> Mount Vernon, August 18, 1799.
>
> Dear Sir:
>
> . . . It is demonstratively clear, that on this Estate (Mount Vernon) I have more working Negros by a full moiety, than can be employed to any advantage in the farming system, and I shall never turn Planter thereon.
>
> To sell the overplus I cannot, because I am principled against this kind of traffic in the human species. To hire them out, is almost as bad, because they could not be disposed of in families to any advantage, and to disperse the families I have an aversion. What then is to be done? Something must or I shall be ruined; for all the money (in addition to what I raise by Crops, and rents) that have been *received* for Lands, sold within the last four years, to the amount of Fifty thousand dollars, has scarcely been able to keep me a float.
>
> Under these circumstances, and thorough conviction that half the workers I keep on this Estate, would render me greater *nett* profit than I *now* derive from the whole, has made me resolve, if it can be accomplished, to settle Plantations on one of my other Lands.[2]

1. Flexner, *Anguish and Farewell*, 444.
2. Fitzpatrick, ed., *Writings*, 37:338–39.

All of his earlier life had been geared to growth and expansion, to the acquisition of land and slaves. In his sunset years, for the first time, Washington began to talk in terms of retrenchment. He said that he wanted to divest himself of the responsibility of operating his farms, and he gave every indication that he wished to be rid of his slave property. During the second term of his presidency, Washington had written a long and elaborate letter to a correspondent in England, the agriculturist Arthur Young, broaching his ideas on leasing out the Mount Vernon farms and giving his reasons for embarking in this new direction:

> Philadelphia, December 12, 1793.
> Sir:
> . . . All my Landed property East of the Apalachian Mountains is under Rent, except the Estate called Mount Vernon. This, hitherto, I have kept in my own hands; but from my present situation; from my advanced time of my life; from a wish to live free from care, and as much at my ease as possible during the remainder of it; and from other causes which are not necessary to detail, I have, latterly, entertained serious thoughts of letting this estate also, reserving the Mansion house farm for my own residence, occupation, and amusement in agriculture.[3]

Washington followed up this private initiative a few years later, circulating an advertisement among his friends and correspondents:

> Philadelphia, February 1, 1796.
> TO BE LET
> AND POSSESSION GIVEN IN AUTUMN
> The Farms appertaining to the Mount Vernon Estate, in Virginia; four in number; adjoining the Mansion House Farm. Leases will be given for the term of fourteen years to *real* farmers of *good* reputation, and none others need apply.
> The largest of these, called River Farm, contains 1207 acres of ploughable land; 879 of which, are in seven fields, nearly of a size, and under good fences; 212 acres (in one enclosure) are, generally in a common grass pasture; and 116 acres more, are in *five* grass lots, and an orchard (of the best grafted fruit) all of them contiguous to the dwelling house and barn. On the premises, are a comfortable dwelling house (in which the Overlooker resides) having three rooms below, and one or two above; an old barn (now in use) and a brick one building 60 by 30 feet; besides ends and wings, sufficient for stabling 20 working horses, and as many oxen; and an excellent brick dairy, with a fine spring in the middle of it. Thirty black labourers (men and women) being the usual number which have been employed on this farm, are, with their children, warmly lodged chiefly in houses of their own building.

3. Ibid., 33:175.

In similar fashion he described the other three farms—Union, Dogue Run, and Muddy Hole—composing the Mount Vernon estate, the slaves on these farms being always referred to as "black labourers." Then, in a separate advertisement, "Terms on Which the Farms at Mount Vernon May Be Obtained," also dated February 1, 1796, Washington stipulated his conditions with respect to the slaves: "Although the admission of Slaves with the Tenants will not be absolutely prohibited; It would, nevertheless, be a pleasing circumstance to exclude them; If not entirely, at least in a great degree: To do which, is not among the least inducements for dividing the farms into small lots."[4]

The satisfactory disposition of his slaves was never far from Washington's mind. He had touched on the delicate subject, and some of the potential difficulties involved, in the December 12, 1793, letter to Arthur Young: "Many of the Negroes, male and female, might be hired by the year as labourers, if this should be preferred to the importation of that class of people; but it deserves consideration how far the mixing of whites and blacks together is advisable; especially where the former, are entirely unacquainted with the latter." He clarified this point, and expanded on it, in a subsequent letter to Young written on November 9, 1794:

> From not being so explicit as I ought to have been in my letter of   my intention, respecting the Negros which reside on my farms, did not sufficiently appear to you. It was not my meaning (if it was so understood) to make it a *condition* that they should be annexed as an appendage thereto. I had something better in view for them than that. To accomodate, not to incumber the farmer, was the idea I meant to convey to you, that is, that he might, or might not as his inclination or interest should dictate, hire them, as he would do any other labourers which his necessity wd. require him to employ.[5]

Washington's concern for the future welfare of the Mount Vernon slaves is mentioned again in a letter to William Pearce:

> Philadelphia, March 20, 1796.
>
> Mr. Pearce:
> . . . One great object with me, is to separate the Negros from the Land; without making the condition of the former worse than it now is: whereas, if I was to rent the farm as they now stand, with the Negros &ca. on Shares, or divide them, negros &ca. as you have suggested there would be a great deal of attention required, and perhaps risque and abuse to be run, and after all perpetual complaints perhaps from the Negros that would be hired of ill usage in a variety of ways which would make one uneasy, and defeat in all probability the main objects which I aim at, viz, tranquillity with a *certain* income. Notwithstanding these observations, and this explanation

4. Ibid., 33:433–34, 444.
5. Ibid., 33:181, 34:21.

The layouts of the five farms that constituted the Mount Vernon estate—Union, Dogue Run, Muddy Hole, River, and Mansion House—and the careful itemization of how the various sections of land in each of the four working farms were utilized show how thoughtfully Washington planned the cultivation of his crops. (Courtesy of the Huntington Library, San Marino, California)

123

FARMS, AND THEIR CONTENTS.

UNION FARM.			MUDDY-HOLE FARM.		
Field, No. I.	. .	120 acres.	Field, No. I.	. .	63 acres.
" II.	. .	129 "	" II.	. .	68 "
" III.	. .	121 "	" III.	. .	52 "
" IV.	.	120 "	" IV.	. .	54 "
" V.	. .	110 "	" V.	. .	65 "
" VI.	.	116 "	" VI.	.	80 "
" VII.	. .	125 "	" VII.	. .	74 "
Meadow,	. . 42		Clover lots,	. .	20 "
"	. . . 25				—
	— 67 "				476
Clover lots,	. .	20 "			
	— 928				

DOGUE RUN FARM.			RIVER FARM.		
Field, No. I.	. .	70 acres.	Field, No. I.	. .	120 acres.
" II.	. .	74 "	" II.	. .	120 "
" III.	. .	74 "	" IV.	. .	125 "
" IV.	.	71 "	" IV.	.	132 "
" V.	. .	75 "	" V.	. .	132 "
" VI.	.	73 "	" VI.	.	130 "
" VII.	. .	80 "	" VII.	. .	120 "
Meadow,	. . 38	"	Pasture,	. . .	212 "
"	. . . 18	"	Orchards, &c.	. .	84 "
"	. . . 12	"	Clover lots,	. . .	32 "
"	. . . 10	"			— 1207
"	. . . 36	"	Union Farm,	. .	928
	— 114 "		Dogue Run Farm,	.	649
Clover lots,	.	18 "			—
	— 649		Total of the four farms,		3260

of my wishes, I shall be very glad, as I have observed before, to receive any suggestions you may think proper to make; to know the sentiments of others, if they are communicated to you; and to know the propositions of all who make them to you whether for the whole farms, or large or small parts of them without the Negros &ca., or in the same manner, the Negros and stock going along with the Farms.[6]

The former president also recognized that the African American population, stimulated by the rhetoric of the Revolution and encouraged by the abolitionist movement, was becoming more difficult to manage. In a letter dated September 14, 1798, addressed to Alexander Spotswood he reflected:

The reason why I doubted about employing an Overseer at the latter Farm, is, that as Union and Dogue run Farms are under one Overseer this year, and the latter conducted in a great measure by the foreman, I had some thoughts of entrusting it solely to him next year, under the direction of the Steward, but when I perceive but too clearly that Negros are growing more and more insolant and difficult to govern, I am more inclined to incur the expense of an Overseer than to hazard the management, and peace of the place to a Negro; provided I can get a good Overseer on moderate terms.[7]

The ultimate solution to the slavery issue, as Washington came to realize and to accept in the closing years of his life, rested in legislative acts of emancipation that would free all enslaved Americans. He strongly expressed this conviction, together with some personal advice on runaways, in a letter to his nephew Lawrence Lewis:

Mount Vernon, August 4, 1797.

Dear Sir:

Your letter of the 24th ulto has been received, and I am sorry to hear of the loss of your servant; but it is my opinion [that] these elopements will be MUCH MORE, before they are LESS frequent: and that the persons making them should never be retained, if they are recovered, as they are sure to contaminate and discontent others. I wish from my soul that the Legislature of this State could see the policy of a gradual Abolition of Slavery; it would prevt. much future mischief.[8]

Flexner, in the second volume of his Washington biography, notes that the general "continued sporadically, whenever opportunity offered, his efforts to rent the farms on terms that would not include the slaves, but, as his declining years passed, the end remained unachieved." Washington himself had apparently reached the conclusion by mid-1797 that the effort was futile. In a letter to the Earl of Buchan, in England, he said: "I was not sanguine in my hope of obtaining

6. Ibid., 34:501–2.
7. Ibid., 36:444–45.
8. Ibid., 37:338–39.

tenants from Great Britain, for my Farms of the estate on which I reside, although the experiment was made." And to Stephen Milburn, a potential renter of the River Farm, he was even more decisive: "Having in a great measure given up the idea of Renting my Farms (from an apprehension that I could not dispose of the whole of them, and that unless I did this my objects wd. not be answered) I was not as explicit as I might have been in my answers to some of the questions you asked on friday last."[9]

Unsuccessful in finding suitable tenants for his farms, Washington turned to another avenue to try to dispose of some of his surplus slaves. He wrote to Benjamin Dulany, the son-in-law and executor of Penelope Manley French, an elderly widow from whom Washington had leased in 1786 approximately five hundred acres of land, known as "French's Farm," which included the labor of her slaves,[10] and which he now proposed to return to her control:

> Mount Vernon, July 15, 1799.
>
> Sir:
>
> As I grow no Tobacco, and probably never shall, I have it in contemplation to make some material changes in the oeconomy of my Farms.
>
> To accomplish this object, a reduction of the present force on them is necessary; of course, the means by which it is to be effected, must have undergone consideration.
>
> Presuming then that it might be agreeable to Mrs. French, or to you, to whom they will ultimately revert, I am induced by a scene of propriety and respect; and from a persuasion that every humane owner of that species of property would rather have it in his own keeping, than suffer it to be in the possession of others, to offer you all the Negros I hold, belonging to that Estate.
>
> And as an evidence of my disposition to act fairly, and liberally, in the business; the whole of them, old, middle aged and young, shall be produced to three disinterested and judicious men, one to be chosen by Mrs. French or yourself, one by me, and the third by those two. The judgment of whom (after comparing the old with the young, and the chances of increase and decrease) shall be conclusive as to the annuity which is to be allowed me, or mine, for, and during the term for which they, at present, stand engaged.
>
> That you may be enabled to form an opinion of their usefulness, from the kind of Negros I am making you an offer of, I enclose a list of them, with remarks, which and their ages, I believe to be accurate; and the reason for giving them at this season of the year, is, that, if either Mrs. French or yourself is disposed to accede to the offer, you may have time to make arrangements accordingly.

9. Flexner, *Anguish and Farewell,* 445; Washington to the earl of Buchan, Mount Vernon, July 4, 1797, and Washington to Milburn, Mount Vernon, May 15, 1797 (Fitzpatrick, ed., *Writings,* 35:487, 445).

10. Freeman, *George Washington: A Biography,* 6:53–54.

For the same reason, an answer, so soon as you can conveniently decide upon the measure, would be very agreeable.[11]

There was no immediate reply to this communication, and Washington's next letter to Dulany took on a tone of near desperation in his eagerness to conclude a deal for the slaves:

> Mount Vernon, September 12, 1799.
>
> Sir:
>
> If Mrs. French or yourself, have come to any determination respecting the proposal I made in a letter addressed to you on the 15th of July last, it would be obliging to inform me of the result; as the season is fully advanced when my arrangements for the ensuing year must be made.
>
> Knowing that Mrs. French had rented her Farm, I did not [illegible] expect that it would have suited her to take the Negros, at any rate unless believing, as no doubt the case would be, that obtaining them in the aggregate, on the terms they were offered, she might derive considerable profit by again hiring them out individually; whilst a number of promising boys and girls would soon be in a situation to encrease her income [illegible] it respectful, and proper however, to couple her name with yours, when the proposal (alluded to before) was made.
>
> I certainly conceived, that as they would, ultimately, descend to you, or yours, that it would be [in] your interest to take them on the terms they were offered; as well, knowing that you had very valuable lands to settle them on, in the vicinity of the Federal City (on both sides of the River) where every thing raised would in a little time commd. a ready market, as for the reason just given, namely, individual hiring; which it would always be in your power to do, as likely Negros of the description I gave you, are always in request.[12]

None of Washington's proposed schemes for easing the burden of managing his Mount Vernon farms and his slave property proved to be workable. He died on December 14, 1799, at the age of sixty-seven, with his Mount Vernon estate, including his slaveholdings, intact. Flexner summarizes Washington's predicament, and his final postmortem resolution on slavery: "When he drew up his will in July 1799 . . . The provisions he worked out [for freeing his slaves after his and Martha's death] reveal that the old man was unable to visualize any practical solution to the dilemma involved in bringing freedom to black Mount Vernon [during his lifetime]."[13]

---

11. Fitzpatrick, ed., *Writings,* 37:307–8.
12. Ibid., 37:359–60.
13. Flexner, *Anguish and Farewell,* 445.

II. PERSONALITIES

8

PHILLIS WHEATLEY

D URING THE colonial period, Washington's dealings with slaves were almost exclusively within the parameters of a carefully systematized, legally prescribed, and socially accepted master-slave relationship. As he rode off to war in the spring of 1775, his comfortable and long-established world of masters and slaves would be challenged for the first time in his life. Some of the challenges were inherent in the forces unleashed by the dramatic events of the revolutionary era. Others were more intimate, directly involving individuals who apparently succeeded in touching an emotional chord. The outwardly austere and reserved Washington was often surprisingly vulnerable to appeals to his humanitarian side. Perhaps the most profound and lasting effect of these transient experiences was to heighten Washington's awareness that the enslaved African Americans were deserving of a better future in the new nation than their current state of perpetual bondage. The five personalities described in this and the following chapters were chosen because their documented stories offer perceptive insights into Washington's attitudes toward slaves and slave issues.

Several months after he arrived in Cambridge to assume command of the American forces besieging the British in Boston, Washington received in the mail a letter with an enclosure. The correspondence came from an unlikely source—a female slave—and the contents were even more unexpected—a poem written in his honor:

> SIR,
> I Have taken the freedom to address your Excellency in the enclosed poem, and entreat your acceptance, though I am not insensible of its inaccuracies. Your being appointed by the Grand Continental Congress to be Generalissimo

of the armies of North America, together with the fame of your virtues, excite sensations not easy to suppress. Your generosity, therefore, I presume, will pardon the attempt. Wishing your Excellency all possible success in the great cause you are so generously engaged in. I am,

Your Excellency's most obedient humble servant,

PHILLIS WHEATLEY.

Providence, Oct. 26, 1775.[1]

Phillis Wheatley was a child prodigy, a poetess of international renown, a black African, and a slave. Her intellectual range and prowess and her literary attainments had created a minor sensation in Boston. She was living proof that black Africans were not barbarians or members of an inferior race. Nor were they destined to be "hewers of wood and carriers of water." All of the commonly held assumptions about blacks belonging to a lower order that helped form the philosophical basis for justifying slavery were contradicted in the personage of Phillis Wheatley.

As a frail girl of only seven or eight years of age, she had been abducted from her native African village by slave traders and shipped to Boston on the slave galley the *Phillis,* arriving in that city on July 11, 1761. Her pathetic appearance at the local slave market won the sympathy of Susanna Wheatley, the wife of the prosperous Boston merchant John Wheatley; Susanna purchased the young orphan girl and took her into the Wheatley home as a member of the household, although legally her status was that of a slave and the property of the Wheatleys. Adopting the surname of her master, as was the usual custom of the times, and given the first name of Phillis (for the ship that had brought her to America), the child rapidly developed her own distinctive personality and showed early signs of her remarkable native talents.[2] John Wheatley testified to her precociousness in a letter dated November 14, 1772: "Without any Assistance from School Education, and by only what she was taught in the Family, she, in sixteen Months Time from her Arrival, attained the English Language, to which she was an utter Stranger before, to such a Degree, as to read any, [of] the most difficult Parts of the Sacred Writings, to the great Astonishment of all who heard her."[3]

"Mary Wheatley [an older daughter of the Wheatleys] . . . became Phillis's friend and her tutor in religion and language, and Phillis proved to be an apt pupil

1. *Papers: Revolutionary War Series,* ed. Abbot and Twohig, 2:242. This letter was first published in the April 1776 issue of *Pennsylvania Magazine* and has since been duplicated in numerous publications.

2. Unlike the other Wheatley slaves, who lived in the carriage house behind the family's King Street residence, Phillis had her own room in the family dwelling. She ate with the family, although when company was present she usually sat at a separate table. She was trained in the social graces and quickly learned to read and write. See Rayford W. Logan and Michael R. Winston, eds., *Dictionary of American Negro Biography,* 640. Also Julian D. Mason Jr., ed., *The Poems of Phillis Wheatley,* 2–3.

3. John C. Shields, ed., *The Collected Works of Phillis Wheatley.*

with a quick mind, studying the Bible, English (language and literature), Latin (language and literature), history, geography, and Christian principles."[4] Phillis Wheatley evidenced a natural aptitude for writing lyric poetry, imitating the style of Alexander Pope, the most fashionable English-language poet of the eighteenth century. The first edition of her poems appeared in pamphlet form in Boston in 1770. Her literary debut transformed the intellectual luminaries of Massachusetts Bay into an admiration society. They came to the Wheatley home on King Street, in the hub of downtown Boston, in a steady stream to listen to Phillis read from the Latin classics, or recite her own poetry, or engage in conversational repartee with the visitors.[5] Their broad endorsement of young Phillis was proudly announced by her publisher in this statement:

> To The PUBLICK.
> As it has been repeatedly suggested to the Publisher, by Persons, who have seen the Manuscript, that Numbers would be ready to suspect they were not really the Writings of PHILLIS, he has procured the following Attestation, from the most respectable Characters in *Boston*, that none might have the least Ground for disputing their *Original.*
>
> WE, whose Names are under-written, do assure the World, that the POEMS specified in the following Page, *were* (as we verily believe) written by PHILLIS, a young Negro Girl, who was but a few Years since, brought an uncultivated Barbarian, from *Africa*, and has ever since been, and now is, under the Disadvantage of serving as a Slave in a Family in this Town. She has been examined by some of the best Judges, and is thought qualified to write them.

His Excellency, THOMAS HUTSCHINSON, *Governor,*
The Hon. ANDREW OLIVER, *Lieutenant-Governor*

The Hon. Thomas Hubbard,	*The Rev.* Charles Cheuney, *D.D.*
The Hon. John Erving,	*The Rev.* Mather Byles, *D.D.*
The Hon. James Pitts,	*The Rev.* Ed. Pemberton, *D.D.*
The Hon. Harrison Gray,	*The Rev.* Andrew Elliot, *D.D.*
The Hon. James Bowdoin,	*The Rev.* Samuel Cooper, *D.D.*
John Hancock, *Esq.;*	*The Rev.* Mr. Samuel Mather,
Joseph Green, *Esq.;*	*The Rev.* Mr. Joon Moorhead,
Richard Carey, *Esq;*	Mr. John Wheatley, *her Master.*[6]

Her reputation in Boston solidly established, Phillis Wheatley traveled to England in 1773, partly for reasons of health, and accompanied by Mary Wheatley's twin brother, Nathaniel. Her reputation preceded her to England, where the publication of her poems was sponsored by the countess of Huntingdon. With her natural poise, intellect, and entertaining conversation, she was a much sought

---

4. Mason, ed., *Poems of Wheatley,* 3.
5. Edward T. James, Janet W. James, and Paul S. Boyer, eds., *Notable American Women, 1607–1950: A Biographical Dictionary,* 3:573–74.
6. Shields, ed., *Works of Wheatley.*

after guest in English society. She hobnobbed with British royalty and acquitted herself everywhere she went with grace and modesty. Brook Watson, the Lord Mayor of London, presented her with an elegant folio edition of *Paradise Lost;* William Legge, the earl of Dartmouth, gave her a vellum-bound copy of *Don Quixote.* Benjamin Franklin, then residing in London, called upon her to pay his respects. He later wrote to his cousin: "Upon your Recommendation I went to see the black Poetess and offer'd her any Services I could do her."[7] The Countess of Huntingdon arranged for the young poetess to be presented at court; but when word came that Mrs. Wheatley in Boston was ill, Phillis decided to return home and was therefore unable to accept the honor.

Phillis returned to Boston to help tend to Mrs. Wheatley until her death in 1774 and to witness the revolutionary fever breaking out into open revolt. Since her feelings were decidedly pro-American, she remained with the Wheatley family when they moved from Boston to Providence, Rhode Island, until the deaths of John Wheatley and his daughter, Mary, in 1778.[8] Her patriotic leanings were expressed in these lines, composed in honor of, and dedicated to, General Washington, and forwarded from Providence to him with her note of October 26, 1775:

> CElestial choir! enthron'd in realms of light,
>   Columbia's scenes of glorious toils I write.
> While freedom's cause her anxious breast alarms,
> She flashes dreadful in refulgent arms.
> See mother earth her offspring's fate bemoan,
> And nations gaze at scenes before unknown!
> See the bright beams of heaven's revolving light
> Involved in sorrows and the veil of night!
>   The goddess comes, she moves divinely fair,
> Olive and laurel binds her golden hair:
> Wherever shines this native of the skies,
> Unnumber'd charms and recent graces rise.
>   Muse! bow propitious while my pen relates
> How pour her armies through a thousand gates:
> As when Eolus heaven's fair face deforms,
> Enwrapp'd in tempest and a night of storms;
> Astonish'd ocean feels the wild uproar,
> The refluent surges beat the sounding shore;
> Or thick as leaves in Autumn's golden reign,
> Such, and so many, moves the warrior's train.
> In bright array they seek the work of war,
> Where high unfurl'd the ensign waves in air.

7. Logan and Winston, eds., *American Negro Biography,* 641; Franklin to Jonathon Williams Sr., London, July 7, 1773 (William B. Willcox, ed., *The Papers of Benjamin Franklin,* 20:291).

8. Logan and Winston, eds., *American Negro Biography,* 641.

Shall I to Washington their praise recite?
Enough thou know'st them in the fields of fight.
Thee, first in place and honours,—we demand
The grace and glory of thy martial band.
Fam'd for thy valour, for thy virtues more,
Hear every tongue thy guardian aid implore!
  One century scarce perform'd its destined round,
When Gallic powers Columbia's fury found;
And so may you, whoever dares disgrace
The land of freedom's heaven-defended race!
Fix'd are the eyes of nations on the scales,
For in their hopes Columbia's arm prevails.
Anon Britannia droops the pensive head,
While round increase the rising hills of dead.
Ah! cruel blindness to Columbia's state!
Lament thy thirst of boundless power too late.
  Proceed, great chief, with virtue on thy side,
Thy ev'ry action let the goddess guide.
A crown, a mansion, and a throne that shine,
With gold unfading, Washington! be thine.[9]

There was no immediate reply from Washington. The general, of course, was burdened with the problems of attempting to create a cohesive army out of farmers and irregular militias with insufficient weapons, supplies, and money; at the same time he worried about how to counter the threat of a powerful, well-equipped, and experienced enemy force camped within easy striking range of his vulnerable positions. Nor was poetry Washington's strong suit; his literary tastes tended toward the more mundane topics of agriculture, politics, and military affairs. Furthermore, he knew that Phillis Wheatley was a black African and a slave. It comes as a surprise, therefore, to find her letter and poem prominently mentioned in flattering terms in a private communication dated February 10, 1776, to Joseph Reed, Washington's close friend, confidant, and military secretary, then residing in Philadelphia:

> I recollect nothing else worth giving you the trouble of, unless you can be amused by reading a Letter and Poem addressed to me by Mrs or Miss Phillis Wheatley—In searching over a parcel of Papers the other day, in order to destroy such as were useless, I brought it to light again—at first, With a view of doing justice to her great poetical Genius, I had a great Mind to publish the Poem, but not knowing whether it might not be considered rather as a mark of my own vanity than as a Compliment to her I laid it aside till I came across it again in the manner just mentioned.[10]

9. G. Herbert Renfro, *Life and Works of Phillis Wheatley*, 32.
10. *Papers: Revolutionary War Series*, ed. Abbot and Twohig, 3:290.

One of the leading political publicists of the American Revolution—Tom Paine (author of *Common Sense*)—obviously recognized a good story when it came across his desk. Linking the black slave poetess, Phillis Wheatley, with General Washington in an adulatory ode of heroic dimensions was made to order copy for the editor of *The Pennsylvania Magazine: or, American Monthly Museum* in Philadelphia. In introducing

POETICAL ESSAYS. 193

X.

Let fingular bleffings America crown ;
May the Congrefs be bleft with immortal renown ;
Each colony live in the true fifterly peace,
Whilft harmony, honour, and riches increafe.
Cuo. Oh ! let freedom, &c.

The following LETTER *and* VERSES, *were written by the famous* Phillis Wheatley, *the African Poetefs, and prefented to his Excellency Gen.* Washington.

SIR,

I Have taken the freedom to addrefs your Excellency in the enclofed poem, and entreat your acceptance, though I am not infenfible of its inaccuracies. Your being appointed by the Grand Continental Congrefs to be Generaliffimo of the armies of North America, together with the fame of your virtues, excite fenfations not eafy to fupprefs. Your generofity, therefore, I prefume, will pardon the attempt. Wifhing your Excellency all poffible fuccefs in the great caufe you are fo generoufly engaged in. I am,

Your Excellency's moft obedient humble fervant,

Providence, Oct. 26, 1775. PHILLIS WHEATLEY.
His Excellency Gen. Wafhington.

CEleftial choir! enthron'd in realms of light,
 Columbia's fcenes of glorious toils I write.
While freedom's caufe her anxious breaft alarms,
She flafhes dreadful in refulgent arms.
See mother earth her offspring's fate bemoan,
And nations gaze at fcenes before unknown!
See the bright beams of heaven's revolving light
Involved in forrows and the veil of night !
 The goddefs comes, fhe moves divinely fair,
Olive and laurel binds her golden hair :
Wherever fhines this native of the fkies,
Unnumber'd charms and recent graces rife.
 Mufe! how propitious while my pen relates
How pour her armies through a thoufand gates :
As when Eolus heaven's fair face deforms,
Enwrapp'd in tempeft and a night of ftorms ;
Aftonifh'd ocean feels the wild uproar,
The refluent furges beat the founding fhore ;
Or thick as leaves in Autumn's golden reign,
Such, and fo many, moves the warrior's train.
In bright array they feek the work of war,
Where high unfurl'd the enfign waves in air.
Shall I to Wafhington their praife recite ?
Enough thou know'ft them in the fields of fight.
Thee, firft in place and honours,—we demand
The grace and glory of thy martial band.
Fam'd for thy valour, for thy virtues more,
Hear every tongue thy guardian aid implore !
 One century fcarce perform'd its deftin'd round,
When Gallic powers Columbia's fury found ;
And fo may you, whoever dares difgrace
The land of freedom's heaven-defended race !
Fix'd are the eyes of nations on the fcales,
For in their hopes Columbia's arm prevails.
Anon Britannia droops the penfive head,
While round increafe the rifing hills of dead.
Ah ! cruel blindnefs to Columbia's ftate !
Lament thy thirft of boundlefs power too late.
 Proceed, great chief, with virtue on thy fide,
Thy ev'ry action let the goddefs guide.
A crown, a manfion, and a throne that fhine,
With gold unfading, WASHINGTON! be thine.

MONTHLY

her letter and poem, Paine wrote: "The following LETTER and VERSES, were written by the famous Phillis Wheatley, the African Poetess, and presented to his Excellency Gen. Washington." Nor could the irony of George Washington, Virginia slave owner, helping to promote the intellectual achievements of a Boston slave woman have been lost on the readers of the *Pennsylvania Magazine*.

Washington's initiative touched off two separate sequences of events. In Philadelphia, Reed may have been sufficiently impressed by Phillis Wheatley's literary accomplishments, and perhaps even more so by Washington's favorable endorsement, that he passed her writings along for publication. Phillis Wheatley's poem and her accompanying note to Washington appeared in print in the April 1776 issue of *Pennsylvania Magazine,* prefaced with the following statement: "The following LETTER and VERSES were written by the famous Phillis Wheatley, the African Poetess, and presented to his Excellency Gen. Washington."[11] Meanwhile, at his headquarters in Cambridge, a second look at the poem written in his honor apparently caused Washington to bestir himself in another direction. Some two weeks after corresponding with Reed, the general wrote a personal letter to the young black poetess, using her first name, as was common practice when addressing a slave, but prefixing it with the title *Mrs.* as a gesture of respect:

Cambridge February 28th 1776.

Mrs Phillis,

Your favour of the 26th of October did not reach my hands 'till the middle of December. Time enough, you will say, to have given an answer ere this. Granted. But a variety of important occurrences, continually interposing to distract the mind and withdraw the attention, I hope will apologize for the delay, and plead my excuse for the seeming, but not real, neglect.

I thank you most sincerely for your polite notice of me, in the elegant Lines you enclosed; and however undeserving I may be of such encomium and panegyrick, the style and manner exhibit a striking proof of your great poetical Talents. In honour of which, and as a tribute justly due to you, I would have published the Poem, had I not been apprehensive, that, while I only meant to give the World this new instance of your genius, I might have incurred the imputation of Vanity. This, and nothing else, determined me not to give it place in the public Prints.

If you should ever come to Cambridge, or near Head Quarters, I shall be happy to see a person so favoured by the Muses, and to whom nature has been so liberal and beneficent in her dispensations. I am, with great Respect, Your obedt humble servant,

G. Washington[12]

The sequel to this incident has been related by the early American woodengraver and historian Benson J. Lossing. According to Lossing, the following scene ostensibly took place at Washington's headquarters in Cambridge during the spring of 1776.

---

11. The poem and letter appeared in the "Poetical Essays" section of *Pennsylvania Magazine: or American Monthly Museum* 2 (April 1776): 193, while Thomas Paine was its editor. See Mason, ed., *Poems of Wheatley,* 164n.

12. *Papers: Revolutionary War Series,* ed. Abbot and Twohig, 3:387.

N:6. *To: M:ª Phillis Wheatley*

Cambridge February 28ᵗʰ 1776.

Mrs Phillis,

Your favour of the 26. of October did not reach my hands till the middle of December. Time enough you will say, to have given an answer ere this. Granted. But a variety of important occurrences, continually interposing to distract the mind and withdraw the attention, I hope will apologize for the delay, and plead my excuse for the seeming, but not real neglect.

I thank you most sincerely for your polite notice of me, in the elegant Lines you enclosed; and however undeserving I may be of such encomium and panegyrick, the stile and manner exhibit a striking proof of your great poetical Talents. In honour of which, and as a tribute justly due to you, I would have published the Poem, had I not been apprehensive, that while I only meant to give the World this new instance of your genius, I might have incurred the imputation of Vanity. This and nothing else, determined me not to give it place in the public Prints.

If you should ever come to Cambridge, or near Head Quarters, I shall be happy to see a person so favoured by the Muses, and to whom Nature has been so liberal and beneficent in her dispensations.

I am, with great Respect,
Your obed: humble servant,
G. Washington.

Only one letter in Washington's entire correspondence is known to have been addressed to a slave. The letter is especially remarkable because Washington wrote to Phillis Wheatley in terms that (except for the familiarity of using "Mrs. Phillis" as his salutation) in no way sound condescending or patronizing. He apologized for failing to respond promptly to her communication of October 1775, and he complimented her profusely on her poetic talents. Finally, he extended an invitation to her to visit him at his headquarters in Cambridge. In spite of his lifelong record as a slave owner who regarded African Americans as little more than chattel property, Washington's note to Wheatley—together with his subsequent efforts to promote her genius—indicates another and brighter side of his character with respect to slaves and slavery. (Courtesy of the Library of Congress, Washington, D.C.)

I can not refrain, however, from noticing the visit of one, who, though a dark child of Africa and a bond-woman, received the most polite attention from the commander-in-chief. This was PHILLIS, a slave of Mr. Wheatley, of Boston. She was brought from Africa when between seven and eight years old. She seemed to acquire knowledge intuitively; became a poet of considerable merit, and corresponded with such eminent persons as the Countess of Huntingdon, Earl of Dartmouth, Reverend George Whitefield, and others. Washington invited her to visit him at Cambridge, which she did a few days before the British evacuated Boston; her master, among others, having left the city by permission, and retired, with his family, to Chelsea. She passed half an

PHILLIS WHEATLEY NEGRO SERVANT to Mr JOHN WHEATLEY of BOSTON.

This silhouette of Phillis Wheatley was originally made to illustrate her book of poems. It is the only known likeness in existence of the African American slave poetess. (Courtesy of Manuscripts and University Archives, Special Collections Department, University of Virginia Library, Charlottesville)

hour with the commander-in-chief, from whom and his officers she received marked attention.[13]

Phillis Wheatley went on to an unhappy marriage and a tragic and premature death.[14] However, her published poems and her correspondence give her the honor of being America's first internationally recognized black intellectual.[15] Her place in history is further assured by the brief linkage with George Washington. She was the only black in the country who ever corresponded with, and subsequently

13. Benson J. Lossing, *The Pictorial Field-Book of the Revolution*, 1:556. Care must be taken in accepting Lossing's description of the events at General Washington's headquarters, which was written long afterward. Unfortunately, Lossing lists no sources, and there is no independent verification of any meeting between Washington and Phillis Wheatley; in *Papers: Revolutionary War Series*, the editors, Abbot and Twohig, comment, "GW apparently met her at his headquarters at Cambridge sometime in March 1776" (2:244n).

14. In April 1778 Phillis Wheatley married a free black man by the name of John Peters. He appears to have been a difficult character who wandered irresponsibly in and out of her life. Two of their three children died quite young. With her husband disinclined to work, Mrs. Peters was forced to support herself and the remaining child while living in a cheap lodging house. Her health finally gave away, and she and the child died in Boston on December 5, 1784. The two were buried in an unmarked grave. A few days later, her former friends and patrons learned of her death from a notice in the *Boston Independent Chronicle*. See James, James, and Boyer, eds., *Notable American Women*, 3:574; Logan and Winston, eds., *American Negro Biography*, 642.

15. According to Renfro, Wheatley's writings "owe their merit not to the fact that an African slave had produced them, but to the superior skill of composition, the delicacy of sentiment, the felicity of expression, and the delightful flow that bespeak no ordinary talent" (*Wheatley*, 26).

apparently met with, the general as an equal—that is, outside a master-slave relationship. The encounter vividly demonstrates that the gulf between the foremost American and the lowly black slave was not so large that it could not be comfortably bridged.

9

BILLY LEE

PLANTATION SLAVES in Virginia did not passively accept their condition of enforced lifelong servitude. They dreamt of freedom. The more daring and desperate slaves plotted insurrection—some even going so far as to contemplate the murder of their oppressors. Others simply chose to run away. And if the vision of freedom proved beyond their reach, then the enslaved African Americans registered their grudges and resentments in less riskier ways: stealing from the master's household; malingering on the job; performing shoddy work; or deliberately disobeying instructions. But relatively few slaves succeeded in gaining their permanent freedom by rebelling, absconding, or protesting. The system was too heavily stacked against them.

One means that did afford an enslaved Virginian the chance to gain the legal status of a free man or woman was manumission by the master or mistress—generally given as a reward for loyal and faithful service. But this was not an easy concession for the slave owner to make. To manumit a slave required breaking with Virginia's established slaveholding tradition and imposed a considerable financial sacrifice, due both to the loss of valuable property and to the legal requirement that freed slaves had to be supported. For Washington in particular, it was a painful choice. Washington, of course, had recognized the aspirations for freedom of his slaves and for years had denied them their goal. But finally—like other enlightened Virginia plantation proprietors—he listened to his conscience and bowed to humanitarian principles. He freed his slaves. The long road that led to manumission at Mount Vernon begins with the story of Billy Lee.

Prominently displayed at the National Gallery of Art in Washington, D.C., is undoubtedly the most famous contemporary painting of George Washington and

The Washington Family, by Edward Savage. (Courtesy of National Gallery of Art, Washington, D.C.)

his immediate family. The American artist Edward Savage worked on the canvas of *The Washington Family* for almost a decade, completing it in Philadelphia in 1796. George Washington, and presumably the other people who are portrayed, sat for Savage on a number of occasions in 1789, 1790, and 1796, while Washington was president of the United States and resided first in New York City and later in Philadelphia. Both the painting and the various prints that were reproduced from engravings of the original were highly regarded by the Washingtons and widely acclaimed by the general public. An especially interesting aspect of this portrait is the inclusion of a mulatto slave named Billy Lee.[1]

1. Wendy C. Wick, *George Washington, an American Icon: The Eighteenth-Century Graphic Portraits,* 41–44, 122. Because Billy Lee was never positively identified by Edward Savage or by anyone else directly associated with *The Washington Family,* the assumption that the face and half figure in the background belong to him is based primarily on the expert opinion of Wick, curator of prints at the National Portrait Gallery in Washington, D.C., where the portrait currently hangs. In *George Washington, an American Icon* Wick twice mentions Billy Lee by name: "Washington's personal virtues as a family man were suggested as well by depicting him surrounded by his wife, his black servant Billy Lee, and two of Martha's grandchildren, Eleanor Parke Custis and George Washington

It was not coincidence that Washington permitted the presence of his trusted body servant and constant companion for better than thirty years in this intimate family portrait. Although technically a slave, because of his loyalty to his master and his long and faithful service, Billy Lee (also known as Will or William) was accorded a special and prominent position in the Washington household, which brought him a place in *The Washington Family* and in several other contemporary paintings of the general, as well as valuable favors not normally accorded to slaves. Among the hundreds of Mount Vernon slaves—most of them known only by their names, ages, marital status, and occupations—Billy Lee is the only one for whom details of his character and personality, his activities and interests, and his career have survived and can be traced with some degree of accuracy. In addition, we have the advantage of knowing what Billy Lee looked like and what he wore, at least on formal occasions.

The earliest mention of Billy Lee appears in Washington's ledger account for 1768. On May 3 of that year, Washington recorded the purchase of a certain "Mulatto Will," a teenage boy, from Mrs. Mary Lee, the widow of Col. John Lee of Westmoreland County, for the price of sixty-one pounds and fifteen shillings.[2] Several years later, Billy Lee's name began to crop up in Washington's diary, indicating that the young African American was accompanying Washington on his periodic trips to Williamsburg and on various cross-country journeys:

> May 21, 1770. "GW today spent 3s. at Ruffin's ferry and somewhere on his route bought a pair of shoes costing 6s. for the mulatto manservant Billy, who accompanied him. . . ."
> Oct. 8, 1770. "Vale. Crawford joined us, & he and I went to Colo. Cresaps leaving the Doctr. at Pritchards with my boy Billy who was taken sick."
> Sept. 6, 1774. "On this day GW spent 15s. for shoes, etc., for William Lee, his body servant, who accompanied him to Philadelphia.[3]"

Washington was a passionate horseman, called by many the finest rider in Virginia. Thomas Jefferson considered him to be the "best horseman of his age."[4] He had to be proficient, for he spent much of his life on horseback: surveying,

---

Parke Custis" (43–44). "Edward Savage's *Washington Family* print depicted the President surrounded by his wife, her grandchildren, Eleanor Custis and George Washington Parke Custis, and the servant Billy Lee" (122). Rumors that the face and figure in the Savage portrait belong to someone other than Billy Lee remain unsubstantiated and have not appeared in print in any recognized professional publication; furthermore, it is highly unlikely that Washington would have permitted a strange black man to be included in this intimate family portrait in which he took such a keen personal interest. Thus, the most persuasive evidence currently available points to Billy Lee.

2. Ledger A—1750–1774, 261, Mount Vernon Library.

3. *Diaries*, ed. Jackson and Twohig, 2:238n, 278, 3:276n.

4. Jefferson to Dr. Walter Jones, Monticello, January 2, 1814 (William A. Bryan, *George Washington in American Literature, 1775–1865*, 49).

exploring the wilderness, fighting the French and the Indians, supervising the work on his plantations, foxhunting, traveling on business and on pleasure, or simply exercising. The Revolutionary War found Washington in the saddle almost constantly; he led his troops, rallied them in battle, gave orders to his officers, reconnoitered the enemy positions, and reviewed his men on parade. And riding at his side or close behind him, from the time that he was purchased until well after the end of the war, was Billy Lee. The two men shared the excitement of the chase and the hardships of the battlefield.

Washington's horsemanship can perhaps be better appreciated from this excerpt from the notebook of a French officer, the Marquis de Chastellux:

> The weather being fair, on the 26th [of November 1780], I got on horseback, after breakfasting with the General. He thoughtfully gave me the horse he had been riding on two days earlier and which I had greatly commended. I found the horse as good as he was handsome but above all, perfectly well broken and well trained, having a good mouth, easy in hand, and stopping short in gallop without bearing the bit. I mention these minute particulars, because it is the General himself who breaks in all his own horses, and because he is a very excellent and bold horseman, leaping the highest fences, and going extremely quick, without standing upon his stirrups, bearing on the bridle, or letting his horse run wild.[5]

Considering that Washington was already well into middle age when these observations were recorded, it is not hard to imagine what it must have been like to keep up with him when he was younger and in the prime of life. But Billy Lee was there, right next to Washington, riding hard and fast and holding his own:

> The habit was to hunt three times a week, weather permitting. . . . The general usually rode in the chase a horse called *Blueskin*, of a dark iron-gray color, approaching to blue. This was a fine but fiery animal, and of great endurance in a long run. Will, the huntsman, better known in Revolutionary lore as Billy, rode a horse called *Chinkling*, a surprising leaper, and made very much like its rider, low, but sturdy, and of great bone and muscle. Will had but one order, which was to keep with the hounds; and, mounted on *Chinkling*, a French horn at his back, throwing himself almost at length on the animal, with his spur in flank, this fearless horseman would rush, at full speed, through brake or tangled wood, in a style at which modern huntsmen would stand aghast.[6]

George Washington Parke Custis, the grandson of Martha Washington, lived at Mount Vernon from infancy until his step-grandfather and his grandmother passed away. In 1826 he began to compose his *Recollections and Private Memoirs of*

5. Chastellux, *Travels in North America*, 1:111.
6. George W. P. Custis, *Recollections and Private Memoirs of Washington*, 386–87.

"The time which Colonel Washington could spare from his building and agricultural improvements between the years 1759 and 1774, was considerably devoted to the pleasures of the chase. . . . During the season, Mount Vernon had many sporting guests from the neighborhood, from Maryland, and elsewhere. Their visits were not of days, but weeks; and they were entertained in the good old style of Virginia's ancient hospitality. Washington, always superbly mounted, in true sporting costume, of blue coat, scarlet waistcoat, buckskin breeches, top boots, velvet cap, and whip with long thong, took the field at daybreak, with his huntsman, Will Lee, his friends and neighbors"—George Washington Parke Custis, *Recollections and Private Memoirs of Washington,* 384–85. (A copy of *A Hunting Piece,* published in London in 1778, hangs in Washington's library at Mount Vernon; courtesy of the Mount Vernon Ladies' Association)

Washington, which is the only firsthand account that describes in any detail Billy Lee's active years as Washington's huntsman and body servant, as well as offering glimpses of Billy during the Revolution. For example, amid the bloody fighting and confusion during the Battle of Monmouth came a bit of battlefield humor with Billy Lee as its centerpiece:

> A ludicrous occurrence varied the incidents of the twenty-eighth of June [1778]. The servants of the general officers were usually well-armed and mounted. Will Lee, or Billy, the former huntsman, and favorite body-servant of the chief, a square muscular figure, and capital horseman, paraded a corps

of valets, and riding pompously at their head, proceeded to an eminence crowned by a large sycamore-tree, from whence could be seen an extensive portion of the field of battle. Here Billy halted, and, having unslung the large telescope that he always carried in a leathern case, with a martial air applied it to his eye, and reconnoitred the enemy. Washington having observed these manoeuvres of the corps of valets, pointed them out to his officers, observing, "See those fellows collecting on yonder height; the enemy will fire on them to a certainty." Meanwhile the British were not unmindful of the assemblage on the height, and perceiving a burly figure well-mounted, and with a telescope in hand, they determined to pay their respects to the group. A shot from a six-pounder passed through the tree, cutting away the limbs, and producing a scampering among the corps of valets, that caused even the grave countenance of the general-in-chief to relax into a smile.[7]

Billy Lee was also at Yorktown, to participate in the final campaign against Lord Cornwallis:

The headquarters were under canvass during the siege and after the surrender of Yorktown. The marquées of the commander-in-chief were pitched in the rear of the grand battery, just out of the range of the enemy's shells. . . . The late Doctor Eneas Manson, of New Haven, who was then attached to the medical staff of the American army, informed me that while vigorous assaults upon two or three English redoubts were in progress, Washington left his marquée, and with Lincoln, Knox, and one or two other officers, disengaged at the time, stood within the grand battery, watching every movement through the embrasures. When the last redoubt was captured, Washington turned to Knox, and said, "The work is done, and *well* done;" and then called to his servant, "Billy, hand me my horse."[8]

Billy Lee figured inadvertently in an unusual and significant episode during the Revolution that was directly tied in with his wartime role as Washington's body servant and valet. In May or June 1777, a pamphlet was published in London that had been secretly prepared by British officials to damage and discredit Washington in the eyes of the public. The pamphlet purported to include

certain letters of Washington written in 1776, to his friends and relatives in Virginia. . . . Were the letters genuine, they would be of interest as showing that Washington was playing a part as commander in chief of the American army, leading a cause for which he had little or no sympathy, and under the burden and discouragement of which, even at this early period of the war, he was becoming disheartened, and longing for a full reconciliation with the mother country. A two-fold object could be accomplished, were this the case. It would strengthen the war party in England, give aid to the

7. Ibid., 224.
8. Ibid., 279, 279n.

ministry to push the issue, and endorse the idea that the contest would be speedily terminated by the complete overthrow of the rebellion in the Colonies, and the reestablishment of the authority of king and Parliament in those dependencies. . . . on reaching America, the letters might discredit Washington with the American army and the people, and by occasioning suspicions of his integrity, introduce dissensions into the councils of the "rebels."

The packet of letters supposedly had been captured by the British following the fall of Fort Lee, New Jersey, on November 20, 1776. The letters were actually forgeries, but the derogatory information concerning Washington was so cleverly woven into a pattern of true facts—British intelligence obviously had access to a spy who was knowledgeable about Washington's personal relationships and family affairs—that the casual reader found them quite plausible. The introduction to these "spurious letters attributed to Washington" began with an anonymous first-person narrative.

> Among the prisoners at Fort Lee, I espied a mulatto fellow, whom I thought I recollected, and who confirmed my conjectures by gazing very earnestly at me. I asked him if he knew me. At first, he was unwilling to own it; but, when he was about to be carried off, thinking, I suppose, that I might perhaps be of some service to him, he came and told me that he was Billy, and the old servant of General Washington. He had been left there on account of an indisposition which prevented his attending his master. I asked him a great many questions, as you may suppose; but found very little satisfaction in his answers. At last, however, he told me that he had a small portmanteau of his master's; of which, when he found that he must be put into confinement, he intreated my care. It contained only a few stockings and shirts; and I could see nothing worth my care, except an almanack, in which he had kept a journal, or diary, of his proceedings since his first coming to New York: there were also two letters from his lady, one from Mr. Custis, and some pretty long ones from a Mr. Lund Washington, and in the same bundle with them, the first draughts, or foul copies, of answers to them. I read these with avidity; and being highly entertained with them, have shewn them to several of my friends, who all agree with me, that he [Washington] is a very different character from what they had supposed him. I never knew a man so much to be pitied.[9]

This introduction was a logical attempt to explain how Washington's traveling bag, with his personal letters and diary, had come into the possession of the British in the first place. The propaganda may have been effective in helping to inflame Tory opinion against the rebels and their commander in chief, but the story found few takers in America. Anyone who knew Washington quickly perceived a glaring

9. The pamphlet bears the imprint of J. Bew, a London bookseller in Paternoster Row. See Worthington C. Ford, ed., *The Spurious Letters Attributed to Washington*, 5–7.

flaw that gave the lie to the forgeries: Washington, usually mounted on horseback when outdoors, was a highly visible figure throughout the war, and everyone who saw him could not help but notice the black man riding along with him wherever he went. The master and his slave were inseparable, and any rumor or claim that parted them was clearly a fabrication. The British letters, therefore, were shrugged off for what they were: blatant forgeries.

The matter of the "spurious letters" lay dormant until 1797. Up to that time, Washington had remained relatively secure from partisan attack. But toward the end of his second and final term as president, both his policies and his person came under severe fire. Emerging party politics and the opportunity for succession provided by his coming retirement from public service were undoubtedly behind the efforts to impugn the aging president. Digging for ammunition with which to damage his reputation, Washington's foes and rivals attempted to regurgitate several of the slanders initially put forward in the bogus British wartime letters. To counter this threat to his reputation as a high-minded public servant, a sensitive and touchy subject with Washington, he wrote two lengthy memorandums explaining the background of the "spurious letters" and the role of Billy Lee in proving their falsehoods. A former military aide, Lt. Col. Benjamin Walker, was the recipient of the first:

Philadelphia, January 12, 1797.

Dear Walker:

. . . If you read the *Aurora* of this City, or those Gazettes which are under the same influence, you cannot but have perceived with what malignant industry, and persevering falsehoods I am assailed, in order to weaken, if not destroy, the confidence of the Public.

Amongst other attempts to effect this purpose, spurious letters, known at the time for their first publication (I believe in the year 1777) to be forgeries, to answer a similar purpose in the Revolution, are, or extracts from them, brought forward with the highest emblazoning, of which they are susceptible, with a view to attach principles to me which every action of my life have given the lie to. But *that* is no stumbling block with the Editors of these Papers and their supporters. And now, *perceiving* a disinclination on my part, perhaps *knowing*, that I had determined not to take notice of such attacks, they are pressing this matter upon the public mind with more avidity than usual; urging, that my silence, is a proof of their genuineness.

Although I never wrote, or ever saw one of these letters until they issued from New York, in Print; yet the Author of them must have been tolerably well acquainted in, or with some person of my family, to have given the names, and some circumstances which are grouped in the mass, of erroneous details. But of all the mistakes which have been committed in this business, none is more palpable, or susceptible of detection than the manner in which it is said they were obtained, by the capture of my Mulatto Billy, with a Portmanteau. *All the Army,* under my immediate command, could contradict this; and I believe most of them know, that no Attendant of mine, or a particle of my baggage ever fell into the hands of the enemy during the whole course of the War.[10]

A second letter, in a similar vein, was sent to Timothy Pickering, Washington's secretary of state at the time, with the request that it "may be deposited in the office of the department of state, as a testimony of the truth to the present generation and to posterity."[11]

Billy Lee returned from the war unscathed. But in the subsequent years of peaceful retirement at Mount Vernon, he seems to have become accident-prone. His first serious mishap took place during a surveying trip with Washington. The circumstances are related in Washington's diary entry of April 22, 1785: "after having run one course & part of another, My Servant William (one of the Chain Carriers) fell, and broke the pan of his knee, wch. put a stop to my Surveying; & with much difficulty I was able to get him to Abingdon, being obliged to get a sled to carry him on, as he could neither Walk, stand, or ride." Some three years later, Billy went down again, severely damaging his other leg. He was now, for all practical purposes, a complete cripple. Washington described the most recent misfortune in this brief journal notation: "Having sent my Waiter Will to Alexandria to the Post Office he fell at Mr. Porters door and broke the pan of his other Knee & was not able to return."[12]

Now that he was barely able to walk or ride, Billy Lee's usefulness as a servant was materially diminished. Nevertheless, when Washington was elected president in 1789, Billy was a member of the party traveling to New York City for the presidential inauguration. He got only as far as Philadelphia, however, where he had to be left behind for medical treatment.

> On 19 April Tobias Lear, who was on his way to New York with Billy, wrote to Clement Biddle in Philadelphia [Washington's old friend and his factor in that city]: "Will appears to be in too bad a state to travel at present; I shall therefore leave him—and will be much obliged to you if you will send him on to New York as soon as he can bear the journey without injury, which I expect will be in two or three days—I shall pay his expences. . . . He dresses his knee himself and therefore will stand in no need of a Doctor unless it should grow worse."

Billy Lee's condition was more serious than initially anticipated, as Biddle reported to Washington from Philadelphia on April 27:

10. Fitzpatrick, ed., *Writings,* 35:363–65.
11. Washington to Pickering, Philadelphia, March 3, 1797 (ibid., 35:414–16).
12. *Diaries,* ed. Jackson and Twohig, 4:125, 5:281.

I have frequently called to see Billy he continues too bad to remove—Doctor Smith was uneasy without some other experienc'd Surgeon or Physician to look at his knee, and I called on Doctor Hutchinson. They are of opinion that the present Sore reaches to the joint and that it would be very improper to remove him at least for a week or two, by which time he probably may be fit to send on by the Way of Bordentown but at present that he ought to be kept as still as possible And this prevents his being put to a private House, but you may depend on my care of, and attention to him, and that he shall be sent on without delay when his Surgeons think it safe.[13]

The next communication came from New York City on May 3, as Lear wrote Biddle

that the president "would thank you to propose it to Billy to return to Mount Vernon when he can be removed for he cannot possibly be of any service here, and perhaps will require a person to attend upon him constantly. if he should incline to return to Mt Vernon you will be so kind as to have him sent in the first vessel that sails for Alexa. after he can be removed with safety—but if he is still anxious to come on here the President would gratify him alto' he will be troublesome. He has been an old & faithful Servt. This is enough for the Presidt to gratify him in every reasonable wish."

But Billy was stubborn and determined. "While he was in Philadelphia Biddle had his knee examined by several local physicians including Dr. William Smith . . . and Dr. James Hutchinson . . . Billy improved under the ministrations of the two doctors, and Biddle wrote to Lear, 25 May: 'I shall have a Steel [brace] made this Day by directions of Dr Hutchinson to strengthen Billy's Knee which will not only render his traveling more safe but Enable him in some measure to walk & I shall send him on some Day this Week by way of Bordentown & Amboy of which I shall advise.' "[14]

An expense item in Lear's account book for June 15 notes that Billy, in spite of his lameness, had made his way to New York City to rejoin his master: "By Contingent Exps. pd. for a Hackney Coach to bring Will, Val de Chambre from the Ferry to the House on his arrival in N.Y." A week later, Lear confirmed the safe arrival of Billy Lee in a letter to Biddle, again written on behalf of the president and dated June 22: "Billy arrived here safe & well on wednesday Morning; he seems not to have lost much flesh by his misfortunes."[15]

Not only was Washington willing to put up with Billy Lee's afflictions, he apparently was also prepared to pay his medical bills without an audible murmur.

13. *Papers: Presidential Series,* ed. Abbot and Twohig, 2:133–34n.
14. Ibid., 2:134n.
15. Decatur, *Private Affairs of George Washington,* 27; *Papers: Presidential Series,* ed. Abbot and Twohig, 2:134n.

Biddle wrote to Lear on June 19: "I hope that Billy got safe to New York without accident. . . . I have not been able to get in all the Bills yet but have paid some & shall have the whole Closed to day & shall send them by next post—it will be a heavy expence but I have desired all Concerned to be as moderate as possible but they exceed my Expectations in their Charges."[16]

Biddle was not unaware of Washington's solicitous concern for the welfare of his servant. Earlier, he had been asked by Washington to lend a hand in straightening out Billy Lee's matrimonial dilemma:

> Mount Vernon July 28th 1784
>
> Dear Sir,
>   The Mulatto fellow William who has been with me all the War is attached (married he says) to one of his own colour a free woman, who, during the War was also of my family—She has been in an infirm state of health for sometime, and I had conceived that the connection between them had ceased—but I am mistaken—they are both applying to me to get her here, and tho' I never wished to see her more, yet I cannot refuse his request (if it can be complied with on reasonable terms) as he has lived with me so long & followed my fortunes through the War with fidelity.
>   After promising thus much, I have to beg the favor of you to procure her a passage to Alexandria either by Sea, by the passage Boats (if any there be) from the head of Elk, or in the Stage as you shall think cheapest & best, and circumstances may require—She is called Margaret Thomas als [alias] Lee (the name which he has assumed) and lives at Isaac & Hannah Sills, black people who frequently employ themselves in Cooking for families in the City of Phila.[17]

There are several more indications of Billy Lee's high standing in the Mount Vernon household. For instance, Elkanah Watson, a visitor to Washington's home in January 1785, recalled this sentimental scene: "His servants seemed to watch his eye, and to anticipate his every wish; hence, a look was equivalent to a command. His servant Billy, the faithful companion of his military career, was always at his side. Smiling content animated and beamed on every countenance in his presence." And in the roster of his slaves that Washington compiled in February 1786, the name "Will" appears at the top of the list with the title "Val de Chambre."[18]

Flexner, in his biography of Washington, provides this insight into the nature of Billy Lee's services to the general in the postwar period:

---

16. *Papers: Presidential Series,* ed. Abbot and Twohig, 2:134n.

17. *Papers: Confederation Series,* ed. Abbot and Twohig, 2:14. "No evidence has been found that Margaret Thomas, or Margaret Lee, came to Mount Vernon" (ibid., 14n).

18. Winslow C. Watson, ed., *Men and Times of the Revolution; or Memoirs of Elkanah Watson,* 279; *Diaries,* ed. Jackson and Twohig, 4:277.

As he had in wartime, Washington arose early, with the dawn in summer, by candlelight during the rest of the year. He was instantly attended by his "valet de chambre," Will (also known as Billy Lee), an aging mulatto slave who had been at his side during both his wars. Will was a privileged servant with duties hardly extending beyond serving a master who needed little personal service, and with a gift for procuring, in the byways of the intricate household, liquor that would get him drunk by evening. In the mornings (presumably) Will was sober, if a little bleary-eyed. He had already laid out the costume in which Washington would attend to his farms: on a recorded occasion a plain blue coat, white cashmere waistcoat, black breeches, and black boots.

Washington shaved himself. Then Will brushed his master's long hair, pulled it back tightly in what was considered a "military manner" (as it left no curls at the side), and tied the queue firmly with a ribbon.[19]

Although Washington finally reached the conclusion that he would have to find someone else to take over Billy's duties, he appeared to face the prospect of losing even the limited services of this longtime retainer with genuine regret. As he told Lear, the task of finding a suitable replacement for Billy Lee was not something he was looking forward to:

German Town, November 8, 1793.

My dear Sir:

. . . I do not *yet* know whether I shall get a substitute for William: nothing short of excellent qualities and a man of good appearance, would induce me to do it. and under my present view of the matter too, who would employ himself otherwise than William did; that is as a Butler as well as a Valette for my wants of the latter are so trifling that any man (as Willm. was) would soon be ruined by idleness who had only them to attend to.[20]

A young Mount Vernon slave, Christopher, did eventually gain the coveted position of body servant to Washington, and Billy Lee rapidly faded from sight, now reduced to cobbling shoes.[21]

In the inventory of his slaves that Washington made in June 1799, just prior to his death in December of that same year, the name "Will" was still being carried as part of the "Mansion House" personnel, but there was no longer a title attached to it.[22] More significant, perhaps, it was Christopher, not Billy Lee, who kept the death

---

19. James T. Flexner, *George Washington and the New Nation, 1783–1793,* 42.

20. Fitzpatrick, ed., *Writings,* 33:151.

21. According to Decatur, "Christopher, one of the young Mount Vernon slaves, was the understudy for the famous Billy Lee as Washington's body-servant and, later on, after William became incapable of work, took his place in the household" (*Private Affairs of George Washington,* 21). On Billy Lee cobbling shoes, see Washington to Pearce, Philadelphia, May 18, 1794 ("George Washington and Mount Vernon," 74).

22. Fitzpatrick, ed., *Writings,* 37:257.

watch by Washington's bedside during the general's final hours. The truth is that Billy Lee was a crippled alcoholic living out his days as a humble shoemaker in an outbuilding on the Mount Vernon estate. But Billy Lee never tired of recapturing the excitement, the glory, and the heroics of the bygone military campaigns of the Revolutionary War in which he had participated in the service of his master:

> Among many interesting relics of the past, to be found in the last days at Mount Vernon, was old Billy, the famed body-servant of the commander-in-chief during the whole of the War of the Revolution. Of a stout athletic form, he had from an accident become a cripple, and, having lost the power of motion, took up the occupation of a shoemaker for sake of employment. Billy carefully reconnoitred the visitors as they arrived, and when a military title was announced, the old body-servant would send his compliments to the soldier, requesting an interview at his quarters. It was never denied, and Billy, after receiving a warm grasp of the hand, would say, "Ah, colonel, glad to see you; we of the army don't see one another often in these peaceful times. Glad to see your honor looking so well; remember you at headquarters. The new-time people don't know what we old soldiers did and suffered for the country in the old war. Was it not cold enough at Valley Forge? Yes, was it; and I am sure you remember it was hot enough at Monmouth. Ah, colonel, I am a poor cripple; can't ride now, so I make shoes and think of the old times; the gineral often stops his horse here, to inquire if I want anything. I want for nothing, thank God, but the use of my limbs."
>
> These interviews were frequent, as many veteran officers called to pay their respects to the retired chief, and all of them bestowed a token of remembrance upon the old body-servant of the Revolution.[23]

Washington, too, had a long memory. He saw beyond the sad events in Billy Lee's later life and focused instead on the daring and challenging trials of the Revolution, when they had ridden together in eight years of hard campaigning, when Billy had proved his worth in loyalty and devotion, in stamina and courage. As Washington plainly states in his will, it was the recollection of these and earlier years of comradeship that prompted him to include Billy Lee among those receiving bequests:

> And to my Mulatto man William (calling himself William Lee) I give immediate freedom; or if he should prefer it (on account of the accidents which have befallen him, and which have rendered him incapable of walking or of any active employment) to remain in the situation he now is, it shall be optional in him to do so: In either case however, I allow him an annuity of thirty dollars during his natural life, which shall be independent of the victuals and cloaths he has been accustomed to receive, if he chuses the last alternative; but in full, with his freedom, if he prefers the first;—& this I give him as a testimony

---

23. Custis, *Recollections,* 450–51.

of my sense of his attachment to me, and for his faithful services during the Revolutionary War.[24]

Although legally a free man and at liberty to come and go as he pleased, Billy Lee chose to stay on in his familiar surroundings. The American painter Charles Willson Peale—who painted a number of portraits of Washington over the years, the first in May 1772 when Washington was still a colonel in the Virginia militia—passed by Mount Vernon in 1804 on a sentimental visit and met with Billy: "The travelers made a pilgrimage to Mount Vernon, Peale full of reminiscences of his visits there in the General's lifetime. All that remained of the family was one slave, old Billy Lee, Washington's body servant through the war, whom Peale found in an outbuilding, a cripple now, cobbling shoes. The two sat down alone together and talked of past days and of the important subject of good health."[25]

Confirmation of Billy Lee's continued presence at Mount Vernon is found in occasional entries in the account books of Judge Bushrod Washington, George Washington's nephew and the executor of his estate. The last such notation is dated December 31, 1824: "Paid for Billy Omitted September 20th. 1824 . . . $33.14."[26] But heavy drinking took its toll on Billy Lee, and his death must have come as a welcome relief to his long years of pain and suffering. George Washington Parke Custis recalled:

> I visited Mount Vernon in October, 1858, where I saw an old mulatto, named Westford, who had been a resident there since August, 1801. He was raised in the family of Judge Bushrod Washington, who came into possession of Mount Vernon, by inheritance, after the death of Mrs. Washington. Westford knew Billy well. His master having left him a house, and a pension of one hundred and fifty dollars a year, Billy became a spoiled child of fortune. He was quite intemperate at times, and finally *delirium tremens*, with all its horrors, seized him. Westford frequently relieved him on such occasions, by bleeding him. One morning, a little more than thirty years ago, Westford was sent for to bring Billy out of a fit. The blood would not flow. Billy was dead![27]

The Mount Vernon handbook adds this postscript: "Near the Washington Tomb is a burial ground identified as having been used by slaves and free blacks in the eighteenth and nineteenth centuries. A monument marking the site was erected by the Mount Vernon Ladies' Association in 1929, and a new memorial honoring those who served in slavery at Mount Vernon, was dedicated in 1983.

24. John C. Fitzpatrick, ed., *The Last Will and Testament of George Washington and Schedule of His Property*, 4.

25. Charles C. Sellers, *Charles Willson Peale*, 316.

26. Executor's Account Book—Washington Estate, 8, Mount Vernon Library.

27. Custis, *Recollections*, 157n.

William Lee (*circa* 1750–1828), George Washington's personal servant during the Revolutionary War, is among those known to have been buried here."[28]

The Washington Family by Edward Savage reflects a rather tall and imposing Billy Lee, in bright red vest with polished brass buttons, long formal tailcoat, and white jersey, standing beside and slightly behind the chair in which Martha Washington is seated. His black hair is tied back in a bun, his forehead is high and broad, and a strong Roman nose accentuates well-formed eyes, heavy brows, a jutting chin, and a fulsome mouth. Washington's tastes were known to incline toward the elegant and fastidious, and judging from the painting, Billy Lee met the highest standards. In appearance and in dress, at least, he was a fitting companion for the general. It is interesting to note that Washington usually referred to Billy as "my servant," sometimes as "my mulatto man" or "my fellow," but never as "my slave."

To these subjective conclusions, drawn from a two-hundred-year-old image, can be added some objective deductions. Keeping pace, as Billy Lee obviously did, with a mounted Washington during his most active and hectic years called for a

Billy Lee was undoubtedly the most widely publicized slave in eighteenth-century America—thanks to his intimate relationship with the commander in chief and to the talent of John Trumbull, the historical painter of the Revolution who portrayed both men in *George Washington*. In addition to his artistic talent, Trumbull had the distinct advantage of knowing his subjects well, having served as one of Washington's military aides during the summer of 1775. The portrait was completed in London in 1780. It was engraved in mezzotint and copies were circulated throughout Europe and America to great popular acclaim. (Courtesy of the Metropolitan Museum of Art)

28. *Mount Vernon: A Handbook,* 120.

man of equivalent riding skill and endurance. Following the general into battle, where the bullets and bayonets were real and deadly, called for an uncommon degree of courage. And learning to adapt to the high-level social and professional gatherings that were Washington's milieu required intelligence, poise, and sensitivity. Clearly, Billy Lee, in his heyday, was no humble, subservient creature, no ordinary run-of-the-mill slave. Although black, a bondsman, and probably illiterate, without formal training or education, Billy Lee was a personality in his own right who earned the respect, confidence, and devotion of his master by serving him loyally and well. Elswyth Thane refers to him as "Billy . . . the best of them all—the body servant who was to accompany Washington all through the war and share every hardship, softening so far as he was able by his devoted service the fatigue and anxieties of the Commander-in-chief."[29]

If Billy Lee had been a white man, he would have had an honored place in American history because of his close proximity to George Washington during the most exciting periods of his career. But because he was a black servant, a humble slave, he has been virtually ignored by both black and white historians and biographers. The major African American bibliographies or encyclopedias, if they mention Billy Lee at all, do so only perfunctorily, and biographers of Washington tend to emphasize Billy's decline in later life. But when Billy was mounted on a horse, he was the equal of any horseman. When he was slung low over Chinkling, galloping at breakneck speed through the woods and meadows following the pack of hounds in pursuit of the fox and then sounding his horn when the fox had been cornered, he was the equal of any huntsman. And when he rode alongside Washington in the thick of battle, ready to hand over to the general a spare horse or his telescope or whatever else might be needed, he was acting as Washington's military aide. This is the man Washington knew and appreciated, respected and honored. This is the Billy Lee whom Washington remembered and gave testimony to "for his faithful services during the Revolutionary War." The gift of manumission was Washington's open acknowledgment that Billy Lee and the other Mount Vernon slaves who would follow him to freedom deserved a rightful place alongside white men in a future multiracial society.

29. Elswyth Thane, *Potomac Squire,* 93.

10

ONEY JUDGE

IN HIS elevated status as Washington's favorite slave and body servant, Billy Lee was obviously satisfied and content with his lot. Most of the other Mount Vernon slaves did not share his good fortune or his willingness to accept the bonds of slavery. They still cherished the hope of a brighter future for themselves outside the confines of servitude. One such restless soul was Oney Judge—a young seamstress in Martha Washington's sewing circle. The details of Oney's elopement from Mount Vernon are vague and uncertain; we have only Washington's version, and that seems highly biased.

Washington was exceedingly angry and upset at Oney's escape, and he was vindictive. He viewed running away as an act of disloyalty as well as a gross violation of his chattel property rights. He wanted Oney Judge returned to Mount Vernon—whether she came willingly or was brought back forcibly—and he was not fussy about the methods employed to recover the fugitive. Trickery, deception, and coercion were all acceptable means for rounding up runaways, as far as Washington was concerned. What counted with him were not the legalities or the ethics of the recovery efforts but only the final results.

A frustrated master, however, had to contend with a female slave who had a mind of her own. Having made good her flight from Mount Vernon, Oney Judge was determined to retain her newly won freedom. This unusual woman had the spunk to try to bargain with President Washington for her liberty. But Washington was not prepared to bargain. A foiled kidnapping plot and a failed negotiation left Oney the clear winner. In New Hampshire she found the sanctuary and security—including marriage—that she had sought. Washington was forced to swallow his disappointment and to accept as inevitable the loss of Martha's pet seamstress.

The search for the fugitive commenced with a confidential letter dated September 1, 1796, from President Washington to his secretary of the treasury, Oliver Wolcott Jr., asking him to look into reports that the missing slave girl had been seen in Portsmouth, New Hampshire.

> Thursday Morning, September 1, [1796].
>
> Dear Sir:
>
> Enclosed is the name, and description of the Girl I mentioned to you last night. She has been the particular attendant on Mrs. Washington since she was ten years old; and was handy and useful to her being perfect Mistress of her needle.
>
> We have heard that she was seen in New York by someone who knew her, directly after she went off. And since by Miss Langden, in Portsmouth; who meeting her one day in the Street, and knowing her, was about to stop and speak to her, but she brushed quickly by, to avoid it.
>
> By her being seen in New York (if the fact be so) it is not probable she went immediately to Portsmouth by Water from this City; but whether she travelled by land, or Water to the latter, it is certain the escape has been planned by some one who knew what he was about, and had the means to defray the expence of it and to entice her off; for not the least suspicion was entertained of her going, or having formed a connexion with any one who could induce her to such an Act.
>
> Whether she is Stationary at Portsmouth, or was there *en passant* only, is uncertain; but as it is the last we have heard of her, I would thank you for writing to the Collector of that Port, and him for his endeavours to recover, and send her back: What will be the best method to effect it, is difficult for me to say. If enquiries are made openly, her Seducer (for she is simple and inoffensive herself) would take the alarm, and adopt instant measures (if he is not tired of her) to secrete or remove her. To seize, and put her on board a Vessel bound immediately to this place, or to Alexandria which I should like better, seems at first view, to be the safest and lease expensive. But if she is discovered, the Collector, I am persuaded, will pursue such measures as to him shall appear best, to effect those ends; and the cost shall be re-embursed and with thanks besides.
>
> If positive proof is required, of the identity of the person, Miss Langden who must have seen her often in the Chamber of Miss Custis, and I dare say Mrs. Langden, on the occasional calls on the girl by Mrs. Washington, when she has been here, would be able to do this.
>
> I am sorry to give you, or any one else trouble on such a trifling occasion, but the ingratitude of the girl, who was brought up and treated more like a child than a Servant (and Mrs. Washington's desire to recover her) ought not to escape with impunity if it can be avoided.[1]

The president's request was duly relayed to Joseph Whipple, the collector of customs in Portsmouth, who promptly responded with a brief note of

---

1. Washington to Wolcott, Philadelphia, September 1, 1796 (Fitzpatrick, ed., *Writings*, 35:201–2).

acknowledgment to Wolcott: "I have to acknowledge the receipt of your letter of the 1.st instant and to Assure you that I shall with great pleasure execute the Presidents wishes in the matter to which it relates—I have just ascertained the fact that the person mentioned is in this Town."[2] About a month later Whipple reported:

Having discovered her place of residence I engaged a passage for her in a Vessel preparing to Sail for Philadelphia avoiding to give alarm by calling on her untill the Vessel was ready—I then caused her to be sent for as if to be employed in my family—After a cautious examination it appeared to me that she had not been decoyed away as had been apprehended, but that a thirst for compleat freedom which she was informed would take place on her arrival here & (in) Boston had been her only motive for absconding.—

It gave me much Satisfaction to find that when uninfluenced by fear she expressed great affection & Reverence for her Master & Mistress, and without hesitation declared her willingness to return & to serve with fidelity during the lives of the President & his Lady if she could be freed on their decease, should she outlive them, but that she should rather suffer death than return to Slavery & liable to be sold or given to any other person.—Finding this to be her disposition & conceiving it would be a pleasing circumstance both to the President & his Lady should she go back without compulsion I prevailed on her to confide in my obtaining for her the freedom she so earnestly wished for—She made preparation with cheerfulness to go on board the Vessel which was to have sailed in a few hours and of her own accord proposed concealing her intention of returning from her acquaintance Lest they should discourage her from her purpose.—I have recited this detail to show the girls good disposition when expressing her uncontrollable Sentiments and acting without bad advisers—I am extremely sorry to add, as I conceive the Girl is a valuable Servant to her Mistress, that the Vessel being detained by a contrary wind, in the course of the next day her intentions were discovered by her acquaintance who dissuaded her from returning and the Vessel sailed without her.

I am informed that many Slaves from the Southern States have come to Massachusetts & some to New Hampshire, either of which States they consider as an Asylum; the popular opinion here in favor of universal freedom has rendered it difficult to get them back to their masters:—In the present case of the Presidents servant continuing inflexible & will not return voluntarily, which at present there is no prospect of, I conceive it must be the legal & most effectual mode of proceeding that a direction should come from an Officer of the Presidents Household to the Attorney of the United States in New Hampshire & that he adopt such measures for returning her to her master as are authorized by the Constitution of the United States—and I shall be happy to facilitate the business to the utmost of my power in obedience to whatever

2. Whipple to Wolcott, Portsmouth, N.H., September 10, 1796 (Washington Papers, microfilm, ser. 4, pt. 2, reel 109, Manuscript Division, Library of Congress, Washington, D.C.).

shall be the pleasure of the President and it is with great regret that I give up the prospect of executing the business in the favourable manner that I at first flattered myself it would be done.[3]

Washington himself answered Whipple's letter. He was obviously annoyed at the miscarriage of his plans for having Oney Judge shanghaied and surreptitiously shipped back to Mount Vernon and urged Whipple to try again, though not at the risk of provoking a public protest—he would rather the girl should have her freedom than create a civil disturbance. Washington walked a fine line in separating his conduct as president of the United States from his responsibilities as a plantation proprietor attempting to recover a fugitive slave. Forced to make a choice, he was careful to place the national interest ahead of his own. But Oney would not have her way without a struggle. Washington set forth his case for her return in this lengthy letter to Whipple in Portsmouth:

> Philadelphia, November 28, 1796.
>
> Sir:
>
> Upon my return to this City, the latter end of October, after an absence of some weeks at Mount Vernon, Mr. Wolcott presented me with your letter of the 4th. of that month.
>
> I regret that the attempt you made to restore the Girl (Oney Judge as she called herself while with us, and who, without the least provocation absconded from her Mistress) should have been attended with so little Success. To enter into such a compromise with *her,* as she suggested to *you,* is totally inadmissable, for reasons that must strike at first view: for however well disposed I might be to a gradual abolition, or even to an entire emancipation of that description of People (if the latter was in itself practicable at this moment) it would neither be politic or just to reward *unfaithfulness* with a premature preference; and thereby discontent before hand the minds of all her fellow-servants who by their steady attachments are far more deserving than herself of favor.
>
> I was apprehensive (and so informed Mr. Wolcott) that if she had any previous notice more than could be avoided of an attempt to send her back, that she would contrive to elude it; for whatever she may have asserted to the contrary, there is no doubt in this family of her having been seduced, and enticed off by a Frenchman, who was either really, or pretendedly deranged, and under that guise, used to frequent the family; and has never been seen here since [the] girl decamped. We have indeed, lately been informed thro' other channels that she went to Portsmouth with a Frenchman, who getting tired of her, as is presumed, left her; and that she had betaken herself to the needle, the use of which she well understood, for a livelihood.
>
> About the epoch I have mentioned she herself was very desirous of returning to Virginia; for when Captn. Prescot was on the point of sailing from

---

3. Whipple to Wolcott, Portsmouth, N.H., October 4, 1796 (ibid.).

Portsmouth for the Federal City with his family, she offered herself to his lady as a waiter, told her she had lived with Mrs. Washington (without entering into particulars), and that she was desirous of getting back to her native place and friends. Mrs. Prescot either from not wanting a Maid Servant, or presuming that she might have been discarded for improper conduct, declined (unlucky for Mrs. Washington) taking her.

If she will return to her former service without obliging me to use compulsory means to effect it her late conduct will be forgiven by her Mistress, and she will meet with the same treatment from me that all the rest of her family (which is a very numerous one) shall receive. If she will not you would oblige me, by resorting to such measures as are proper to put her on board a Vessel bound either to Alexandria or the Federal City. Directed in either case, to my Manager at Mount Vernon; by the door of which the Vessel must pass, or to the care of Mr. Lear at the last mentioned place, if the Vessel should not stop before it arrives at that Port.

I do not mean however, by this request, that such violent measures should be used as would excite a mob or riot, which might be the case if she has adherents, or even uneasy Sensations in the Minds of well disposed Citizens; rather than either of these should happen I would forego her Services altogether, and the example also which is of infinite more importance. The less is said beforehand, and the more celerity is used in the act of shipping her when an opportunity presents, the better chance Mrs. Washington (who is desirous of receiving her again) will have to be gratified.

We had vastly rather she should be sent to Virginia than brought to this place [Philadelphia], as our stay here will be but short; and as it is not unlikely that she may, from the circumstances I have mentioned, be in a state of pregnancy. I should be glad to hear from you on this subject.[4]

From Whipple's subsequent report to the president, it seems that along with her freedom Oney Judge had found true love in New Hampshire, in the arms of a free mulatto: "I have deferred answering your letter some days to find out the present retreat of the Girl and yesterday discovered that she was lodged at a Free-Negros—that she is published for marriage agreeably to our law in such cases to a mulatto."[5] Oney Judge's marriage was confirmed by this official notice in the New Hampshire town records:

Greenland, January 8 1797

This may Certify that Mr. John Harris and Miss Oney Gudge was Published in this Town by Thos. Philbrook T. Clerk
The above persons were married by

4. Fitzpatrick, ed., *Writings*, 35:296–98.

5. Whipple to Washington, Portsmouth, N.H., December 22, 1796 (Washington Papers, microfilm, ser. 4, pt. 4, reel 110, Manuscript Division, Library of Congress).

Saml. Haven Clerk
Tho. Philbrook T. Clerk[6]

Whatever the moral overtones, under the prevailing laws Washington had every legal right to try to recover his fugitive slave property. But his willingness to engage in ethically questionable subterfuges shows him at his worst. There is an old saying to the effect that slavery degrades the master as much as it does the slave. Washington apparently was no exception to this maxim.

The sad reflection on Washington's character of this episode is that as late as 1797—a scant two years before his death—he still could not bring himself to come to terms with the realization that the enslaved African Americans' dream of freedom was firm and unshakable. Only when he drew up his will was Washington reconciled and prepared to concede the point that Oney Judge had bargained for— freedom from slavery.

6. New Hampshire Town Records, Greenland, vol. 1, 1749–1820, New Hampshire State Library, Concord. There are no other known records or documents relating to Oney Judge or to her husband, John Harris.

11

The Marquis de Lafayette

G EORGE WASHINGTON first made the acquaintance of the Marquis de Lafayette at a dinner held at the City Tavern in Philadelphia on August 1, 1777. Lafayette was immediately captivated by Washington, who was the guest of honor, and later wrote in his memoirs: "though he was surrounded by officers and private citizens, the majesty of his countenance and of his figure made it impossible not to recognize him; he was especially distinguished also by the affability of his manners and the dignity with which he addressed those about him." It seems that the attraction was mutual: "When they were about to separate, Washington took LaFayette aside, spoke to him very kindly, complimented him upon the noble spirit he had shown and the sacrifices he had made in favor of the American cause, and then told him that he should be pleased if he would make the quarters of the Commander-in-Chief his home, establish himself there whenever he thought proper, and consider himself at all times as one of his family."[1] Thus began a lifelong friendship that would have a profound impact on the course of American history as well as bring about a remarkable questioning of Washington's conventional views on the institution of slavery.

Although Lafayette was only nineteen years old when he met Washington, with negligible military experience, he did have some impressive credentials. The marquis had inherited from his Gallic forebears the ancestral title along with extensive landholdings, great personal wealth, and social and political leverage. Furthermore, he had married into one of France's most powerful and prestigious

1. Charlemagne Tower Jr., *The Marquis de La Fayette in the American Revolution*, 1:214–15.

families of the ancien régime, the Noailles.[2] And he had in his pocket a commission designating him a major general in the Continental army, duly authorized by the Continental Congress on the basis of a promise made to the marquis the previous year by Silas Deane, the official American representative in Paris. Lafayette's standing in the nobility and his court connections, which the American diplomats in Paris were eager to exploit in promoting an alliance with France, were the motivation for agreeing to award such a high rank to the boy soldier.[3]

All of this was of only passing interest to Washington. The British were preparing to bloody him again and to chase him out of Philadelphia. His urgent concern was to avoid an overwhelming and disastrous defeat of his outnumbered troops, which could spell the disintegration of his command. The young marquis, however, saw the pending confrontation as a welcome opportunity. He had come to America that summer driven by visions of grandeur. Unlike so many of the other foreign mercenaries who had flocked to Washington's headquarters, Lafayette had no interest in material rewards or emoluments. He had come to America to fight for liberty, to win glory for himself, and to punish "perfidious Albion." He was flattered to be able to ride proudly beside Washington on parade through the streets of Philadelphia, decked out in his brand-new major general's uniform.[4] But he was also sensible and intelligent enough to realize that his title and position were strictly honorary. He would have to earn the right to exercise the prerogatives of leadership that went with his rank.

The Battle of Brandywine, on September 11, 1777, gave Lafayette that chance. Washington sent him into combat as a volunteer, and the marquis fought bravely and well under difficult conditions in which the Continentals were once more

---

2. According to Andreas Latzko, as an infant Lafayette "had been held over the font by his rich grandfather, the Marquis de la Rivière [and] . . . entered in the register as the very great and very puissant Lord, Monseigneur Maria Joseph Paul Yves Roch Gilbert du Motier, Marquis de LaFayette, Baron de Vissac, Seigneur de St. Romain" (*Lafayette: A Life,* 4). On the death of his mother and grandfather in April 1770, he "became a rich heir by entail, sole owner of the whole of the landed properties of the Counts of La Rivière . . . lord over an estate of three and a half million francs" (ibid., 14). On April 11, 1774, at the Hotel de Noailles, rue St.-Honoré, Lafayette married Mademoiselle Marie-Adrienne-Françoise de Noailles, daughter of the Duc d'Ayen, Maréchal du Camp et Armées du Roi, afterward Duc de Noailles (Tower, *La Fayette,* 1:12).

3. Undaunted by an initially cool reception, the young Frenchman had petitioned the Continental Congress, asking to serve in the American military at his own expense and as a volunteer rather than an officer. His modest and unusual proposal garnered congressional attention, his credentials were examined, and on July 31, 1777, Lafayette was voted the commission of major general, though he was not given an active command (*Dictionary of American Biography,* vol. 5, pt. 2, 536). Deane said that Lafayette's "high birth, his alliances, the great dignities which his family hold at his Court, his considerable estates in this realm, his personal merit, his reputation, his disinterestedness, and above all, his zeal for the liberty of our provinces, are such as have only been able to engage me to promise him the rank of major-general in the name of the United States" (Tower, *La Fayette,* 1:35).

4. See Latzko, *Lafayette,* 59.

forced to retreat. Lafayette was wounded in the leg by an enemy sharpshooter during the encounter but gallantly continued the struggle and refused to leave the field.[5] It was this "baptism of fire" that won him the admiration and acceptance of his fellow officers and soldiers. When Washington encountered the young Frenchman limping but still in action, he ordered him to retire to have his wound dressed. "Treat him as though he were my son," Washington reportedly told the surgeons.[6]

Lafayette, while convalescing in Bethlehem, Pennsylvania, wrote a letter to his wife in which he informed her of the warm friendship that had sprung up with the American general:

> Be at ease about the treatment of my wound, for all the doctors in America are aroused in my behalf. I have a friend who has spoken to them in a way to ensure my being well cared for, and that is General Washington.
>
> That inestimable man, whose talent and virtue I admire—the better I know him the more I venerate him—has been kind enough to become my intimate friend.
>
> His tender interest in me quickly won my heart; I am established in his household and we live together like two brothers in mutual intimacy and confidence. This friendship makes me most happy in this country.
>
> When he sent his chief surgeon to me, he told him to care for me as though I were his son, and, having heard that I wished to join the army too soon, he wrote me a letter full of tenderness in which he urged me to wait until I was entirely cured.[7]

Washington was a reserved man with few close friends (outside his circle of relatives) and even fewer intimates. The Marquis de Lafayette was among those privileged to belong to the innermost circle. The simplest and most logical explanation for their special affinity toward each other is that Lafayette needed a father figure—his natural father having been killed by the British in one of the many skirmishes of the Seven Years' War before Lafayette was born—and Washington, childless in his marriage, craved a son of his own. Lafayette invariably referred to Washington as his "spiritual father" and to himself as the general's "adopted son."[8] As for Washington, he made no secret of the fact that he felt happy and comfortable in that role.

The two men could not have been more different. In addition to the disparity in their ages (Washington was forty-five in 1777 and Lafayette was his junior by twenty-five years), they were of diametrically opposite temperaments. Lafayette was impulsive, dashing, headstrong, enthusiastic, filled with romantic ideals, and

---

5. Ibid.
6. See Brand Whitlock, *La Fayette,* 1:92.
7. Letter of October 16, 1777 (ibid., 1:95).
8. See Gottschalk, ed., *Letters of Lafayette to Washington,* ix, xiv.

generously endowed with Gallic charm. Washington was outwardly cold and austere, inwardly cautious and conservative, ever meticulous, pragmatic, and punctilious, and his emotions were almost always under tight control. Hence, it is probable that Lafayette's spirited hopes and aspirations stimulated Washington, while Washington's disciplined nature served to rein in Lafayette's extravagant exuberance.

The one common thread that ran through the inconsistencies of character and temperament was total dedication to the principle of liberty. Washington thought of liberty at first in terms that excluded blacks, since by background and conditioning he regarded slaves as chattel property. Lafayette, who probably had never laid eyes on a black man or woman until he came to America, protested vehemently when he learned that liberty there meant freedom only for the whites, with the overwhelming majority of the African Americans destined to be held in perpetual bondage: "I would never have drawn my sword in the cause of America, if I could have conceived that thereby I was founding a land of slavery."[9] Washington would not be deaf to the marquis's admonitions and proselytizing on the issue of slavery once Lafayette realized the true state of affairs. In fact, he was to become Lafayette's chosen, if somewhat reticent, partner in a plan to emancipate the slaves.

From the very beginning Lafayette had faith in Washington as a man of character and integrity and appeared to take it for granted that the future president would never abandon the ideals for which the Revolution was being fought. In the midst of the bleak and depressing winter days at Valley Forge, which Lafayette shared with Washington and the stalwarts of the Continental army, he managed these optimistic lines to his father-in-law, the Duke d'Ayen, in France: "Our General is a man truly made for this revolution, which could not be successfully accomplished without him. I see him more closely than any man in the world and I see that he is worthy of the adoration of his country. . . . I admire more each day the beauty of his character and of his soul. . . . his name will be revered in all ages by all lovers of liberty and humanity."[10]

Lafayette aided the cause of freedom in many ways, including generous personal financial contributions toward sustaining the Revolution. (Louis Gottschalk quotes a figure of around seven hundred thousand livres, or about $1 million.)[11] He also used his political and social contacts in France with very effective results. Rosy communiqués from the field and eloquent arguments and persistent pleadings for assistance, in person and via correspondence, at the Court of Versailles

9. Lafayette to Thomas Clarkson (William C. Nell, *The Colored Patriots of the American Revolution,* 388).

10. Quoted in Whitlock, *La Fayette,* 1:13.

11. Louis Gottschalk, *Lafayette Joins the American Army,* 332.

were invaluable in convincing the French to intervene openly and actively on the side of the Americans. Lafayette created single-handedly the image in France of George Washington as a brilliant and victorious leader; he identified so closely with the general that he himself became known the length and breadth of his native land as *le Washington français*.[12]

When the French commanders arrived in North America to begin combined operations with their new ally, it was Lafayette who handled the delicate liaison between them and their American counterparts, and especially with Washington.[13] As the inevitable misunderstandings arose, Lafayette was called upon to exercise his considerable diplomatic skills to soothe ruffled feathers and massage the super-sensitive egos on both sides. Thanks in part to his ministrations, the frictions were held to a minimum and the degree of cooperation, by and large, was satisfactory.

Soldiering came naturally to Lafayette. He also profited from being a fast learner. The young Frenchman, who performed with valor in a number of the major engagements of the war, so impressed Washington that he was entrusted with the independent command of the Continental troops in Virginia in the spring of 1781. Lafayette was given the hazardous assignment of parrying the advances and threatened thrusts of Lord Cornwallis, whose seasoned veterans were operating in the southern theater. He managed his role in this game of tactical warfare so well that the overconfident Cornwallis was expertly maneuvered into a corner at Yorktown. In that untenable position, blockaded by the French fleet and besieged by the massed armies of the Americans and the French, Cornwallis was finally forced to capitulate.

On a note of triumph Lafayette returned to France, to be feted and toasted everywhere he went. When the general treaty of peace between England and the United States was signed in Paris, on January 20, 1783, Lafayette found himself in Cádiz, in the company of the Count d'Estaing, who commanded the French squadron then based in the Spanish port. Lafayette immediately asked d'Estaing to dispatch a fast-sailing vessel to Philadelphia with the momentous news. To the president of Congress he wrote a short, formal note:

> Cadix, 5 February, 1783.
>
> SIR,
>
> Having been at some pains to engage a vessel to go to Philadelphia, I now find myself happily relieved by the kindness of Count d'Estaing. He is just now pleased to tell me, that he will dispatch a French ship, and, by way of compliment on the occasion, he has made choice of the *Triumph*. So that I am not without hopes of giving Congress the first tidings of a general peace; and

12. Gottschalk, ed., *Letters of Lafayette to Washington*, xvii.
13. Ibid., xii, xiv.

I am happy in the smallest opportunity of doing any thing, that may prove agreeable to America.

I have the honor to be, &c.

LAFAYETTE.[14]

The marquis also took the opportunity to send a long, personal letter to Washington.

Cadiz, February the 5th, 1783

My dear General

. . . I rejoice at the blessings of a peace where our noble ends have been secured. Remember our Valley Forge times, and from a recollection of past dangers and labours, we still will be more pleased at our present comfortable situation—What a sense of pride and satisfaction I feel when I think of the times that have determined my engaging in the American cause! . . .

At the prospect of a peace, I had prepared to go to America—you know me too well, my dear General, not to be sensible of the pleasure I anticipated in the hope to embrace you, and to be reunited with my fellow soldiers. . . . Happy, ten times happy will I be in embracing my dear General, my father, my best friend whom I love with an affection and a respect which I too well feel, not to know it is impossible for me to express it.

Then, apparently out of the blue, came a startling suggestion to emancipate the slaves:

Now, my dear General, that you are going to enjoy some ease and quiet, permit me to propose a plan to you which might become greatly beneficial to the Black Part of Mankind. Let us unite in purchasing a small estate where we may try the experiment to free the Negroes, and use them only as tenants—such an example as yours might render it a general practice, and if we succeed in America, I will chearfully devote a part of my time to render the method fashionable in the West Indias. If it be a wild scheme, I had rather be mad that way, than to be thought wise on the other tack.

The letter closed with some sound and prophetic advice:

Your influence, my dear General, cannot be better employed than in inducing the people of America to strengthen their federal Union—it is a work in which it behooves you to be concerned—I look upon it as a necessary measure. . . . Now is the time when the powers of Congress must be fixed, the boundaries determined, and Articles of Confederation revised—It is a work in which every well wisher to America must desire to be concerned— It is the finishing stroke that is wanting to the perfection to the Temple of Liberty.[15]

14. Worthington C. Ford, ed., *The Writings of George Washington, 1782–1785*, 10:197n.
15. Gottschalk, ed., *Letters of Lafayette to Washington*, 259–61.

Washington, who had been impatiently marking time at his headquarters in Newburgh, New York, while the hostilities were winding down, was delighted to receive from Lafayette the first official confirmation of the formal conclusion to the war. In his reply the general's restrained style just barely conceals his joy:

> Head Qrs., Newburgh, April 5, 1783
>
> My dear Marqs.:
>
> It is easier for you to conceive than for me to express the sensibility of my Heart at the communications in your letter of the 5th. of Feby. from Cadiz. It is to these communications we are indebted for the only acct. yet recd of a general Pacification. My mind upon the receipt of this news was instantly assailed by a thousand ideas, all of them contending for pre-eminence, but believe me my dear friend none could supplant, or ever will eradicate that gratitude, which has arisen from a lively sense of the conduct of your Nation: from my obligations to many illustrious characters of it, among whom (I do not mean to flatter, when) I place you at the head of them.

He went on to respond to Lafayette's plan to free the slaves in America:

> The scheme, my dear Marqs. which you propose as a precedent, to encourage the emancipation of the black people of this Country from that state of Bondage in wch. they are held, is a striking evidence of the benevolence of your Heart. I shall be happy to join you in so laudable a work; but will defer going into a detail of the business, 'till I have the pleasure of seeing you.[16]

Taken at face value, the above should stand as proof of Washington's growing commitment to the abolition of slavery. Regrettably, the historical record demonstrates otherwise. His good intentions did not translate into tangible, meaningful actions. As it turned out, he gave lip service, and nothing more, to emancipation. Instead of leadership, he retreated quickly and quietly behind his preferred shield of benign neutrality. But the fact that Lafayette had managed to extract a written promise from Washington on such a sensitive issue speaks for the depth of their friendship and the powerful influence the young man exerted over his older comrade.

In spite of Washington's obvious hesitation, Lafayette continued with undiminished zeal in his efforts to encourage his participation in the crusade to abolish slavery. The next opportunity presented itself in the summer of 1784, when Lafayette made the first of two triumphal tours of the new nation. The brightest moments of his six-month visit were those he spent with Washington at Mount Vernon: "on the 17th [of August 1784], he drove into the park at Mount Vernon where Washington was waiting. They spent eleven days together, riding

16. Fitzpatrick, ed., *Writings*, 26:297, 300.

about over the plantation in the drowsy heat of a Virginia summer, or sitting at the end of lazy afternoons on the wide veranda overlooking the Potomac, while Mrs. Washington made the tea." The two old friends enjoyed long and leisurely conversations covering a wide range of topics, from politics to wartime reminiscences. They also touched on the subject of slavery, and "the Marquis urged his plan of emancipation; Washington was sympathetic, but thought the time hardly ripe; how was one to work a Virginia plantation without negro hands?"[17]

While in America, Lafayette strived to focus attention on the slavery issue and used his prestige and popularity at every opportunity to try to sway public

If the Marquis de Lafayette had had his way, he probably would have been delighted to set free all of the slaves in the United States. That, of course, was impossible. But when James Armistead (born circa 1748, the slave of William Armistead of New Kent County, Virginia) approached him in Richmond in November 1784 asking for a testimonial that might help him to gain his freedom, the Frenchman was pleased to oblige. He wrote: "This is to Certify that the Bearer by the Name of James Has done Essential Service to Me While I Had the Honour to Command in this State. His Intelligence from the Ennemy's Camp Were Industriously Collected and Most faithfully delivered. He Perfectly Acquitted Himself With Some Important Commissions I Gave Him and Appears to me Entitled to Every Reward His Situation Can Admit of. Done Under My Hand, Richmond November 21st 1784 Lafayette." Lafayette's recommendation carried sufficient weight to move the Virginia House of Delegates to purchase and emancipate James, who, in gratitude to his benefactor, assumed Lafayette as his surname. The Virginia legislature later also granted James a pension in recognition of his wartime services as a spy and courier for the Americans. The original engraving showing a bust portrait of James Lafayette with the Marquis de Lafayette's inscription beneath it was very likely executed in Richmond sometime after 1784 by an unknown artist. (Courtesy of the Virginia Historical Society, Richmond)

17. Whitlock, *La Fayette*, 1:285–86.

opinion. In an address before the Virginia House of Delegates, he "extolled the patriotism of Virginia in her time of trial. He carefully uttered the words 'Federal union' as he praised the state for shedding the blood of her sons 'in defense of her sister states.' With the problem of the enslaved Virginians in mind, he prayed that Virginia would 'continue to give to the world unquestionable proofs of her philanthropy and her regard to the liberties of all mankind.'" Lafayette also met in Richmond with a slave by the name of James, who had been a servant in the household of Lord Cornwallis but had acted as a secret agent for the marquis in 1781, turning over to him valuable information relating to the military plans and movements of the British. James now asked Lafayette for some suitable recognition of his "essential services," prompting him to write a testimonial bearing witness that James had "industriously collected and most faithfully delivered" intelligence of the enemy's dispositions and had "perfectly acquitted himself with some important commissions." Two years later, in 1786, the Virginia legislature voted James, who had chosen the surname Lafayette, his freedom.[18]

The final parting between Washington and Lafayette was an emotional one. Washington accompanied the marquis to Annapolis before bidding him an affectionate farewell. Soon afterward the general set down his feelings on paper:

> Mount Vernon 8th Decr 1784.
>
> My Dr Marqs,
>   In the moment of our separation upon the road as I travelled, & every hour since—I felt all that love, respect & attachment for you, with which length of years, close connexion & your merits, have inspired me. I often asked myself, as our Carriages distended, whether that was the last sight, I ever should have of you? And tho' I wished to say no—my fears answered yes.[19]

After his return to France, Lafayette wrote Washington of his progress in bringing about emancipation within the French colony of Cayenne, the capital city of present-day French Guiana on the northeast coast of South America. Some months later, in 1786, the marquis wrote: "an other secret I intrust to you, my dear General, is that I have purchased for hundred and twenty five thousand French livres a plantation in the Colony of Cayenne and am going to free my Negroes in order to make that experiment which you know is my hobby horse."[20]

Washington responded to this news with unabashed admiration. In contrast to Lafayette's enterprising initiative, he could only express frustration and

18. Louis Gottschalk, *Lafayette between the American and the French Revolution, 1783–1789*, 126–27.
19. *Papers: Confederation Series*, ed. Abbot and Twohig, 2:175.
20. Lafayette to Washington, Sarguemines, France, July 14, 1785; Lafayette to Washington, Paris, February 6, 1786 (Gottschalk, ed., *Letters of Lafayette to Washington*, 309).

disappointment at the lack of progress in America in changing public opinion or in securing abolitionist legislation:

> Mount Vernon 10th May 1786.
>
> My Dear Marquis,
>
> The benevolence of your heart my Dr [dear] Marqs is so conspicuous upon all occasions, that I never wonder at any fresh proofs of it; but your late purchase of an Estate in the Colony of Cayenne with a view of emancipating the slaves on it, is a generous and noble proof of your humanity. Would to God a like spirit would diffuse itself generally into the minds of the people of this country, but I despair of seeing it—some petitions were presented to the [Virginia] Assembly at its last Session, for the abolition of slavery, but they could scarcely obtain a reading. To set them [the slaves] afloat at once would, I really believe, be productive of much inconvenience & mischief; but by degrees it certainly might, & assuredly ought to be effected, & that too by Legislative authority.[21]

The rest of the story falls short of the expectations raised by the earlier exchanges on emancipation between Washington and Lafayette. The Frenchman went on to become a leading spokesman for abolition; the American sat and pondered, a captive of the plantation society to which he belonged and the slave-labor system on which he was economically dependent. The two men remained the very best of friends and continued to correspond until Washington's death in 1799, but the ability of the marquis to pull Washington along with him into the mainstream of the abolitionist movement diminished following their final their parting in Annapolis. Each went his own way.

Perhaps there would have been a different ending if Lafayette had remained in America instead of returning to France and if he had continued to exert his remarkable influence with Washington in persuading the general to play an active leadership role in the emancipation struggle. The Quakers—including a prominent Quaker merchant and plantation proprietor in Virginia, Robert Pleasants—had already demonstrated that freeing the plantation slaves and teaching them to become yeomen farmers on their own parcels of land was feasible and practical. The program that Lafayette was attempting to install on his newly purchased plantation in Cayenne could probably have been promoted just as well in Virginia and other southern regions of America—particularly if Washington had given it his personal blessing and the example of his own participation. But this was not to be.

For his part, Lafayette was instrumental in helping to found the first French society for the elimination of the slave trade. In 1788 he asked Alexander Hamilton

---

21. *Papers: Confederation Series,* ed. Abbot and Twohig, 4:41–44.

to enroll him in the emancipation campaign in the United States and was promptly named an honorary member of the New York Society for Promoting the Manumission of Slaves. Benjamin Franklin, as president of the Philanthropic Society of Philadelphia, called on Lafayette for his personal assistance and influence at the Court of Versailles in gaining support for the society's antislavery petition in France. In England, at his own request, Lafayette became a corresponding member of the British Committee for the Abolition of the Slave Trade.[22] As for the experiment in Cayenne, it proved successful to the extent that, as Lafayette insistently pointed out, the colony as a whole experienced none of the violence between whites and blacks that occurred in the rest of the French West Indies when legalized slavery finally ended in those French possessions.[23]

If Washington was aware of Lafayette's later antislavery activities, he would have had to learn of them from sources other than the marquis, since for reasons that remain unexplained the topic of slavery virtually disappeared from their correspondence. Lafayette may have considered it futile to push his friend beyond certain tolerable limits; or perhaps the subject had become a painful source of embarrassment. Whatever their reasons, slavery was no longer an issue of discussion between them. In the closing decades of the eighteenth century Lafayette became hopelessly entangled in the political intrigues and quicksands of the French Revolution,[24] while Washington was hard put to cope with the demanding political role of "founding father" and elected leader of the new American republic.

22. Gottschalk, *Lafayette between the Revolutions*, 370–71.
23. See Melvin D. Kennedy, *Lafayette and Slavery*, 5.
24. Between 1792 and 1797, Lafayette was held in several foreign prisons. After his release, he and his family remained in exile until 1799, when they returned to France and settled at La Grange, about forty miles outside Paris (*Dictionary of American Biography*, vol. 5, pt. 2, 538).

12

JOHN LAURENS

Henry Laurens was a wealthy South Carolina merchant and planter who owned a large number of slaves on his rice and indigo plantations and, like Washington, considered them for many years to be essential to his lifestyle and his economic well-being. He was also an early and prominent advocate of independence and a respected friend of George Washington. Laurens's organizational skills and leadership abilities paved the way for his election in November 1777 as the third president of the Continental Congress, succeeding John Hancock.[1] His son John was a dedicated idealist: brilliant, enterprising, compassionate, and courageous. Educated in England and Switzerland, where he was exposed to the humanist philosophy of the Enlightenment that pronounced individual rights to be the cornerstone of the new natural order, John Laurens was welcomed as a volunteer aide to General Washington. He thus joined an elite circle of young men, including the Marquis de Lafayette, who composed the commander in chief's intimate military family during the years 1778–1779.

It was from this vantage point that John Laurens formulated the idea he quietly broached to his father in a letter dated January 14, 1778:

> I barely hinted to you, my dearest father, my desire to augment the Continental forces from an untried source. I wish I had any foundation to ask

---

1. Henry Laurens, as one of the leading merchants of Charleston in the 1760s, had amassed his fortune buying and selling slaves. He also employed gangs of slaves to work his land in South Carolina and Georgia, estimated to total around twenty thousand acres. "His ideas on this subject [slavery] underwent a gradual but steady change which transformed him from the enthusiastic importer of Africans in the '50s to the advocate of universal emancipation in 1776" (David D. Wallace, *The Life of Henry Laurens*, 444–45).

for an extraordinary addition to those favours which I have already received from you. I would solicit you to cede me a number of your able bodied men slaves, instead of leaving me a fortune.

I would bring about a two-fold good; first, I would advance those who are unjustly deprived of the rights of mankind to a state which would be a proper gradation between abject slavery and perfect liberty, and besides I would reinforce the defenders of liberty with a number of gallant soldiers. Men, who have the habit of subordination almost indelibly impressed on them, would have one very essential qualification of soldiers. I am persuaded that if I could obtain authority for the purpose, I would have a corps of such men trained, uniformly equip'd and ready in every respect to act at the opening of the next campaign.[2]

Two weeks later he wrote that his plan had received Washington's tacit approval: "You ask, what is the general's opinion, upon this subject? He is convinced, that the numerous tribes of blacks in the southern part of the continent, offer a resource to us that should not be neglected. With respect to my particular plan, he only objects to it, with the arguments of pity for a man who would be less rich than he might be."[3]

Henry Laurens fell in with his son's scheme and a year later, on March 16, 1779, put the proposition directly to Washington: "Our affairs in the Southern department [are] in more favorable light, than we had viewed them in a few days ago; nevertheless, the Country is greatly distressed, and will be more so, unless further reinforcements are sent to its relief. had we Arms for 3000 such black Men, as I could select in Carolina I should have no doubt of success in driving the British out of Georgia and subduing East Florida before the end of July."[4] These were brave but empty words, which Washington promptly shrugged off with a polite, noncommittal, and disingenuous reply:

> Middle brook, [New Jersey], March 20, 1779.
> Dear Sir:
> The policy of our arming Slaves is, in my opinion, a moot point, unless the enemy set the example; for should we begin to form Battalions of them, I have not the smallest doubt (if the War is to be prosecuted) of their following us in it, and justifying the measure upon our own ground; the upshot then must be, who can arm fastest, and where are our Arms? besides, I am not clear that a discrimination will not render Slavery more irksome to those who remain in it; most of the good and evil things of this life are judged of by comparison; and I fear a comparison in this case will be productive of much discontent in those who are held in servitude; but as this is a subject that has

2. John Laurens, *The Army Correspondence of Colonel John Laurens in the Years 1777–8*, 108.
3. John Laurens to Henry Laurens, Valley Forge, Pa., February 2, 1778 (ibid., 117–18).
4. Fitzpatrick, ed., *Writings*, 14:267n.

never employed much of my thoughts, these are no more than the first crude Ideas that have struck me upon the occasion.[5]

In spite of Washington's apparent misgivings, it seemed for a time that the tide of events in the South favored Laurens's proposal. South Carolina was in desperate straits in 1779. Not only were the British sending in their best troops, supported by the native Tories, but they were actively inciting the slaves and border Indians to join in the fight against the rebels. Faced with frequent raids and the ever-present fear of uprisings by their own restless slaves, the patriotic white planters were disinclined to leave their plantations to assist the organized militia. Consequently, the war in the South degenerated into a bitter internecine struggle that ravaged the countryside, with the Royalists the obvious beneficiaries. In the winter of that forlorn year, John Rutledge, the governor of South Carolina, sent his emissaries to Philadelphia to plead with the Continental Congress for soldiers, supplies, and money. Having none of these to give, the frustrated legislators instead passed resolutions recommending, among other things, that the Southerners recruit their own slaves as an immediate and practical solution to their pressing manpower needs.

Taking his cue from Congress, Washington dispatched the enthusiastic John Laurens, newly commissioned a lieutenant colonel, to Charleston to personally present his proposition for African American recruitment to the South Carolina Assembly. His instructions were drafted by Alexander Hamilton, the youthful secretary and military aide to the commander in chief. In the official covering note, addressed to John Jay, president of the Continental Congress, Hamilton added his own private assessments, which almost certainly bore Washington's approval, of the short- and long-term benefits of making Continental soldiers out of slaves:

> [Middlebrook, New Jersey, March 14, 1779]
>
> Dear Sir,
>
> Col Laurens, who will have the honor of delivering [to] you this letter, is on his way to South Carolina, on a project, which I think, in the present situation of affairs there, is a very good one and deserves every kind of support and encouragement. This is to raise two three or four battalions of negroes; with the assistance of the government of that state, by contributions from the owners in proportion to the number they possess. If you should think proper to enter upon the subject with him, he will give you a detail of his plan. He wishes to have it recommended by Congress to the state; and, as an inducement, that they would engage to take those battalions into Continental pay.
>
> It appears to me, that an expedient of this kind, in the present state of Southern affairs, is the most rational, that can be adopted, and promises

5. Ibid., 14:267.

very important advantages. Indeed, I hardly see how a sufficient force can be collected in that quarter without it; and the enemy's operations there are growing infinitely serious and formidable. I have not the least doubt, that the negroes will make very excellent soldiers, with proper management; and I will venture to pronounce, that they cannot be put in better hands than those of Mr. Laurens. He has all the zeal, intelligence, enterprise, and every other qualification requisite to succeed in such an undertaking. . . . I frequently hear it objected to the scheme of embodying negroes that they are too stupid to make soldiers. This is so far from appearing to me a valid objection that I think their want of cultivation (for their natural faculties are probably as good as ours) joined to that habit of subordination which they acquire from a life of servitude, will make them sooner become soldiers than our White inhabitants. Let officers be men of sense and sentiment, and the nearer the soldiers approach to machines perhaps the better.

I foresee that this project will have to combat much opposition from prejudice and self-interest. The contempt we have been taught to entertain for the blacks, makes us fancy many things that are founded neither in reason nor experience; and an unwillingness to part with property of so valuable a kind will furnish a thousand arguments to show the impracticability or pernicious tendency of a scheme which requires such a sacrifice. But it should be considered, that if we do not make use of them in this way, the enemy probably will; and that the best way to counteract the temptation they will hold out will be to offer them ourselves. An essential part of the plan is to give them their freedom with their muskets. This will secure their fidelity, animate their courage, and I believe will have a good influence upon those who remain, by opening a door to their emancipation. This circumstance, I confess, has no small weight in inducing me to wish the success of the project; for the dictates of humanity and true policy equally interest me in favour of this unfortunate class of men. . . .

If arms are wanted for these troops and no better way of supplying them is to be found, we should endeavour to levy a contribution of arms upon the militia at large. Extraordinary exigencies demand extraordinary means. I fear this Southern business will become a very *grave* one.[6]

Moral fervor and the weight of rational arguments, however, were not strong enough to overcome the entrenched opposition of the Southern slave interests. John Laurens and his friends and supporters in the North were speedily disabused of their high hopes. In the words of the Southern historian Edward McCrady, the advice of Congress "was heard in South Carolina with indignation and rejected with scorn." It is said that Henry Laurens, upon receiving the news that the South Carolina legislature had given short shrift to his son's petition, could not resist a bit of sarcastic I-told-you-so: "I learn [that] your black Air Castle is blown up with contemptuous huzzas." On this sour note, the curtain rang down on

6. Harold C. Syrett, ed., *The Papers of Alexander Hamilton,* 2:17–19.

the first phase of John Laurens's single-minded campaign "to transform the timid slave into a firm defender of liberty and render him worthy to enjoy it himself."[7]

There was a hiatus of about two years during which Laurens's project was shelved as other matters occupied his time and attention. The British were increasingly moving the war into the South, as John Laurens reported to Washington:

> Charleston, February 14, 1780
>
> DEAR GENERAL,
>
> The day before yesterday, we had certain intelligence of the arrival of forty-five sail at North Edisto. A debarkation immediately commenced on Simmon's Island; and an advanced corps, it is said, of five hundred, proceeded the following day to John's Island. The Vigilant and two galleys are at Port Royal. Private accounts say that General Prevost is left to command at Savannah; that his troops consist of the Hessians and Loyalists that were there before, reenforced by a corps of blacks and a detachment of savages. It is generally reported that Sir Henry Clinton commands the present expedition. It appears to me to be the British policy to transfer the theatre of the war to this vulnerable part of the Continent.[8]

Lieutenant Colonel Laurens fought with conspicuous courage and gallantry at the Battle of Charleston in May 1780 and was captured by the British when the city and its army of five thousand defenders were forced to surrender. Paroled and set free, he was selected by Washington, and unanimously confirmed by Congress in December 1780, to travel to France as the special American minister to the Court of Versailles. His energetic and skillful diplomacy at the court was credited with helping to bring the French into the war as full-fledged allies and, perhaps equally important, with helping to loosen French purse strings controlling the flow of desperately needed money and supplies. He also had a key role in laying the groundwork for the crucial French naval cooperation in the victorious Yorktown campaign. Laurens managed to return from France in time to take part in this final major battle of the Revolution; as a token of the high esteem in which he was held, he was designated by Washington as his personal representative in negotiating and accepting the capitulation of Lord Cornwallis.

His determination undiminished by the passage of time, and fortified by his recent triumphs, John Laurens revived his earlier concept of enlisting enslaved African Americans in the South. He had in mind to use them in the planned military drive to eliminate the remaining British presence in South Carolina. Laurens

---

7. Edward McCrady, *The History of South Carolina in the Revolution, 1780–1785,* 314; Sara B. Townsend, *An American Soldier: The Life of John Laurens,* 133, 130.

8. Jared Sparks, ed., *Correspondence of the American Revolution: Being Letters of Eminent Men to George Washington,* 2:402.

communicated with the general from his native state on December 10, 1781: "I think they [the British] may be forced to evacuate Charles Town [Charleston] in the course of the present campaign—provided the Council of this State (South Carolina) will enter vigorously into the measure of reinforcing General Greene with a well chosen Corps of black levies."[9] Washington reacted favorably in his reply on February 18, 1782: "[British] Reinforcements may undoubtedly be expected, and I know of nothing which can be opposed to them with such a prospect of success as the Corps you have proposed should be levied in Carolina." And he gave his young friend an added boost a month later in a letter written on March 22: "I am sorry that the raising of the black corps, hung in suspence when you last wrote; but hope if your Assembly then about to sit adopted the measure, it is now in a degree of forwardness, and may be useful to the public cause."[10]

John Laurens directed his prodigious energies once again toward winning legislative approval for his proposal. His next letter to Washington reflected his continued optimism, despite certain setbacks:

> Bacon's Bridge, S.C., May 19, 1782
>
> MY DEAR GENERAL,
> . . . The plan, which brought me to this country [South Carolina], was urged with all the zeal which the subject inspired, both in our Privy Council and Assembly; but the single voice of reason was drowned by the howlings of a triple-headed monster, in which prejudice, avarice, and pusillanimity were united. It was some degree of consolation to me, however, to perceive that truth and philosophy had gained some ground; the suffrages in favor of the measures being twice as numerous as on a former occasion. Some hopes have been lately given [to] me from Georgia; but I fear, when the question is put, we shall be outvoted there with as much disparity as we have been in this country.[11]

The refusal of the recalcitrant Southerners to place the public good ahead of narrow sectional and private interests brought forth a rare display of temper by the commander in chief in his reply to Laurens:

> Head Quarters, July 10, 1782.
>
> My Dr. Sir:
> The last Post brought me your Letter of the 19 May. I must confess that I am not at all astonished at the failure of your Plan. That spirit of Freedom which at the commencement of this contest would have gladly sacrificed every thing to the attainment of its object has long since subsided, and every selfish Passion has taken its place; it is not the public but the private Interest which

9. Washington Papers, microfilm, ser. 4, reel 82, Manuscript Division, Library of Congress.
10. Fitzpatrick, ed., Writings, 24:4, 88n.
11. Sparks, ed., Correspondence, 2:506.

When Lt. Col. John Laurens was killed in August 1782 at the age of twenty-seven in a minor skirmish with the British in a rice field in South Carolina, the budding antislavery movement lost one of its most zealous and determined advocates. Laurens had succeeded in persuading General Washington to allow him to pursue his plan to recruit the slaves of the Deep South for the Continental army with the explicit promise of freedom in return for their services. The young crusader was in the midst of an uphill battle with the entrenched slave owners in the South Carolina and Georgia legislatures when his life was cut short. (Courtesy of the South Carolina Historical Society, Charleston)

influences the generality of Mankind nor can the Americans any longer boast an exception; under these circumstances it would rather have been surprizing if you had succeeded nor will you I fear succeed better in Georgia.[12]

The outcome of the debate in South Carolina was never in serious doubt. The arguments that Lieutenant Colonel Laurens again presented to the state legislature stood no chance against the united and solid wall of the slave owners' lobby. But the failure was not for want of trying. The young zealot was still challenging the odds, and the opposition, and was still brightly optimistic when he penned his last letter to Washington on June 12, 1782: "The approaching session of the Georgia Legislature, and the encouragement given me by Governor [Richard] Howley, who has a decisive influence in the counsels of that country, induce me to remain in this quarter for the purpose of taking new measures on the subject of our black

12. Fitzpatrick, ed., *Writings*, 24:421.

levies. The arrival of Colonel Baylor, whose seniority entitled him to the command of the light troops, afford me ample leisure for pursuing the business in person; and I shall do it, with all the tenacity of a man making a last effort on so interesting an occasion."[13]

Barely three months after these lines were written, John Laurens, only twenty-seven years of age, was killed in a minor skirmish with a British patrol near Charleston. Washington received the sad news in a report from Maj. Gen. Nathanael Greene:

> Ashley Hill, S.C., August 29, 1782
>
> SIR,
>
> Since I wrote to your Excellency, a day or two ago, Lieutenant-Colonel Laurens has been killed in an action on the Combahee River, about fifty miles south of our camp. The enemy made a detachment into that quarter, with a number of armed vessels, empty sloops and schooners, with about five hundred infantry, to collect rice. General Gist, with the light troops, in which Lieutenant-Colonel Laurens held a command, was detached to oppose them. Inclosed is a copy of General Gist's letter containing an account of the different operations. Colonel Laurens's fall is glorious; but his fate is much to be lamented. Your Excellency has lost a valuable Aid-de-camp, the army a brave officer, and the public a worthy and patriotic citizen.[14]

Washington responded: "The Death of Colo Laurens I consider as a very heavy misfortune, not only as it affects the public at large, but particularly so to his Family, and all his private Friends and Connections, to whom his amiable and useful Character had rendered him peculiarly dear."[15]

John Laurens's death was a serious blow to the budding antislavery movement, for there was no one else of his stature and caliber from the Deep South who was so committed to the cause of freedom for the slaves. Nor was there anyone among Washington's military subordinates, except for the Marquis de Lafayette, who ranked so high in the general's affections. Although Washington had been skeptical from the outset, he nevertheless had permitted his junior officer to proceed with his scheme for enlisting slaves as soldiers and then emancipating them. Just how far Washington actually would have gone in supporting Laurens is sheer conjecture. Whatever liberalizing influence John Laurens may have had on Washington ceased when he was struck down by the enemy's bullets.

Henry Laurens wrote to his son on September 21, 1779, these prophetic lines: "If you succeed [in your efforts to free the slaves] you will lay the cornerstone for

---

13. Sparks, ed., *Correspondence*, 3:515.
14. Ibid., 3:529–30.
15. Washington to Nathanael Greene, Verplanks Point, N.Y., October 18, 1782 (Fitzpatrick, ed., *Writings*, 25:271).

accomplishing a prediction of your Grandfather and your name will be honorably written and transmitted to posterity; but even the attempt without perfect success will, I know, afford you unspeakable self-satisfaction. The work will at a future date be efficaciously taken up, and then it will be remembered who began it in South Carolina."[16]

16. Wallace, *Life of Laurens,* 451.

III. THE REVOLUTIONARY WAR

13

AFRICAN AMERICAN RECRUITS

A s t h e tensions between England and her thirteen American colonies grew more heated, the word *slavery* was frequently employed in the debates describing the deteriorating relationship. For the white Americans, *slavery* meant the perceived tyranny of the crown over their lives. And the expression *freedom from slavery* meant casting off (or loosening) the political, economic, and social shackles imposed on them by British imperial policies.

For the enslaved African Americans, the slavery rhetoric of the white revolutionaries had its own special meaning. The slaves were not particularly interested in the ideological issues being argued by the white advocates on either side. Their overriding concern was with their personal freedom, with eliminating the legal chains that bound them to a condition of enforced lifelong servitude. "This yearning for freedom was common among those in bondage and its roots ran deep. The contagion of freedom had long infected blacks, reaching epidemic proportions with the outbreak of war against England . . . all blacks during the Revolutionary era shared a common goal—the pursuit of freedom and equality."[1]

The enslaved African Americans were quick to recognize the opportunities that the impending hostilities afforded them in gaining their freedom. The newborn black militancy raised the hopes of the British authorities and at the same time caused fear and consternation among Southern slave owners. "British military leaders and Crown officials viewed with intense interest the aggressive behavior of slaves and the apprehension it excited in their owners. Although the motives of the London government were complex, from the beginning of the conflict the

---

1. Benjamin Quarles, *Black Mosaic: Essays in Afro-American History and Historiography,* 48.

North ministry was tempted by the idea of using the slave population in some capacity to crush southern resistance."[2]

The African American population in numbers alone constituted a tempting manpower pool: "In sheer numbers blacks composed in 1774 a larger proportion of the total population than they ever would again: 500,000 out of 2,600,000, or nearly 20 percent." The British had little hesitancy in recruiting the enslaved African Americans for service in the British ranks. "Blacks [had] fought in mixed companies in all of the colonial wars." The Americans of 1775 had inherited a different perspective and outlook in their military order: "Yet on one point, the use of the Negro for military service, policy became uniform throughout the colonies. Slave or free, Negroes were excluded from the militia, save as noncombatants or in unusual emergencies. This policy of semiexclusion became so prevalent as to constitute a basic tenet of American military tradition."[3]

Under these circumstances, it was not unexpected that the opening gambit would come from the British side. A formal offer of emancipation was broadcast to the African American population of Virginia in the fall of 1775:

> By his Excellency the Right Honourable JOHN, Earl of DUNMORE, His Majesty's Lieutenant and Governour-General of the Colony and Dominion of VIRGINIA, and Vice-Admiral of the same.
> A PROCLAMATION
> . . . and I do hereby further declare all indented servants, Negroes, or others, (appertaining to Rebels,) free, that are able and willing to bear arms, they joining His Majesty's Troops, as soon as may be, for the more speedily reducing this Colony to a proper sense of their duty to His Majesty's crown and dignity.[4]

Lord Dunmore's edict produced the desired effect: African Americans flocked to the royal colors and were promptly enlisted as soldiers and military laborers. Within a month there were about three hundred former slaves in British uniform, their livery triumphantly inscribed across the front with the slogan "Liberty to Slaves!"; and they proudly bore the official designation of their benefactor: "Lord Dunmore's Ethiopian Regiment." Although there had been advance rumors of Dunmore's intended proclamation, when it was finally announced it shocked and outraged the Americans. The Continental Congress saw this action as an attempt to tear up "the foundations of civil authority and Government within the said Colony [Virginia]." John Hancock, president of the Congress, relayed the

2. Sylvia R. Frey, *Water from the Rock: Black Resistance in a Revolutionary Age,* 54. Lord Frederick North (1732–1792) was the British prime minister during most of the period of the American Revolution.

3. Quarles, *Black Mosaic,* 50; Frey, *Water from the Rock,* 77; Quarles, *Black Mosaic,* 25.

4. Peter Force, ed., *American Archives: Fourth Series,* 3:1385.

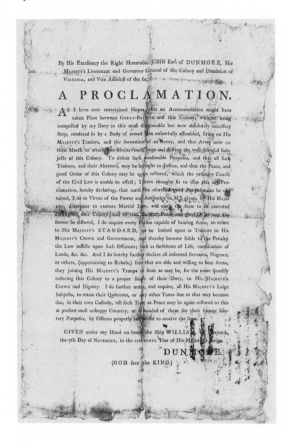

Lord Dunmore's proclamation opened the door for slaves to win their freedom by serving as soldiers in the Revolutionary War. His initiative on the British side was quickly imitated by the Americans. (Manuscripts and University Archives, Special Collections Department, University of Virginia Library, Charlottesville)

news to George Washington at his headquarters in Cambridge on December 2, 1775: "This Day we Receiv'd Advice from Northampton in Virginia, that Lord Dunmore has Erected his Standard at Norfolk, proclaim'd Martial Law, invited the Negroes to Join him, and offer'd them Freedom, for which purpose he has issued a proclamation from on board the Ship where he Resides; and that Two Counties have been Obliged to Submitt to him—However I hope such measures are taking as will speedily and effectually Repel His Violences and secure the peace & safety of that Colony."[5]

The news clearly disturbed and angered Washington. He wrote to Joseph Reed, his close friend and military secretary, on December 15:

> If the Virginians are wise, that Arch Traitor to the Rights of Humanity, Lord Dunmore, should be instantly crushd, if it takes the force of the whole Colony

5. Benjamin Quarles, *The Negro in the American Revolution,* 26–28; Force, ed., *Archives,* 3:1941; *Papers: Revolutionary War Series,* ed. Abbot and Twohig, 2:469.

to do it. otherwise, like a snow Ball in rolling, his army will get size—some through Fear—some through promises—and some from Inclination joining his Standard—But that which renders the measure indispensably necessary, is, the Negros; for if he gets formidable, numbers of th(e)m will be tempted to join who will be affraid to do it without.[6]

To his colleague Richard Henry Lee, serving in the Continental Congress as a delegate from Virginia, Washington wrote on December 26 that if Dunmore "is not crushed before Spring, he will become the most formidable Enemy America has—his strength will Increase as a Snow ball by Rolling; and faster, if some expedient cannot be hit upon to convince the Slaves and Servants of the Impotency of His designs."[7]

The conventional wisdom of the Southern slave-owning community, reflected in Washington's attitude, was that the African Americans were inferior beings. They were not qualified or suited to the martial arts. To place weapons in their hands was an insult to the ruling class as well as a dangerous precedent and a threat to the established order. Even the wartime emergency and the pressing need for manpower did nothing, at least initially, to change the general's mind-set.

In 1755, when Washington was a young colonel of the Virginia Regiment charged with protecting the frontier settlements against raids by the French and their Indian allies, he had few qualms about enlisting slaves for military duties. He sent a note to his subordinate, Capt. Peter Hog, on December 27, 1755, which included the following directive: "I think it will be advisable to detain both Mulatto's and Negroes in your Company; and employ them as Pioneers or Hatchet-men."[8] But the orders that issued from Washington's headquarters at Cambridge after he had taken command of the Continental army in July 1775 demonstrated a continuing low regard for African Americans:

> From the Number of Boys, Deserters, & Negroes which have been listed in the Troops of this Province, I entertain some Doubts whether the Number [of new recruits] required can be raised here.
>
> You are not to enlist any deserter from the Ministerial [British] Army, nor any stroller, negro, or vagabond, or person suspected of being an enemy to the liberty of *America*, nor any under eighteen years of age.
>
> Neither Negroes, Boys unable to bare Arms, nor old men unfit to endure the fatigues of the campaign, are to be inlisted.

6. *Papers: Revolutionary War Series*, ed. Abbot and Twohig, 2:553.
7. Ibid., 2:611.
8. *Papers: Colonial Series*, ed. Abbot and Twohig, 2:236.

> Any person therefore (Negroes excepted, which the Congress do not incline to inlist again) coming with a proper Order and will subscribe [to] the Inlistment, shall be immediately supplied.[9]

Washington's exclusionary policy had widespread support. The Massachusetts Committee of Safety, acting on its own initiative, had already passed the following resolution, dated May 20, 1775: "*Resolved,* That it is the opinion of this Committee, as the contest now between *Great Britain* and the Colonies respects the liberties and privileges of the latter, which the Colonies are determined to maintain, that the admission of any persons as Soldiers into the Army now raising, but only such as are Freemen, will be inconsistent with the principles that are to be supported, and reflect dishonour on this Colony; and that no slaves be admitted into this Army upon any consideration whatever."[10]

The South was even more adamant in its determination to keep the military the exclusive province of white men. South Carolina historian Edward McCrady wrote:

> The planters, of course, were opposed to a measure which might take from them the ablest and most intelligent of their slaves. But, far beyond this, there was an instinctive repugnance and aversion to the idea of calling upon slaves to rescue the liberties of freemen. And still further and deeper was their resentment at the proposition that, having given these negroes their freedom, they were to be clothed and treated in all respects as other soldiers. This suggestion was an offence to the rank and file of the army, militia, volunteer, and regular alike.[11]

However, Edward Rutledge of South Carolina, one of the standard-bearers of southern convictions in the Continental Congress, went too far when he suggested forcing the discharge of the African Americans who were currently serving in the army. A motion to that effect, on September 26, 1775, "was strongly supported by many of the Southern delegates; but the opposition was so powerful and so determined, that 'he [Rutledge] lost his point.' "[12]

At a council of war of the general officers of the Continental army held at the Cambridge headquarters on October 8, 1775, with General Washington presiding, questions relating to the enlistment of African Americans were brought

9. Washington to the President of Congress (John Hancock), Cambridge, July 10–11, 1775 (*Papers: Revolutionary War Series,* ed. Abbot and Twohig, 1:90); Force, ed., *Archives,* 2:1630; General Orders by General Washington, Cambridge, November 12 and October 31, 1775 (*Papers: Revolutionary War Series,* ed. Abbot and Twohig, 2:269, 354).

10. Force, ed., *Archives,* 2:762.

11. McCrady, *History of South Carolina in the Revolution,* 501.

12. George Livermore, *On Negroes as Slaves, as Citizens, and as Soldiers,* 101.

up for consideration and resolution: "10th Whether it will be adviseable to re-
inlist any Negroes in the new Army—or whether there be a Distinction between
such as are Slaves & those who are free?" The response, as recorded in the
minutes of the Council, was negative on both counts: "Agreed unanimously
to reject all Slaves, & by a great Majority to reject Negroes altogether."[13] The
issue surfaced again about a week later, during a conference in Cambridge with
General Washington, various state officials, and three visiting delegates from
the Continental Congress in Philadelphia: Thomas Lynch of South Carolina,
Benjamin Franklin of Pennsylvania, and Benjamin Harrison of Virginia. "The
Delegates now proceeded to confer with General *Washington,* as well on sundry
matters mentioned in his letters to the Congress, upon which no order had been
made, as also upon other matters occurring in the course of this business, viz: . . .
7th. Ought not Negroes to be excluded from the new enlistment, especially such
as are slaves? all were thought improper by the Council of Officers. . . . *Agreed,*
That they be rejected altogether."[14]

The knowledge that African American recruits had acquitted themselves well
in earlier engagements with the British—and one man, Salem Poor, had performed with such conspicuous bravery at the Battle of Charlestown (Bunker
Hill) that he had been cited in an extraordinary petition by his commanding
officers—seemingly went unnoticed by Washington. But the fear ignited by Lord
Dunmore's proclamation—that armed slaves would soon be fighting on the side
of the British—led to a reluctant yet complete reversal on Washington's part.
On December 30, 1775, he authorized a general order setting forth these new
instructions to his recruiting officers: "As the General is informed, that Numbers
of Free Negroes are desirous of inlisting, he gives leave to the recruiting Officers,
to entertain them, and promises to lay the matter before the Congress, who he
doubts not will approve of it."[15]

The very next day Washington communicated his revised opinion to the
president of the Congress, together with his proposed program for reenlisting
African American recruits in the Continental army. He also emphasized to the
Congress that he held the British to blame for his sudden change of heart: "it
has been represented to me that the free negroes who have Served in this Army,
are very much disatisfied at being discarded—as it is to be apprehended, that
they may Seek employ in the ministerial Army—I have presumed to depart from
the Resolution respecting them, & have given Licence for their being enlisted,

---

13. *Papers: Revolutionary War Series,* ed. Abbot and Twohig, 2:125.
14. Force, ed., *Archives,* 3:1161. See also Livermore, *Negroes,* 101.
15. *Papers: Revolutionary War Series,* ed. Abbot and Twohig, 2:620. On Salem Poor, see Quarles,
Negro in the American Revolution, 9–11.

if this is disapproved of by Congress, I will put a Stop to it." The Continental Congress quickly rubber-stamped the modified enlistment policy recommended by the commander in chief: "that the free negroes who have served faithfully in the army at Cambridge, may be re-inlisted therein, but no others."[16]

It is interesting to note that in a subsequent general order to his recruiting officers, dated February 21, 1776, Washington specifically forbade the enlistment of enslaved African Americans in line with his prior instructions from the Congress, but he said nothing that would restrict the recruiters from signing up free black volunteers: "The General being anxious to have the established Regiments, compleated, with all possible expedition, desires the Colonels, and commanding Officers, forthwith to send an Officer from each incompleat Company, into the Country, upon the recruiting service; who are expressly forbid enlisting any Boys— Old Men—or Slaves."[17]

Actually, the point was moot. According to generally accepted procedure and existing law, a slave could not be recruited without the written permission of his master, but this technicality was, by and large, ignored in practice. Once the commander in chief had opened the door, officially acknowledging the acceptance of African Americans into military service, their active recruitment turned into a spirited business, irrespective of their slave or free status. Benjamin Quarles, in *The Negro in the American Revolution,* concludes that "when manpower needs became acute, whether in the volunteer forces, the militia, or the Continental troops, hesitancies and fears were put into the background and the Negro was mustered in."[18]

Six months after Lord Dunmore's proclamation, with African American participation on both sides of the conflict a reality, Washington still made plain his distaste for having to fight a war involving "Slaves and Savages" and "foreign mercenaries."[19] Yet, as a pragmatic and down-to-earth leader, he was well aware that the war would have to be fought and won with every man and method available to him. He was soon listening to suggestions for incorporating entire African American units into the Continental army, perhaps spurred by an urgent message from Maj. Gen. Nathanael Greene of an apparent British plan to form an independent regiment of African Americans in New York: "A Negro belonging to one Strikeer at Gravesend was taken prisoner as he says last Sunday at Coney Island, Yesterday he made his escape, and was taken prisoner by the Rifle Guard.

16. *Papers: Revolutionary War Series,* ed. Abbot and Twohig, 2:623, 625n.
17. Ibid., 3:350.
18. Quarles, *Negro in the American Revolution,* xxvii, 13.
19. Washington to the Massachusetts General Court, New York City, July 11, 1776 (*Papers: Revolutionary War Series,* ed. Abbot and Twohig, 5:270).

He reports Eight hundred Negroes Collected on Statten Island, this day to be formd into a Regiment."[20] This report was later shown to be unfounded.

While the British may have been a step ahead, the Americans were close behind in developing plans for the large-scale recruitment of African Americans. To Rhode Island belongs the credit for being the first state to meld successfully a cohesive group of slaves into the overall war effort. Brig. Gen. James Varnum, who had been assigned staff responsibility for the recruitment and reenlistment of soldiers, took the initiative in proposing to Washington that a separate all-black Rhode Island battalion be formed, to be led by white officers:

Camp, January 2, 1778

Sir,—

The two Battalions from the State of Rhode Island being Small, & there being a Necessity of the State's furnishing an additional Number to make up their Proportion in the continental Army; the Field Officers have represented to me the Propriety of making one temporary Battalion from the two, so that one entire Corps of Officers may repair to Rhode Island, in order to receive & prepare the Recruits for the Field. It is imagined that a Battalion of Negroes can be easily raised there. Should that Measure be adopted—or Recruits obtained upon any other Principle, the Service will be advanced.[21]

Washington forwarded the proposal to Gov. Nicholas Cooke of Rhode Island, together with his own brief covering note authorizing the recruitment program: "Inclosed you will receive a Copy of a Letter from Genl. Varnum to me, upon the means which might be adopted for completing the Rhode Island Troops to their full proportion in the Continental Army. I have nothing to say, in addition to what I wrote the 29th of last Month on this important subject, but to desire that you will give the Officers employed in this business all the assistance in your power." The matter was promptly placed before the February 1778 session of the Rhode Island General Assembly, and an act was duly passed, though not without some vocal opposition.[22]

Whereas, for the preservation of the rights and liberties of the United States, it is necessary that the whole powers of Government should be exerted in recruiting the Continental battalions; and whereas His Excellency Gen. Washington hath inclosed to this State a proposal made to him by Brigadier-General Varnum, to enlist into the two battalions, raising by this State, such slaves as should be willing to enter into the service: and whereas, history affords us frequent Precedents of the *wisest*, the *freest*, and *bravest* nations

20. Greene to Washington, Long Island, N.Y., July 21, 1776 (ibid., 5:414).

21. Washington Papers, microfilm, ser. 4, reel 46, Manuscript Division, Library of Congress.

22. Washington to Cooke, Valley Forge, January 2, 1778 (Fitzpatrick, ed., *Writings*, 10:257); Philip S. Foner, *History of Black Americans: From Africa to the Emergence of the Cotton Kingdom*, 326.

having liberated their Slaves, and inlisted them as Soldiers to fight in Defence of their Country; and also, whereas, the Enemy, with a great force, have taken Possession of the Capital and of a great Part of this State; and this State is obliged to raise a very considerable Number of Troops for its own immediate Defence, whereby it is in a Manner rendered impossible for this State to furnish Recruits for the said two Battalions, without adopting the said Measure so recommended:

It is Voted and Resolved, That every able-bodied *negro,* mulatto, or *Indian* man slave, in this State, may inlist into either of the said two battalions to serve during the continuance of the present war with Great Britain: that every slave so inlisting shall be entitled to and receive all the bounties, wages, and encouragements allowed by the Continental Congress to any soldier inlisting into their service.

It is further Voted and Resolved, That every slave so inlisting shall, upon his passing muster before Col. Christopher Greene, be immediately discharged from the service of his master or mistress, and be absolutely FREE, as though he had never been incumbered with any kind of servitude or slavery.[23]

General Washington was informed straightaway, in a personal letter from Governor Cooke, of Rhode Island's historic step in offering full freedom to those enslaved African Americans willing to enlist in the Continental army and to fight for the American cause. The governor noted, "The number of slaves in this State is not great; but it is generally thought that three hundred and upwards will be enlisted." Governor Cooke's optimism was slightly premature. "Eventually his prophecy was fulfilled, but from February 23 to August 3 the state raised only seventy recruits from its new source of supply."[24]

While the enterprising Rhode Island experiment with wholesale African American enlistments was in progress, Washington persisted in expressing his resentment of the British tactics that had lured slaves and Indians into the war in the first place: "The enemy have set every engine at work, against us, and have actually called savages and even our own slaves to their assistance." At the same time, he was obviously searching for further ways to harness slave manpower to the patriot effort—without, if possible, jeopardizing the existing structure of slavery:

The difficulty of getting waggoners and the enormous wages given them, would tempt one to try any expedient to answer the end on easier and cheaper terms. Among others, it has occurred to me, whether it would not be eligible to hire Negroes in Carolina, Virginia and Maryland for the purpose. They ought however to be freemen, for slaves could not be sufficiently depended on. It is to be apprehended [that] they would too frequently

23. Livermore, *Negroes,* 118–19.
24. Cooke to Washington, Providence, February 23, 1778 (ibid., 121–22); Paul F. Dearden, *The Rhode Island Campaign of 1778: Inauspicious Dawn of Alliance,* 23.

desert to the enemy to obtain their liberty; and for the profit of it, or to conciliate a more favorable reception, would carry off their waggon-horses with them.[25]

General Washington's reservations notwithstanding, the number of African Americans employed in a wide range of wartime activities was on the rise. Charles Knowles Bolton, in *The Private Soldier under Washington,* observed, "Blacks continued to serve in the army despite all legislative efforts to exclude them; a return of negroes in Washington's command August 24, 1778, shows that seven brigades then had an average of fifty-four in each. A Hessian officer said in 1777: 'One sees no regiment in which there are not negroes in abundance, and among them are able-bodied, sturdy fellows.' "[26] And Frank Landon Humphreys described the role of blacks in the context of Connecticut's overall contribution to the War of Independence:

> Two months after the battle of Monmouth, in 1778, Adjutant-General Scam-
> mell made a return of such [black] troops then in the army. They were
> enrolled in fourteen different regiments and represented several States. Five
> hundred and eighty-six were in active service, out of a total muster of seven
> hundred and fifty-two. There were about one hundred of them scattered
> throughout the fifty or more companies in the Connecticut Line. When the
> above consolidation took place however, going into effect on January 1, 1781,
> the Connecticut negro soldiers appear to have been brought together into one
> company in Colonel Butler's regiment and put under the nominal command
> of Col. [David] Humphreys. It is a tradition that he was one of the first men
> in the country to recognize the possibilities of the negro as a soldier, and by
> his own influence and that of his faithful body-servant, Jethro Martin, among
> people of his own race, created much enthusiasm for the cause of freedom
> among the negroes of Connecticut.[27]

Connecticut was second to Rhode Island in actively organizing a program to recruit blacks for military service. "Close to three hundred black soldiers can be unmistakenly identified as serving either in Connecticut's regiments of the Continental Army or with the State militia. . . . These . . . soldiers made up less than two percent of Connecticut's Revolutionary troops. While this is a small percentage, it should be noted that blacks made up only three percent of Connecticut's population and that almost all of the black enlistees served in the Continental Army which saw more duty than the State militia."[28]

25. Washington to the Committee of Congress, Valley Forge, January 29, 1778 (Fitzpatrick, ed., *Writings,* 10:400–401).

26. Charles K. Bolton, *The Private Soldier under Washington,* 22.

27. Frank Landon Humphreys, *Life and Times of David Humphreys,* 1:191–92.

28. David O. White, *Connecticut's Black Soldiers, 1775–1783,* 8.

Although General Washington was not directly involved in the formation of the Connecticut black units, his close friend and military aide Col. David Humphreys was, and it can be assumed that the commander in chief was kept fully informed of their status and activities. "Connecticut's actual black company was the Second Company of the Fourth Regiment which was formed in 1781. The nominal head of this unit was Colonel David Humphreys. He never actually commanded the unit, since he was an aide-de-camp to General Washington from 1781–1783, the entire time that it was active. All of the officers and noncommissioned officers in the company were white, and all of the privates were black. . . . It [the Second Company] was treated on an equal footing with the other companies in that it was given the same amounts per man in provisions and pay."[29]

The British continued to aggressively recruit African Americans, thereby putting pressure on the Americans to step up their own enlistment drives. Benjamin Quarles reports, "It has been estimated . . . that 5,000 Negro soldiers served in the patriot forces"; yet "The number of Negroes who fled to the British ran into the tens of thousands." John Cadwalader, who was serving in the Maryland legislature, wrote to Washington on June 5, 1781: "We have resolved to raise, immediately, seven hundred and fifty negroes, to be incorporated with the other troops; and a bill is now almost completed." The Marquis de Lafayette, leading the Continental soldiers in Virginia, emphasized to his commander in chief the necessity of competing with the British for the services of African American horsemen. "Nothing But a treaty of alliance with the Negroes Can find Out dragoon Horses, and it is By those means the Enemy Have Got a formidable Cavalry." And Maj. Gen. Nathanael Greene reported: "I have recommended to this State [South Carolina] to raise some black regiments. To fill up the regiments with whites is impracticable, and to get reenforcements from the northwards precarious, and at least difficult, from the prejudices respecting the climate. Some are for it; but the far greater part of the people are opposed to it."[30]

The efforts to enlist Southern slaves, particularly by Lieutenant Colonel Laurens, were to no avail. Neither South Carolina nor Georgia ever sanctioned the use of slaves as soldiers, in spite of the urgent pleadings of Greene, John and Henry Laurens, and other wartime figures. Yet Washington, a Southerner himself, demonstrated his ability to rise above certain inborn and ingrained prejudices. His acceptance of African Americans as Continental soldiers was, of course, prompted

29. Ibid., 32.

30. Quarles, *Negro in the American Revolution,* xxix, 119; Sparks, ed., *Correspondence,* 3:331; Lafayette to Washington, Malvern Hill, Va., July 20, 1781 (Stanley J. Idzerda, ed., *Lafayette in the Age of the American Revolution,* 4:256); Greene to Washington, South Carolina, January 24, 1782 (Livermore, *Negroes,* 148).

by a fear of how the British might, and in fact did, utilize slave manpower. But he was also influenced by the combined voices of the select group of men who were close to him during the war and whom he trusted, respected, and relied upon. They included young liberal-minded progressives like Nathanael Greene, the Marquis de Lafayette, Alexander Hamilton, John Laurens, and David Humphreys, as well as other officers who, for a variety of reasons, argued convincingly in favor of recruiting African Americans as soldiers, organizing them into military units, and eventually freeing them.

The Revolutionary War brought genuine freedom to many former enslaved African Americans, both those who fought on the American side as well as those who were enlisted by the British. "Slaves were more than passive observers or victims of the War of Independence. Both sides used them as frontline soldiers, or more often in a variety of ancillary roles; much the larger numbers were engaged on the British side. Many slaves saw opportunities for seeking individual freedom during the Revolutionary war, and as many as fifty thousand may have been evacuated with the British forces in the closing stages—although some later returned."[31] As commander in chief, Washington was responsible for authorizing the entry of African Americans into the Continental army as full-fledged soldiers. Along with their freedom, they gained a renewed sense of pride, a stake in their country, and hope for the future. It was a significant and irrevocable step on the long and difficult road to racial equality.

31. Peter J. Parish, *Slavery: History and Historians,* 17.

14

COMBAT VETERANS

T HE NUMEROUS plantation slaves of the South were regarded by the British as useful pawns in their efforts to put down the rebellion in that region. In their propaganda, they held out the hope and promise of freedom to the enslaved African Americans. But it was soon obvious that the British had not come as liberators. They were motivated strictly by self-interest and by practical military and economic considerations. Sylvia Frey explains: "The adoption of an official policy designed to encourage black desertion to the British would rob the South of its labor force and ultimately wreck its economy, at the same time crippling the rebel war effort. Black runaways could be employed in the production of supplies, relieving the army of its dependence on European food shipments, or could be trained and armed for combat." The slaves who flocked to the British standard in the South were not disappointed—except in one important respect. They were not considered fit to be combat soldiers. "Although some [British] officers continued to urge the full military use of blacks as 'indispensably necessary' to the war effort in the South, there is virtually no evidence that they ever saw combat." Instead, they were exploited as menials: "unskilled blacks dug the latrines and cleaned the streets and did most of the manual labor necessary to support the army."[1]

The enslaved African Americans in the South were not given weapons or allowed to fight in the Revolution due to the prejudices of both the Southerners and the British. Men who had been armed, trained, disciplined, and hardened in battle

1. Sylvia R. Frey, *The British Soldier in America: A Social History of Military Life in the Revolutionary Period*, 18–19.

would no longer be content to return to their prescribed condition of meek and submissive servitude. They would demand not only their freedom but also equality and respect, as well as the status and recognition accorded to other British combat veterans. Furthermore, the danger of insurrections by armed slaves was seen as a serious threat to the social order. The Southerners, of course, correctly interpreted that the granting of these privileges would work to undermine the entire social and economic structure on which their slave society was based. Therefore, one has to look outside the South and British military hegemony for evidence of organized activity involving African American combat veterans.

While there were similar racial prejudices and traditions in the North, they were less deep-seated than those in the South. For one thing, the Northern economy was not nearly as dependent on slave labor as was the plantation economy of the South. For another, the leaders in the North were more liberal-minded. Thus, once General Washington in Cambridge had made his decision in principle early in 1776 to allow the enlistment of African Americans in the Continental army, he placed no restrictions or limitations on how they were to be employed. The orders went down to the commanders in the field, who promptly received the new African American recruits and welcomed them as badly needed additions to their depleted ranks. The African American soldiers were integrated into regular fighting regiments, given muskets and bayonets, taught to use them, drilled and officered, and prepared for military action. The era of the professional African American combat veteran had begun.

Of the approximately five thousand African American soldiers who served in the Continental army and the various state militias under the general command of George Washington, none were officers and none were individually cited or mentioned in dispatches by the commander in chief for personal heroism or distinction on the battlefield. Nevertheless, the combat records of the African American fighting men in the Revolution bear adequate testimony to their valor and bravery. From beginning to end, they participated in the armed encounters with the enemy and they shared the victories and glory—and the sacrifices and bloodshed—with their white comrades. It is fair to say that the African American combat veterans earned their freedom and the esteem of their countrymen by their wartime feats.

The most conspicuous African American unit was the First Rhode Island Regiment of 1777. On August 29, 1778, barely six months after these former slaves (together with free negroes, mulattoes, and Narragansett Indians) had been recruited and mustered into the Continental army as a result of state legislative action, they were exposed to enemy gunfire and bayonets at the hard-fought Battle of Rhode Island. Historian Samuel G. Arnold gives this account of the battlefield action in which the black regiment was engaged and in which it distinguished itself by its staying power, its professionalism, and its courage:

> For nearly seven hours the battle raged with but little intermission. . . . The carnage was frightful. Down the slope of Anthony's Hill, a western continuation of Quaker Hill, the Hessian columns and British infantry twice rushed to the assault and were repulsed in the valley with great slaughter. . . . A third time the enemy, with desperate courage and increased strength, attempted to assail the redoubt, and would have carried it but for the timely aid of two continental battalions despatched by [Maj. Gen. John] Sullivan to support his almost exhausted troops. It was in repelling these furious onsets, that the newly raised black regiment, under Col. Greene, distinguished itself by deeds of desperate valor. Posted behind a thicket in the valley, they three times drove back the Hessians who charged repeatedly down the hill to dislodge them.[2]

Paul F. Dearden adds this comment: "In truth, the newly recruited 'green' troops did hold back a number of British attacks, but as these assaults swelled in intensity and took on a definite form, it became necessary for Nathanael Greene to engage the American right wing and ultimately hold that portion of the field where the redoubt lay. While the First Rhode Island made a contribution, it can hardly claim all the laurels for the defense of the American right. . . . Christopher Greene's regiment had lost two dead, nine wounded, and eleven missing."[3]

Several contemporary observations by high-ranking professional soldiers single out the black Rhode Island troops for favorable comment. The first of these is from the diary of the Marquis de Chastellux: "The 5th [of January, 1781] I did not set out till eleven, although I had a thirty-mile journey to Lebanon. At the ferry-crossing I met with a detachment of the Rhode Island regiment, the same corps we had with us all last summer, but they have since been recruited and clothed. The majority of the enlisted men are Negroes or mulattoes; but they are strong, robust men, and those I saw made a very good appearance."[4] Baron Ludwig von Closen, a German-born officer attached to the French army as an aide to General Rochambeau, reviewed the Americans in the summer of 1781 while they were camped in Westchester, New York, preparing to move south for the Yorktown campaign, and noted in his diary:

> [July 4, 1781] On the 4th, M. de Rochambeau sent me with Colonel *Cobb* to find General Washington, whom we joined in White Plains where his army was resting, while he was selecting a camp site there. . . . I had a chance to

---

2. Samuel G. Arnold, *History of the State of Rhode Island and Providence Plantations*, 2:427.
3. Dearden, *Rhode Island Campaign*, xiii–xiv, 127.
4. Chastellux, *Travels in North America*, 1:229.

see the American army, man for man. It was really painful to see these brave
men, almost naked, with only some trousers and little linen jackets, most of
them without stockings, but, would you believe it? very cheerful and healthy
in appearance. A quarter of them were negroes, merry, confident, and sturdy.
[July 9, 1781, near Dobbs Ferry] On the 9th, all the American army presented
arms; General Washington invited our headquarters staff to come to see it.
The whole effect was rather good. . . . Three-quarters of the Rhode Island
regiment consists of negroes, and that regiment is the most neatly dressed,
the best under arms, and the most precise in its maneuvers.[5]

Because of its esprit de corps and the bravery in combat of its individual soldiers,
the Rhode Island battalion was the best known all-black unit in the Revolutionary
War. The first muster of the battalion was taken on July 6, 1778: it numbered four
companies with 19 commissioned officers and 144 noncommissioned officers
and privates; another company was added later, bringing the total numerical
strength to 226 officers and enlisted men. Col. Christopher Greene of Rhode
Island was placed in command. He was a cousin of Maj. Gen. Nathanael Greene
and a distinguished and decorated veteran combat officer.

[Colonel Greene] had already commanded some four hundred Negro troops
at Fort Mercer on the Delaware, where between October 22 and November 20
[1777] the black Continentals had successfully held off waves of attacks by
superior numbers of Hessians and British regulars. Faced by overwhelming
odds, Colonel Greene had abandoned the fort and withdrawn with the
surviving black soldiers in good order. He had been commended by Congress,
and his assignment to head the Rhode Island black battalion was a logical
aftermath. . . . After the Rhode Island engagement [in August of 1778], the
battalion fought in the South and then was moved back to the North. On
4 May 1781, during a surprise attack by a Tory regiment at Points Bridge,
Croton River, New York, the black battalion lost part of its men in a futile
attempt to save the life of its commander, Colonel Greene.[6]

As George Livermore notes, "Among the traits which distinguished this regiment
was their devotion to their officers: when their brave Col. Greene was afterwards
cut down and mortally wounded, the sabres of the enemy reached his body only
through the limbs of his faithful guard of blacks, who hovered over him and
protected him, every one of whom was killed, and whom he was not ashamed to
call his children."[7]

Lt. Col. Jeremiah Olney took over the command of the Rhode Island battalion
and held it until the end of the war. Under his leadership, the all-black regiment

5. Evelyn M. Acomb, ed., *The Revolutionary Journal of Baron Ludwig von Closen, 1780–1783,* 89,
91–92.

6. Foner, *Africa to the Cotton Kingdom,* 327–28, 341.

7. Livermore, *Negroes,* 154.

Jean-Baptiste-Antoine de Verger (1762–1851) was a sublieutenant in the Royal Deux-Ponts Regiment in the French Expeditionary Army commanded by the Comte Rochambeau that was sent to America in 1780–1783 to assist the patriots fight the English during the Revolutionary War. In addition to being a professional soldier, de Verger was also a talented and accomplished artist who made many military portrayals and maps. His drawings of American foot soldiers from the Yorktown campaign of 1781 include a black light infantryman of the First Rhode Island Regiment, the only known authentic contemporary rendering of a black soldier in the Continental army. (From Howard C. Rice Jr. and Anne S. K. Brown, eds., *The American Campaigns of Rochambeau's Army 1780, 1781, 1782, 1783*, vol. 1, facing 142; courtesy Anne S. K. Brown Military Collection, Brown University)

continued to live up to its reputation in the battles of Red Bank, Yorktown, and Fort Oswego.[8] On discharging his men in Saratoga, New York, on June 13, 1783, Colonel Olney issued these final garrison orders:

> The happy day having at length arrived when the Officers and men engaged for the war are to be disbanded, the liberties and Independence of America being (through their extraordinary sufferings and exertions in conjunction with the other troops in the field) fully established and acknowledged by our enemy, the commandant, though happy on the occasion, cannot dismiss these brave officers and men he has so long had the honor to command without experiencing the keenest sensibility at a parting scene, and to acknowledge the very great share of merit they have acquired in faithfully persevering in the best of causes, in every stage of service, with unexampled fortitude and patience through all the dangers and trials of a long and severe war, and he is at the same time extremely happy in the opportunity to declare his entire

8. Foner, *Africa to the Cotton Kingdom*, 327.

approbation of their valor and good conduct displayed on every occasion when called to face the enemy in the field.[9]

It is not an easy task for the historian to link George Washington with the African American soldiers in his command. However, in the case of the black Rhode Island Regiment, it is a documented fact that Washington was instrumental in helping to create the unit in the first place. Also, he was present when these men passed in impressive review before the assembled dignitaries near Dobbs Ferry, as recounted by Baron Ludwig von Closen, and there can be little doubt that he saw them in action when they took part in the siege of Yorktown. Many of these same black combat veterans were never given their proper due when they returned home. They became mere footnotes in the historical record. Nevertheless, they left a considerable impression on their military contemporaries and fellow Americans, who were well aware of their patriotism and gallant exploits.

There were, of course, other all-black units that participated in the Revolution. "In Massachusetts two Negro companies were formed, one under Major Samuel Lawrence and the other—the Bucks of America—under Middleton, a Negro commander." In Connecticut, "Several companies of the 6th Battalion Connecticut Forces were formed into a separate company, known as the Colonial's or 6th Company. The company numbered at its first muster three officers (all evidently white) and fifty-two enlisted men. The black company fought as a separate unit until November 1782, after which the men were distributed among the white companies of the battalion."[10] But none of these military units were as visible or as prominent in the War of Independence as the Rhode Island Regiment, and certainly none were as closely involved with the commander in chief.

Washington did see his share of individual African American combat soldiers. John Hope Franklin and Alfred A. Moss Jr., in *From Slavery to Freedom: A History of African Americans,* report that "two Negroes, Prince Whipple and Oliver Cromwell, were with General Washington when he crossed the Delaware on Christmas Day 1776."[11] A more detailed account of the activities of these two black soldiers is provided in *The Negro Almanac:*

> One of George Washington's most loyal comrades-in-arms was Prince Whipple, a black man born in Amabon, Africa. . . . [Whipple] succeeded in joining the Continental forces as a bodyguard to General Whipple of New Hampshire, whose name he took, and served in many of General Washington's

9. "The Negro in the Military Service of the United States 1639–1886," microfilm, reel 10-35-1, chapter 1, 288, National Archives and Records Service, Washington, D.C.

10. John Hope Franklin and Alfred A. Moss Jr., *From Slavery to Freedom: A History of African Americans,* 77; Foner, *Africa to the Cotton Kingdom,* 328.

11. Franklin and Moss, *From Slavery to Freedom,* 77–78.

By His Excellency

GEORGE WASHINGTON, Esq;

General and Commander in Chief of the Forces of the United States of America.

THESE are to CERTIFY that the Bearer hereof *Brister Baker Soldier* in the *Second Connecticut* Regiment, having faithfully ferved the United States *from April 8th 777 to June 8th 788* — and being inlifted for the War only, is hereby DISCHARGED from the American Army.

GIVEN at HEAD-QUARTERS the *8th June 1783*

G Washington

By His Excellency's Command,

J. Trumbull Jun Secy

REGISTERED in the Books of the Regiment,

Certify Adjutant,

THE above *Baker* has been honored with the BADGE of MERIT for *Six* Years faithful Service. *H Swift Col.*

HEAD-QUARTERS, June *12th* 1783

THE within CERTIFICATE fhall not avail th Bearer as a Difcharge, until the Ratification of the definitiv Treaty of Peace; previous to which Time, and until Proclama tion thereof fhall be made, He is to be confidered as being o Furlough.

GEORGE WASHINGTON.

This discharge certificate from the Continental army, personally signed by General Washington, was issued on June 8, 1783, to Brister Baker, an African American slave and a soldier in the Second Connecticut Regiment who was "honored with the BADGE of MERIT for Six Years faithful Service." "Bristol [Brister?] Baker of New Haven fought in three Connecticut regiments from 1777 until his discharge in 1783. The next year his owner emancipated him and wrote of Baker: '. . . [he] has been a good Soldier and frugal of his Interest and capable of Business Equal to most white men in Way of Husbandry, and being as he says but about 38 years old, thinking that it is reasonable that he should be set free as he has been fighting for the Liberties of the Country.' Baker lived as a free man in New Haven for nine years until he died in 1793. His estate, similar to many black veterans of the war, was meager, but it did include the bounty land that he had received from the government as partial payment for his military service" (David O. White, *Connecticut's Black Soldiers, 1775–1783*, 25). (Courtesy of the New Jersey Historical Society, Newark)

campaigns. After enduring the hardships of the retreat from Long Island, he was one of the soldiers to have the privilege of being in the boat with Washington during the famous Christmas night crossing of the Delaware. This event is commemorated in Emanuel Gottlieb Leutze's inspiring painting of the event. . . .

Oliver Cromwell served in the American revolutionary forces for 6 years and 9 months, much longer than most of the patriots, and saw action in many important battles. Besides being present at the surrender of Cornwallis at Yorktown, he was one of the valiant soldiers who crossed the Delaware River with Washington on Christmas night in 1776.

Born in Columbus, N.J., Cromwell enlisted in the Second New Jersey Regiment, under the command of Colonel Israel Shreve. He participated in the battles of Trenton and Princeton in 1776–1777, Brandywine in 1777,

Monmouth in 1778, and Yorktown in 1781. When he was discharged he
was awarded an Army pension of $96 a year in recognition of his honorable
service.[12]

Finally, Philip S. Foner notes in *History of Black Americans: From Africa to the
Emergence of the Cotton Kingdom:* "While there were no monuments to honor
them, many blacks who served in the American forces received commendations
from their commanding officers. One was Samuel Charlton, a slave from New
Jersey who was entered as a substitute for his master, fought in several battles
including those at Brandywine and Monmouth; stood near Molly Pitcher when
she took her husband's place behind the cannon; and received recognition for his
services from General Washington."[13]

Although Washington mentioned none of the above men or incidents in
his wartime correspondence, and is not on record with any form of official
acknowledgment of the numerous and varied deeds and actions attributed to
the African American combat veterans under his command, the available bits of
evidence, both real and circumstantial, demonstrate that Washington had come
to accept the significant contributions of African American soldiers in helping to
win the War of Independence. The far-ranging services and sacrifices of African
Americans in the cause of freedom spoke louder than words, and, as a result,
the old myth of black inferiority was quietly laid aside. The reality of the African
American combat veteran had taken its place.

12. Harry A. Ploski and James Williams, eds., *The Negro Almanac: A Reference Work on the African-
American,* 5th ed., 822–33, 828.
13. Foner, *Africa to the Cotton Kingdom,* 341.

15

THE COMMANDER IN CHIEF

M UCH HAS been written about George Washington's relationships during the Revolutionary War with the officers and men of the Continental army, but virtually nothing has been said about the commander in chief's contacts with the African American soldiers in his military command. The latter left almost no memoirs on which to draw; nor have biographers and historians been able to uncover meaningful documented accounts. Most of the information on this aspect of Washington's career comes from his own army records and personal correspondence files. While these are sketchy and often fragmented, they do present a limited portrait of Washington in his day-to-day dealings with the African American Continental soldiers.

One illuminating episode concerns an African American soldier, Fortune Stoddard, who had been convicted by the civil courts in Maryland of manslaughter, although the alleged act was seemingly committed in the line of duty. Washington, on learning that the man had been held in jail for an inordinately long time and was now to be sold into slavery again to pay for the cost of his prosecution and incarceration, protested vigorously to the secretary of war, Maj. Gen. Benjamin Lincoln:

Head Quarters, August 5, 1782.

Sir:

I have the honor to inclose [for] you a Letter from Colo. Olney with some other Papers relating to a soldier of the Rhode Island Regiment who has been in confinement in the state of Maryland since last Winter.

As it will be extremely unjust and cruel that the Soldier should be any longer confined or should be sold to pay the Charges of his Prosecution I request you to take the matter up as soon as possible and procure his release.[1]

Fortune Stoddard's freedom depended on the payment of the fees charged against him by the state of Maryland: "Last June Negro Fortune Stoddard had his tryal, he was acquitted of the Murder, but found guilty of Manslaughter. He is ready to be delivered on payment of his fees, which if not speedily done he must be sold agreeable to the laws of this State. The fee will amount (at present) to Twenty five pounds Specie if not more. Every day he remains in custody adds something to the sum. I request you would as speedily as possible favor me with a letter, informing me, whether you intend to pay his fees & by whom the money is to be paid." Secretary Lincoln acted promptly. He wrote to the president of the Continental Congress, "Resolved that the State of Maryland be requested to discharge the said Fortune Stoddard from his confinement and charge the United States with the fees."[2] Presumably, the monies due to the state of Maryland were paid by the Continental Congress, and Fortune Stoddard returned to his military duties as a free man—thanks in no small part to the action of his commander in chief.

More than once, a problem unique to the African American soldiers serving in the Continental army would reach the commander in chief's desk for resolution: were they free men because they were soldiers in the Continental army, or did their former owners still have the right to claim them? Coincidentally, in a letter to Gov. John Hancock of Massachusetts, General Washington used the phrase "equal justice" in referring to such a dispute:

> Head Quarters, October 31, 1780.
>
> Sir:
>
> Upon the representation of Mr. Morey that two Negro Men belonging to him, were detained as Soldiers in the Massachusetts Line contrary to his inclination, I gave directions to Brigadier General [John] Glover to appoint a Board of Officers to enquire into the Justice of his claim and to report the facts with their opinion thereon. A Copy of this Report I now do Myself the honor to inclose to you.
>
> As Mr. Morey is a subject of your State, and the question appears to be how far the several circumstances stated in the Report ought to affect his property I have thought proper to refer the matter to Your opinion; having

---

1. Fitzpatrick, ed., *Writings*, 24:467.

2. Patrick Hamilton to Henry Sherman, Cecil County, Md., July 8, 1782 (copy in the Washington Papers, file no. 48238, Alderman Library, University of Virginia); Lincoln to the Continental Congress, Continental Army Headquarters, Highlands, N.Y., August 9, 1782 (Papers of the Continental Congress, reel 149, fol. 561, National Archives, Washington, D.C.).

no object in view but a desire that *equal justice* may be done to the public and the individual concerned.[3]

A similar case involved Capt. Jonathon Hobby of the Third Massachusetts Regiment, who personally appealed to Washington for help in retrieving his property, "a Negro Man now serving as a soldier." Perhaps Hobby felt that Washington, as a slave owner himself, might be especially sympathetic to his desire to recover his fugitive slave. But the commander in chief rarely allowed his personal feelings to interfere with strict military protocol. He duly referred Captain Hobby's claim to a staff officer, Brig. Gen. Rufus Putnam:

> Head Quarters, February 2, 1783.
> Sir:
> Mr. Hobby having claimed as his property a Negro Man now serving as a soldier in the 3d. Masstts. Regt. you will be pleased to order a Court of Enquiry, consisting of five as respectable Officers as can be appointed in your Brigade, to examine into the validity of the claim, the manner in which the person in question came into [the] service, and the propriety of his being discharged or retained in service, having inquired into the matter with all the attending circumstances, they will report to you their opinion thereon, which you will communicate to me as soon as conveniently may be.
> P.S. All concerned should be notified to attend.[4]

Five days later Washington wrote Hobby informing him of the outcome of the investigation: legally, he was not entitled to the return of his slave. Washington did leave open the possibility of a trade (that is, one body for another), not an unusual suggestion since the substitution system was a widely recognized and frequently used method of fulfilling military obligations. "As the Court of Enquiry upon a revisal of their Proceedings are still of [the] opinion that the Negro man claimed by you is legally holden to serve the term he is inlisted for, and that your only remedy is against the State. The Commander in Chief does not think himself authorized to discharge the Sd Negro, unless another man is obtained by the State, or otherwise, to serve in his room."[5] There is no record of a response by Hobby to Washington's proposal.

As far as can be ascertained, the administration and dispensation of military justice within Washington's command followed the same due process irrespective of whether the soldier was white or black. Two general orders, relating to the same case of homicide involving an African American soldier and taken from the

3. Fitzpatrick, ed., *Writings*, 20:272; italics added.
4. Ibid., 26:90.
5. Ibid., 26:107–8.

commander in chief's wartime files, serve to illustrate the established procedure for dispensing military justice:

GENERAL ORDERS

Head Quarters, Morristown,

Tuesday, March 7, 1780.

At the request of Captain Van Dyck, a Court of Enquiry is to sit tomorrow at Col. Spencer's quarters, who is appointed President of the same, to enquire into the conduct of Captn. VanDyck respecting the death of a Negro man, soldier in Captn. Bernard's Company, Col. Wylly's regiment, who was killed on the night of the 14th. day of January last; Each of the Pennsylvania and Maryland brigades will furnish a Captain who are to sit as members.

GENERAL ORDERS

Head Quarters, Morristown,

Sunday, March 12, 1780

The Court of Enquiry whereof Colonel Spencer is Presidt., having made strict examination into the conduct of Captain Van Dyck respecting the death of a Negro soldier belonging to Captain Bernard's Company in Colonel Wylly's regiment, report as follows, (Vizt.)

> "The Court considering the evidence are fully of [the] opinion that Captain Van Dyck being in the line of his duty, his conduct on the occasion was highly justifiable."

The Commander in Chief approves the judgment of the court, and the Court is dissolved.[6]

African American soldiers, like their white comrades, occasionally found themselves in trouble with the civil authorities. When such incidents came to the attention of the commander in chief, he was quick to take the necessary steps to turn the accused over to the rightful jurisdiction. Joseph Gilpin, a justice of the peace of Cecil County, Maryland, had written to Washington to inform him that a local coroner's inquest had returned a verdict of murder in an investigation centering on an African American soldier, who was now wanted to stand trial:

Head of Elk, Md., December 25, 1781

Sir

I am Sorrowed to Trouble your Excellency On the Present Unfortunate Accident—One of the Inhabitants of this Place hath Been Shot Dead at the House Where a Small Partie of Soldiers had their Bellit [billet]—In Consequence our Coroner hath held a Jury of Inquest of Lawfull Men upon the Body who upon hearing the Hole Evidence Returned on their Inquisition that the Person was Murdered and that the same was Comited by a Negro Soldier in the service of the United States upon which it Became my Duty as one of the Justices of the Peace for the County aforesaid to Commit the

6. Ibid., 18:80–81, 108–9.

offender to the Gaol for tryal—But find him arrested By Martial Law and under Guard and Major Rudolph & Captain Benson has Dought whether the [they] out [ought] to Give him up upon which we have Mutually A Greed to waite your Excellencys further order in the present unhappy affair.[7]

The commander in chief responded to Gilpin's request in this letter of December 30, 1781:

Sir:

I am exceedingly sorry for the accident of which you inform me in yours of the 25th. The only reparation I can make, is to order the Soldier to be immediately given up to the Civil authority, for which purpose I inclose a letter to the commanding Officer to the Head of Elk.

I take it extremely kind of you, Sir, to have made an application to me upon the present occasion. You undoubtedly had a right by Law to have secured the Offender by virtue of your own authority.[8]

The necessary implementing instructions sent to the commanding officer stationed in the town Head of Elk cautioned, "I shall depend upon your taking all possible pains to prevent any accident of the like kind in [the] future."[9]

The commander in chief is also on record on the issue of integrating military formations. In a note to Maj. Gen. William Heath, dated June 29, 1780, he said: "I think it will be best to march Colo. Greenes [Rhode Island] Regt. and the Levies when collected, to the Army, and upon their arrival here, so arrange and model them, as to level the Regiments. The objection to joining Greenes Regiment may be removed by dividing the Blacks in such a manner between the two, as to abolish the name and appearance of a Black Corps."[10] This may have been the first tangible step in American military history leading to the full integration of its armed forces. It might be added that before the end of the war white and black soldiers could be found in virtually all military units (except in the Deep South) fighting side by side.

It seems that African Americans played a role in Washington's intelligence operations. A brief, cryptic entry, without reference or further explanation, in his military correspondence with Maj. Henry "Light-Horse Harry" Lee, dated July 26, 1779, indicates that certain African Americans, whose intimate knowledge of the inland rivers and coastal waterways made them particularly valuable to the Continental army as pilots, were carrying out daring and important secret

7. Washington Papers, microfilm, ser. 4, reel 82, Manuscript Division, Library of Congress.
8. Fitzpatrick, ed., *Writings,* 23:415.
9. Washington to the Continental Officer Commanding at the Head of Elk (Maj. John Rudolph), Philadelphia, December 30, 1781 (ibid., 23:414).
10. Ibid., 19:93.

missions: "I have granted a Warrant for the 1000 Dolls. promised the Negro pilots, and included the 230 expended by you for secret services."[11] This transaction was probably in connection with Major Lee's planned attack against the British outpost at Paulus Hook (now a part of Jersey City), which took place on August 19. Negro pilots might have been involved because this daring and successful commando raid was an amphibious operation over salt marshes and river crossings.

Although not ordinarily under General Washington's direct command, African American seamen carried out hazardous assignments that directly supported the Continental army's offensive and defensive maneuvers. David White points out, "In all of America, there were close to 2,000 black seamen." Many of them were professional pilots. "The navies of the Chesapeake Bay states, Maryland and Virginia, frequently used Negroes as pilots. . . . Negroes who grew up in the counties lying on the [Chesapeake] bay or its tributaries had become skillful in the navigation of these waters."[12] The same can be said of the African Americans living in the other coastal states. Whether as pilots, spies, or messengers, these unofficial freedom fighters with their unique and intimate knowledge of the landscape and seascape were valuable assets to the commander in chief and to the Continental army.

One final task that occupied the commander in chief in the days when the war was winding down was the recovery of the slaves who had fled, or who were being taken away, in the British evacuation. A concerted effort to return fugitive African American soldiers, and runaway slaves who had taken advantage of the wartime crisis, to their rightful owners started almost before the ink had dried on the Yorktown capitulation:

> GENERAL ORDERS
> Head Quarters near York, Thursday, October 25, 1781.
> It having been represented that many Negroes and Mulattoes the property of Citizens of these States have concealed themselves on board the Ships in the harbor; that some still continue to attach themselves to British Officers and that others have attempted to impose themselves upon the officers of the French and American Armies as Freemen and to make their escapes in that manner, In order to prevent their succeeding in such practices All Officers of the Allied Army and other persons of every denomination concerned are directed not to suffer any such negroes or mulattoes to be retained in their Service but on the contrary to cause them to be delivered to the Guards.[13]

Until the last British soldier and civilian—along with the last Negro under their control—had been evacuated from New York City in November 1783 (after

11. Ibid., 15:488.
12. White, *Connecticut's Black Soldiers*, 31; Quarles, *Negro in the American Revolution*, 87.
13. Fitzpatrick, ed., *Writings*, 23:264–65.

the signing of the final peace treaty in Paris), the commander in chief was in the forefront of the negotiations with his British opposite—Sir Guy Carleton—trying to protect the legitimate interests of the American slave owners in their slave property. He was only partially successful in this effort. Thousands of slaves made good their escape with the British. But this concluding action of the conflict indicates that—despite his wartime benevolence and tolerance of the African Americans in his command—in peacetime, George Washington would revert (at least for the moment) to the more comfortable and accustomed role of a staunch guardian of the status quo of the slave system.

The available records show that General Washington was scrupulously correct and honorable in his dealings with the African American soldiers of the Continental army. In terms of military protocol, he accorded them the same rights and privileges that were given to the white soldiers in his command. He recognized that they were human beings, and he came to appreciate their qualities as fighting men. He was also well aware of their willingness to shed their blood and, if necessary, to make the ultimate sacrifice in the cause of freedom and independence. The performance on the battlefields of the African American soldiers left an impression on the commander in chief that perhaps—in the long run—helped to persuade him to modify and change his attitude toward slaves and the institution of slavery.

IV. THE NEW NATION

16

THE CONSTITUTIONAL CONVENTION

THE ARTICLES of Confederation, formally in place since March 1781, had proved an ineffective constitution for governing the new nation. The political leaders of the country soon realized that a lasting union of the thirteen diverse states required the establishment of a strong central government. Following a preliminary meeting of delegates in Annapolis, Maryland, in 1786, the call went out to all of the states to send representatives to gather in Philadelphia in May 1787 to "render the constitution of the Federal Government adequate to the exigencies of the Union." George Washington, summoned from his retirement at Mount Vernon, led the Virginia delegation. The *Pennsylvania Packet* of May 14, 1787, reported the news of Washington's entry into the city: "Yesterday His Excellency General WASHINGTON, a member of the grand convention, arrived here,—He was met at some distance and escorted into the city by the troops of horse, and saluted at his entrance by the artillery. The joy of the people on the coming of this great and good man was shown by their acclamations and the ringing of bells."[1]

On May 25, 1787, with only twenty-nine of the fifty-five appointed delegates in attendance, representing nine states, the Federal Constitutional Convention of 1787 was officially called to order. Washington recorded this terse comment in his diary: "the Members present resolved to organize the body; when, by a unanimous vote I was called up to the Chair as President of the body."[2] That short and dispassionate statement does not begin to convey the influential role that

1. Richard B. Bernstein with Kym S. Rice, *Are We to Be a Nation? The Making of the Constitution,* 105; *Pennsylvania Packet and Daily Advertiser,* May 14, 1787.
2. *Diaries,* ed. Jackson and Twohig, 5:162.

Washington was to play in affecting the course and outcome of the deliberations. Max Farrand, an authority on the federal convention, summarized the impact of Washington's presence:

> He sat on a raised platform, in a large, carved, high-backed chair, from which his commanding figure and dignified bearing exerted a potent influence on the assembly, an influence enhanced by the formal courtesy and stately intercourse of the times. Washington was the great man of his day and the members not only respected and admired him; some of them were actually afraid of him. When he rose to his feet he was almost the Commander-in-Chief again. There is evidence to show that his support or disapproval was at times a decisive factor in the deliberations of the Convention.

Farrand goes on to explain how Washington, although saying very little in his official capacity as presiding officer of the convention, was able to sway the assembled delegates: "in the following three months and a half of the Convention, at which fifty-five members were present at one time or another, the average attendance was only slightly larger than that of the first day. In such a small body personality counted for much, in ways that the historian can only surmise. Many compromises of conflicting interests were reached by informal discussion outside of the formal sessions. In these small gatherings individual character was often as decisive as weighty argument."[3]

What was said by the delegates in their private off-hours conversations over drinks and repast in the taverns of Philadelphia is undocumented. But it can be safely assumed that Washington made known at these intimate and convivial social affairs his views on the controversial issues of the day that were being debated on the floor of the convention. Whether conveyed by direct words, or through a frown, a cold stare, a nod of the head, or a raised eyebrow, the intended wishes of the general were taken into serious consideration and carried over into the formal give-and-take at the State House. Of first priority, Washington wanted meaningful authority to be vested in a strong central government—a government that could exercise real power; that could, if necessary, override divisive sectional interests; and yet that would prove acceptable to the majority of the states. To achieve his primary objective Washington was willing to compromise on lesser issues, including slavery.

It was very clear to the delegates, by virtue of the well-known fact that Washington's slaveholdings ranked among the largest in Virginia,[4] that he would not

---

3. Max Farrand, *The Fathers of the Constitution: A Chronicle of the Establishment of the Union*, 110–11.

4. "Among the largest reported slaveholdings in Virginia in 1782–1783 were: John Tabb, Amelia County, 257 slaves; William Allen, Sussex, 241 slaves; George Chewning, Saint Maryes White Chappell

look kindly on any radical measures that would disturb his holdings or affect his way of life. His strong personal commitment to the status quo of slavery made the topic especially delicate. There was probably not a single representative at the convention who was willing to provoke Washington on this sensitive subject, and certainly none were eager to tempt his displeasure by an outright challenge.[5] His own commitment to slavery notwithstanding, Washington had shown an increasing awareness of the necessity of reconciling the liberal doctrines on which the American experiment in democracy had been established with a system of human bondage. He was, therefore, prepared in principle to entertain arguments regarding plans for the long-term dismantling of the institution of slavery.

There were, of course, proponents on both sides of the slavery question. Under the benign but watchful gaze of their presiding officer, the opposing delegates engaged in a running dialogue over a period of several days. The following are brief extracts of that dialogue, as recorded by James Madison, the unofficial chronicler of the convention proceedings:

[Tuesday, August 21, 1787]

Mr. L— Martin [Luther Martin of Maryland], proposed to vary the sect: 4. art VII so as to allow a prohibition or tax on the importation of slaves. . . . it was inconsistent with the principles of the revolution and dishonorable to the American character to have such a feature in the Constitution.

Mr Rutlidge [John Rutledge of South Carolina] did not see how the impor-tation of slaves could be encouraged by this section. . . . Religion & humanity had nothing to do with this question—Interest alone is the governing principle with Nations—The true question at present is whether the Southn. States shall or shall not be parties to the Union. . . .

Mr. Elseworth [Oliver Ellsworth of Connecticut] was for leaving the clause as it stands. let every State import what it pleases. The morality or wisdom of slavery are considerations belonging to the States themselves. . . .

Mr Pinkney [Charles Pinckney of South Carolina]. South Carolina can never receive the plan if it prohibits the slave trade.

These initial exchanges with regard to the slave trade set the tone and laid down the lines for subsequent confrontations. Bluntly stated, it was a matter of economic interests versus moral considerations, with the Southern states threatening to turn their backs on the Union if they felt that any key element of the system of slavery was endangered. The debate grew more heated and acrimonious the next day:

Parish, 224 slaves; Thomas Nelson, Hanover, 208 slaves; Wilson N. Cary, Fluvanna, 200 slaves; George Washington, Fairfax, 188 slaves" (Washington Papers, Mount Vernon Library).

5. According to Catherine D. Bowen, "Washington's self-discipline [was] legendary, as [was] his anger when aroused" (*Miracle at Philadelphia: The Story of the Constitutional Convention, May to September 1787*, 28). Saul K. Padover noted that George Washington "could freeze the boldest with a look" (*To Secure These Blessings: The Great Debates of the Constitutional Convention of 1787*, 18).

[Wednesday, August 22, 1787]

Art. VII sect 4. resumed. Mr. Sherman [Roger Sherman of Connecticut] was for leaving the clause as it stands. He disapproved of the slave trade: yet as the States were now possessed of the right to import slaves, as the public good did not require it to be taken from them, & as it was expedient to have as few objections as possible to the proposed scheme of Government, he thought it best to leave the matter as we find it. . . .

Col. Mason [George Mason of Virginia]. This infernal traffic originated in the avarice of British Merchants. . . . The present question concerns not the importing States alone but the whole Union. . . . Slavery discourages arts & manufactures. . . . Every master of slaves is born a petty tyrant. They bring the judgment of heaven on a Country. As nations can not be rewarded or punished in the next world they must be in this. By an inevitable chain of cause & effects providence punishes national sins, by national calamities. He lamented that some of our Eastern brethren had from a lust of gain embarked in this nefarious traffic. As to the States being in possession of the Right to import, this was the case with many other rights, now to be properly given up. He held it essential in every point of view, that the Genl. Govt. should have the power to prevent the increase of slavery.[6]

These were some of the harshest words in denunciation of slavery that were reported to have been spoken at the convention. They must have been particularly striking to Washington since the speaker, George Mason, was one of his oldest friends, his political mentor during his formative years, and his next-door neighbor at Gunston Hall. But the words came as no surprise. Colonel Mason, throughout his public career, had been a consistent, pungent, and passionate advocate of antislavery measures. Although Washington had actively joined with Mason in subscribing to the Fairfax Resolves in 1774 to ban the importation of African slaves into Virginia, he was not willing now, in Philadelphia in 1787, to jeopardize political unity for the nebulous vision of a new order. It was not the first time that the two men had diverged at the crossroads of principle and expediency, but it was their most serious clash, one that would result in the permanent rupture of their long years of friendship.[7]

Washington was determined, above all else, to create a powerful and lasting federal union, and to achieve that end he was prepared to come to terms on the issue of slavery. From his pragmatic point of view, this was not a painful sacrifice to place on the altar of *e pluribus unum*. Mason, by contrast, refused to bend on the slave question. Because the Constitution, as finally drawn, incorporated the damaging compromises between the New England states and those of the Deep South on the tariff and the slave trade, he withheld his signature from the

6. Max Farrand, ed., *The Records of the Federal Convention of 1787*, 2:364, 369, 370.
7. Flexner, *Washington and the New Nation*, 135.

document, obstinately asserting that "he would sooner chop off his right hand than put it to the Constitution as it now stands."[8] He forcefully carried his opposition into the ratification debates in Virginia, where, in the climax of a hard and bitter fight, he was outvoted and the Constitution was adopted.

The gauntlet thrown down in Philadelphia by Mason was quickly picked up by convention delegates with widely differing opinions:

> Mr. Elsworth [Oliver Ellsworth of Connecticut].—As he had never owned a slave could not judge of the effects of slavery on character. He said however that if it was to be considered in a moral light we ought to go farther and free those already in the Country. . . . Slavery in time will not be a speck in our Country. Provision is already made in Connecticut for abolishing it. And the abolition has already taken place in Massachusetts. . . .
>
> Mr. Pinkney [Charles Pinckney of South Carolina]—If slavery be wrong, it is justified by the example of all the world. . . . In all ages one half of mankind have been slaves. If the S. States were let alone they will probably of themselves stop importations. He wd. himself as a Citizen of S. Carolina vote for it. An attempt to take away the right as proposed will produce serious objections to the Constitution which he wished to see adopted.
>
> General Pinkney [Gen. Charles Cotesworth Pinckney of South Carolina] declared it to be his firm opinion that if himself & all his colleagues were to sign the Constitution & use their personal influence, it would be of no avail towards obtaining the assent of their Constituents. S. Carolina & Georgia cannot do without slaves. . . . He contended that the importation of slaves would be for the interest of the whole Union. The more slaves, the more produce to employ the carrying trade; The more consumption also, and the more of this, the more of revenue for the common treasury. . . .
>
> Mr. Dickenson [John Dickinson of Delaware] considered it as inadmissible on every principle of honor & safety that the importation of slaves should be authorized to the States by the Constitution. . . . He could not believe that the Southn. States would refuse to confederate on the account apprehended; especially as the power was not likely to be immediately exercised by the Genl. Government. . . .
>
> Genl. Pinkney thought himself bound to declare candidly that he did not think S. Carolina would stop her importations of slaves in any short time, but only stop them occasionally as she now does. . . .
>
> Mr. Rutlidge [John Rutledge of South Carolina]. If the Convention thinks that N.C.; S.C. & Georgia will ever agree to the plan, unless their right to import slaves be untouched, the expectation is vain. The people of those States will never be such fools as to give up so important an interest.[9]

After the oratorical dust had settled, the accusations and ultimatums had come and gone, the proposals and counterproposals had been considered, the delegates

---

8. Helen H. Miller, *George Mason: Gentleman Revolutionary*, 261.
9. Farrand, ed., *Records.* 2:370–73.

eventually reached an understanding that managed to legalize completely the existing institution of slavery while throwing an empty sop in the direction of abolitionist sentiment. Deliberately, the obnoxious nomenclature—*slaves* and *slavery*—was excised entirely from this great body of law. Whatever the motives of the representatives to the federal convention—whether shame, guilt, embarrassment, or discomfiture—these incriminating words do not appear anywhere in the Constitution of the United States. Instead, the more genteel *person* serves as the code word for *slave.*

The issue of slave importation was conveniently postponed for twenty years. Under Section 9 of Article I, the slave trade was authorized to continue practically unmolested: "The Migration or Importation of such Persons as any of the States now existing shall think proper to admit, shall not be prohibited by the Congress prior to the Year one thousand eight hundred and eight, but a Tax or duty may be imposed on such Importation, not exceeding ten dollars for each Person." The Southerners also won the right to count their slaves in apportioning their representation in the House of Representatives, as stated in Section 2 of Article I: "Representatives and direct Taxes shall be apportioned among the several States which may be included within this Union, according to their respective Numbers, which shall be determined by adding to the whole Number of free Persons . . . three fifths of all other Persons." But it was the third concession to the slaveholding interests that would cause such a terrible history of human anguish and suffering. Known to later generations as the Fugitive Slave Law, Section 2 of Article IV states: "No Person held to Service or Labour in one State, under the Laws thereof, escaping into another, shall, in Consequence of any Law or Regulation therein, be discharged from such Service or Labour, but shall be delivered up on Claim of the Party of whom such Service or Labour may be due."[10]

The four delegates from South Carolina—Charles Pinckney, Charles Cotesworth Pinckney (his kinsman), John Rutledge, and Pierce Butler—were all outspoken defenders on the floor of the federal convention of the property rights of the slaveholding South (including, of course, their own South Carolina constituencies). All four men were Revolutionary War veterans and prominent politicians and statesmen, and all of them were on friendly terms with George Washington. The two Pinckneys and John Rutledge were lawyers. Irish-born Major Butler had been a professional soldier in the British army who, in 1775, decided to throw in his lot with the Americans. He married into a prestigious South Carolina family, the Middletons, and soon became wealthy as one of the region's largest plantation proprietors and slave owners.

10. Edward Dumbauld, *The Constitution of the United States,* 67, 185, 415.

Major Butler had a strong vested interest in maintaining the slave system of the South and consequently was one of its most ardent and consistent advocates throughout his long political career, which encompassed terms as South Carolina's first U.S. senator. In Philadelphia in the summer of 1787, "Major Butler played a procrustean role in shaping the slave to fit the fabric of the new constitution." His most memorable contribution to the text of the Constitution was his authorship of the so-called Fugitive Slave Law. "The third time the delegates faced up to the problem of Africans in their midst came in response to a proposal by Pierce Butler. It had long galled the owners to have no legal redress when their slaves escaped and found protection in free states. Major Butler's remedy came to be known as the Fugitive Slave Law. His resolution also demonstrated the reluctance of the delegates to call a slave a slave. . . . The Butler resolution was adopted unanimously, without debate, and appears in the United States Constitution . . . with but little change from Pierce Butler's own version."[11]

Whatever Washington may have thought of the slavery issues being debated and decided at the federal convention, it is interesting to note that the proslavery views that found their way into the Constitution were (coincidentally or not) those most compatible with Washington's own values and beliefs.

The historian John Hope Franklin has a modern-day explanation for these acts of commission, or omission, by the delegates to the convention: "The fathers of the Constitution were dedicated to the proposition that 'government should rest upon the dominion of property.' For the Southern fathers this meant slaves, just as surely as it meant commerce and industry for the Northern fathers. In the protection of this property the Constitution has given recognition to the institution of human slavery, and it was to take seventy-five years to undo that which was accomplished in Philadelphia in 1787."[12] Washington offered his own perspective and interpretation of the work of the convention. In his covering letter of September 17, 1787, forwarding the final draft of the Constitution to Congress for its review and acceptance, he wrote:

> WE have now the honor to submit to the consideration of the United States in Congress assembled, that Constitution which has appeared to us the most adviseable.—
>
> In all our deliberations on this subject we kept steadily in our view, that which appears to us the greatest interest of every true American, the consolidation of our Union, in which is involved our prosperity, felicity, safety, perhaps our national existence. This important consideration, seriously and deeply impressed on our minds, led each State in the Convention to be

11. Malcolm Bell Jr., *Major Butler's Legacy: Five Generations of a Slaveholding Family,* 69, 75, 76.
12. Franklin and Moss, *From Slavery to Freedom,* 144.

less rigid on points of inferior magnitude, than might have been otherwise expected; and thus the Constitution, which we now present, is the result of a spirit of amity, and of that mutual deference and concession which the peculiarity of our political situation rendered indispensable.[13]

If the ghost of George Washington could be summoned to appear and testify before a contemporary committee of Congress investigating the defects and short-comings of the Constitution as it was drawn up in 1787, it would very likely shrug its shoulders and impatiently exclaim: "Honorable committee members: we made the best possible bargain under the most difficult and trying circumstances." And who could plausibly fault that answer? Washington used his authority effectively among the obstreperous delegates to forge a consensus for his goal of a strong federal government. He presided over the successful formulation of a code of laws that has stood the test of time for more than two centuries. Surely he had every right to be proud of the achievements of the federal convention and to be indignant with its critics.

Yet, as Washington himself conceded in his letter to Congress, he and his colleagues had agreed to a series of compromises, that is, "to be less rigid on points of inferior magnitude, than might have been otherwise expected." Unfortunately, the compromises that were reached on slavery proved to have serious consequences. For one thing, they made a mockery of the democratic principles on which the new nation had been founded. For another, they condemned literally millions of helpless African American men, women, and children, to a permanent condition of involuntary servitude. Furthermore, they split the country ideologically and, in the final denouement, came perilously close to wrecking the Union in a brutal and bloody civil war.

13. Farrand, ed., *Records*, 2:666–67.

17

PRESIDENTIAL POLITICS

F ROM THE moment that George Washington was chosen commander in chief of the Continental army by the Continental Congress in Philadelphia on June 16, 1775, until his death at Mount Vernon on December 14, 1799, he was a figure of intense worldwide interest and curiosity who moved continually in the public limelight. During this period of almost a quarter of a century, it was well known throughout the thirteen states and abroad, and Washington did not in any way attempt to disguise or conceal the fact, that he was a substantial slaveholder who used slave labor on his estate in Virginia. While many people may have privately disagreed with the practice of owning slaves, Washington was rarely subject to open criticism on this aspect of his conduct. During the Revolution, personal attacks were directed primarily at his military competence and performance. Immediately following the war, while he lived in retirement at Mount Vernon, his prestige as the victorious citizen-soldier and the leading architect of the new nation was so overpowering that only the most disrespectful dared to say anything derogatory about the revered and beloved general.

Washington became vulnerable to public criticism, however, when he actively entered the national political arena—when he was unanimously chosen in February 1789 to become the first president of the United States. It was not long after that, and in spite of his awesome standing, that he found himself the target of opposing politicians, unfriendly newspaper editors and publishers, and other dissident and hostile elements. In the course of his two terms in office, President Washington was frequently attacked and loudly abused for the policies of his administration, for the actions of his subordinates, and even for his personal behavior, such as his supposedly lavish and aristocratic lifestyle, but seldom was he publicly taken to task for being a slave owner. All around him there swirled a storm of antislavery activity, which he seemed to move above and beyond, almost like an aloof and neutral observer, outwardly untouched and unaffected.

Public opinion in America in the 1780s was being mobilized on a massive scale in what appeared at the time to be a concerted drive to rid the country once and for all of the institution of slavery. Abolitionist societies, pioneered by the Quakers, were organized in the tier of states stretching between and including Massachusetts and Virginia. These societies aggressively promoted programs ranging from outlawing the slave trade to outright emancipation. Bending to these pressures, the individual states proceeded to enact progressive legislation. As early as 1780, with the final outcome of the war with England still undecided, Pennsylvania was impelled to provide for the gradual abolition of slavery. The Pennsylvania statute stated in part that no black person born after 1780 could be held in bondage once he or she had reached the age of twenty-eight. The Commonwealth of Massachusetts, in 1783, became the first state to legally and absolutely abolish slavery. Connecticut and Rhode Island followed suit in 1784 to the extent of agreeing to the gradual elimination of slavery within their respective borders. In 1783 Maryland forbade further traffic in slaves, and manumission acts were passed into law in New York in 1785 and in New Jersey in 1786. In the South, too, the tide of the abolitionist movement was pushing down barriers. In 1786, North Carolina substantially increased the duty on every African slave imported into that state, and in 1787 South Carolina prohibited the importation of slaves for a period of several years.[1] But the most signal victory for the antislavery forces came with the passage of the Northwest Ordinance by the Continental Congress in 1787. A key proviso of the ordinance explicitly declared that slavery, or any other form of involuntary servitude, was forever excluded from all of the territory covered by this farsighted piece of legislation, encompassing a huge area of land bounded by Pennsylvania to the east, the Mississippi River to the west, and the Ohio River to the south.[2]

It was soon clear that the national debate on slavery was going to be introduced into the proceedings of the federal Congress, then just beginning to function in New York City. In May 1789, Josiah Parker of Virginia moved to insert a clause in an

1. The Quakers organized the first antislavery society in 1775; by 1792 there were twelve such societies, in every state from Massachusetts to Virginia. Franklin and Moss, *From Slavery to Freedom*, 80–81.

2. The ordinance "contained an article, based on Jefferson's recommendation in 1784, that the Western territories should be closed to the introduction of slavery, but went beyond Jefferson's recommendation, for while he would have allowed bondage to be legal in the area for sixteen years (until 1800), it banned both slavery and involuntary servitude in the territory from the beginning" (Foner, *Africa to the Cotton Kingdom*, 375).

import bill being considered in the House of Representatives that would impose "a duty on the importation of slaves, of ten dollars each person." He regretted "that the constitution prevented Congress from prohibiting the importation altogether . . . [and] hoped such a duty as he moved for would prevent, in some degree, this irrational and inhuman traffic." The challenge was promptly taken up by James Jackson of Georgia, a fiery personality, an articulate speaker, and one of the most influential members of the House.

> MR. JACKSON said, it was the fashion of the day to favor the liberty of slaves. He would not go into a discussion of the subject; but he believed it was capable of demonstration that they were better off in their present situation than they would be if they were manumitted. What are they to do if they are discharged? Work for a living? Experience has shown us they will not. Examine what has become of those in Maryland; many of them have been set free in that State. Did they turn themselves to industry and useful pursuits? No, they turn out common pickpockets, petty larceny villains. And is this mercy, forsooth, to turn them into a way in which they must lose their lives; for when they are thrown upon the world, void of property and connexions, they cannot get their living but by pilfering. What is to be done for compensation? Will Virginia set all her negroes free? Will they give up the money they cost them, and to whom? When this practice comes to be tried there, the sound of liberty will lose those charms which make it grateful to the ravished ear. But our slaves are not in a worse situation than they were on the coast of Africa. It is not uncommon there for the parents to sell their children in peace; and in war, the whole are taken and made slaves together. In these cases, it is only a change of one slavery for another; and are they not better here, where they have a master, bound by the ties of interest and law, to provide for their support and comfort in old age or infirmity, in which, if they were free, they would sink under the pressure of woe for want of assistance? He would say nothing of the partiality of such a tax; it was admitted by the avowed friends of the measure; Georgia, in particular, would be oppressed. On this account, it would be the most odious tax Congress could impose.

The proslavery arguments of Jackson and his colleagues prevailed. Congressman Parker withdrew his motion, and the House adjourned. The dialogue was resumed the following year, as all the well-known and well-rehearsed arguments, pro and con, were rehashed. Again, Jackson led his side in countering the abolitionists, but this time his tactics were to undermine the credibility of the Quakers: "Are they the only people whose feelings are to be consulted on this occasion? Is it to them we owe our present happiness? Was it they who formed the Constitution? Did they, by their arms or contributions, establish our independence? . . . Do they understand the rights of mankind, and the disposition of Providence, better than others? If they were to consult that book, which claims our regard, they will find that slavery is not only allowed but commanded. Their Saviour, who possessed more benevolence and commiseration than they pretend to, has allowed of it."[3]

On Friday, February 12, 1790, a new element was injected into the debate. In the last public act of his long and distinguished career, Benjamin Franklin, president of the Pennsylvania Society for Promoting the Abolition of Slavery, and the Relief of Free Negroes Unlawfully Held in Bondage, signed his name to a memorial brought before the House of Representatives.[4] Backed by Franklin's prestige, this compassionate document gave fresh hope to the antislavery bloc in Congress. In part it reads:

> That mankind are all formed by the same Almighty Being, alike objects of his care, and equally designed for the enjoyment of happiness, the Christian religion teaches us to believe, and the political creed of Americans fully coincides with the position. Your memorialists, particularly engaged in attending to the distresses arising from slavery, believe it their indispensable duty to present this subject to your notice. They have observed, with real satisfaction, that many important and salutary powers are vested in you for "promoting the welfare and securing the blessings of liberty to the people of the United States;" and as they conceive that these blessings ought rightfully to be administered, without distinction of color, to all descriptions of people, so they indulge themselves in the pleasing expectation, that nothing which can be done for the relief of the unhappy objects of their care will be either omitted or delayed.
>
> From a persuasion that equal liberty was originally the portion, and is still the birth-right of all men; and influenced by the strong ties of humanity, and the principles of their institution, your memorialists conceive themselves bound to use all justifiable endeavors to loosen the bands of slavery, and promote a general enjoyment of the blessings of freedom. Under these impressions, they earnestly entreat your serious attention to the subject of slavery; that you will be pleased to countenance the restoration of liberty to those unhappy men, who alone, in this land of freedom are degraded into perpetual bondage, and who, amidst the general joy of surrounding freemen, are groaning in servile subjection; that you will devise means for removing this inconsistency from the character of the American people; that you will promote mercy and justice towards this distressed race, and that you will step

---

3. Joseph Gales Sr., comp., *The Debates and Proceedings in the Congress of the United States,* 1:336–38, 1224–25, 1229.

4. "It is well known that the last public act of Franklin's career was his signing, as president, of an address to the public from the Pennsylvania Society for Promoting the Abolition of Slavery, and the Relief of Free Negroes Unlawfully Held in Bondage. There can be little doubt that Franklin wrote the address, which contains both abolitionist zeal and ambivalence about the place of free blacks in American society. The address described slavery as 'an atrocious debasement of human nature,' but one whose 'very extirpation, if not performed with solicitous care, may sometimes open a source of serious evils'" (J. A. Leo Lemay, ed., *Reappraising Benjamin Franklin: A Bicentennial Perspective,* 436–37).

to the very verge of the power vested in you for discouraging every species of traffic in the persons of our fellow-men.[5]

The simple logic and the appealing humanity of Franklin's request rallied the abolitionists. But the Southerners fought back. Judge Edanus Burke of South Carolina openly raised the threat of sedition, and James Jackson quickly amplified on this theme: "let me ask the gentleman if it is good policy to bring forward a business at this moment, likely to light up the flame of civil discord; for the people of the Southern States will resist one tyranny as soon as another? The other parts of the Continent may bear them down by force of arms, but they will never suffer themselves to be divested of their property without a struggle." In the face of these bellicose, almost violent Southern objections, the House nevertheless agreed, by a solid majority of forty-three to fourteen, to refer the antislavery petitions to a special committee. The committee worked quietly behind the scenes and on March 23, 1790, released its findings. In essence, the special committee refused to take any meaningful action in response to the abolitionist memorials. Instead, it chose to retreat behind the constitutional restrictions and prohibitions on slavery. The introduction and the first two points of the seven-point report adequately serve to illustrate the committee's self-proclaimed helplessness:

> The Committee to whom were referred sundry memorials from the people called Quakers, and also, a memorial from the Pennsylvania Society for promoting the Abolition of Slavery, submit the following report:
> That, from the nature of the matters contained in these memorials, they were induced to examine the powers vested in Congress, under the present Constitution, relating to the Abolition of Slavery, and are clearly of [the] opinion,
> *First.* That the General Government is expressly restrained from prohibiting the importation of such persons "as any of the States now existing shall think proper to admit, until the year one thousand eight hundred and eight."
> *Secondly.* That Congress, by a fair construction of the Constitution, are equally restrained from interfering in the emancipation of slaves, who already are, or who may, within the period mentioned, be imported into, or born within, any of the said States.[6]

The conclusions of the special committee of the House of Representatives sent an unmistakable message to the Quakers and other abolitionists: they could not look to the federal government in the foreseeable future for any substantial remedial legislation with respect to slavery. The Constitution, at least according to

---

5. *The Writings of Benjamin Franklin,* ed. Albert H. Smyth, 10:66–68; Gales, comp., *Debates and Proceedings,* 1:1197–98.
6. Gales, comp., *Debates and Proceedings,* 1:1199–1200, 1473.

their interpretation, had effectively shackled the legislators. Nor was the executive branch offering any encouragement. Officially, of course, President Washington was not involved in the debates that were proceeding in the House of Representatives. Personally, however, he seemed very pleased that the abolitionists' proposals had expired in Congress. Private correspondence between Washington and his old friend and kinsman Dr. David Stuart in Virginia casts some light on his true feelings. Stuart had written to the president on March 15, 1790: "The late applications to Congress, respecting the slaves, will certainly tend to promote this spirit [of jealousy between the Northern and Southern States]—It gives particular umbrage, that the Quakers should be so busy in this business—That they will raise up a storm against themselves, appears to me very certain." Washington replied: "The Memorial of the Quakers (& a very mal-apropos one it was) has at length been put to sleep from which it is not [illegible] it will awake before the year 1808."[7]

Stuart pursued the subject with Washington in a letter dated June 1790:

> I shall now endeavour to give you, all the information I have been able to collect during my journeys, respecting the present temper of mind of the people of this State [Virginia]. . . . the late transactions of Congress, have soured the Public mind to a great degree, which was just recovering from the fever which the Slave business had occasioned. . . . With respect to the Slave business . . . great advantage(s) had been taken of it . . . by many who wished to purcha[se] slaves, circulating a report that Congress were about to pass an act for their ge[ne]ral emancipation—This occasioned su[ch] an alarm, that many were sold for the merest trifle—That the sellers were of course much enraged at Congress, for taking up a subject which they were precluded by the Constitution from medling with for the present, and thus furnishing the occasion for the alar[m] wc[h] induced them to sell—As the people [of] that part of the Country were before much opposed to the Government, it may naturally be supposed, that this circumstance has embittered them much more against it.

Washington was quick to agree that the Quakers were to blame for the antislavery agitation. But he also scolded those slave owners who were responsible for neglecting and mistreating their slave property and were thereby contributing to the general unrest and the growing pressures for emancipation. "The introductions of the (Quaker) Memorial, respecting Slavery, was to be sure, not only an ill-judged piece of business, but occasioned a great waste of time. The final decision thereon,

7. Stuart to Washington, Virginia, March 15, 1790; Washington to Stuart, New York, March 28, 1790 (*Papers: Presidential Series,* ed. Abbot and Twohig, 5:236, 288). Stuart (1753–circa 1814) was educated in Scotland as a physician. He married Eleanor Calvert Custis, the widow of Martha Washington's son, John Parke Custis, in 1783. Their home in Abingdon lay on the Potomac just above Alexandria. Stuart in 1788 was the delegate from Fairfax Court serving in the Virginia Assembly (ibid., 4n).

however, was as favourable as the proprietors of that species of property could well have expected considering the great dereliction to Slavery in a large part of this Union."[8]

While the members of the House of Representatives jousted sporadically over the slavery issue during the winter months of 1790, President Washington discreetly maintained his official silence. But, interestingly enough, he did consent to meet in private with Warner Mifflin, the leading Quaker spokesman and antislavery advocate of that period. It was a unique opportunity for Mifflin to use his considerable powers of persuasion to try to influence the president to take a public stand in favor of emancipation. The lobbying was to no avail. President Washington stood firm in his refusal to become a partisan in the controversy. Washington did record in his diary the gist of his conversation with Mifflin:

> Tuesday 16th. [March 1790, New York City]
> Exercised on horseback between 10 & 12 Oclock. Previous to this, I was visited (having given permisn.) by a Mr. Warner Mifflin, one of the People called Quakers; active in pursuit of the Measures laid before Congress for emancipating the Slaves. After much general conversation, and an endeavor to remove the prejudices which he said had been entertained of the motives by which the attending deputation from their Society were actuated, he used Arguments to shew the immorality—injustice and impolicy of keeping these people in a state of Slavery; with declarations, however, that he did not wish for more than a graduel abolition, or to see any infraction of the Constitution to effect it. To these I replied, that as it was a matter which might come before me for official decision I was not inclined to express any sentimts. on the merits of the question before this should happen.[9]

As president, Washington was spared the necessity of having to publicly state his convictions on the slavery issue; neither Mifflin nor his abolitionist allies were able to move their antislavery motions and petitions past the Congress, though not for lack of trying. In November 1792, in Philadelphia, the nation's new capital, Mifflin and his cohorts were still fighting an uphill battle against congressional hostility and indifference:

> Mr. [John] STEELE [of North Carolina] called the attention of the House to the memorial and representation of Warner Mifflin on the subject of Negro slavery. Mr. S. said, that after what had passed at New York on this subject, he had hoped the House would have heard no more of it; but, to his surprise, he found the subject was started anew, and had been introduced by a fanatic, who, not content with keeping his own conscience, undertook to become the keeper of the consciences of other men, and in a manner which he deemed

8. Stuart to Washington, June 1790; Washington to Stuart, June 15, 1790 (ibid., 5:460, 525).
9. *Diaries*, ed. Jackson and Twohig, 6:47.

not very decent, had intrusted his opinions into this House. . . . Gentlemen in the Northern States do not realize the mischievous consequences which have already resulted from measures of this kind, and if a stop were not put to such proceedings, the Southern States would be compelled to apply to the General Government for their interference. He concluded by moving "that the paper purporting to be a petition from Warner Mifflin, be returned to him by the Clerk of the House; and that the entry of said petition be expunged from the Journal."

With virtually no supporters left among the House membership, Mifflin's crusade at the federal level quietly died with the return of his latest petition.[10]

Although frustrated and checked in the Congress, the Quakers continued to press on with their aggressive efforts in the state legislatures, at the municipal level, in the courts of law, through the media, and by every other legal means available to free the African Americans from their condition of servitude and to improve their status in society. Pennsylvania, a state founded by Quakers and heavily populated by the sect, was a hotbed of abolitionist activity. President Washington, in a letter to Philadelphia financier Robert Morris, registered this complaint about the unwelcome meddling by the Quakers with the rights of slave owners and their property:

Mt Vernon 12th April 1786

Dr Sir,

I give you the trouble of this letter at the instance of Mr Dalby of Alexandria; who is called to Philadelphia to attend what he conceives to be a vexatious lawsuit respecting a slave of his, which a Society of Quakers in the City (formed for such purposes) have attempted to liberate. The merits of this case will no doubt appear upon trial; but from Mr Dalby's state[ment] of the matter, it should seem that this Society is not only acting repugnant to justice so far as its conduct concerns strangers, but, in my opinion extremely impolitickly with respect to the State—the City in particular; & without being able (but by Acts of tyranny & oppression) to accomplish their own ends. . . . and if the practice of this Society of which Mr. Dalby speaks, is not discountenanced, none of those whose *misfortune* it is to have slaves as attendants will visit the City if they can possibly avoid it; because by so doing they hazard their property—or they must be at the expence (& this will not always succeed) of providing servants of another description for the trip.

I hope it will not be conceived from these observations, that it is my wish to hold the unhappy people who are the subject of this letter, in slavery. I can only say that there is not a man living who wishes more sincerely than I do, to see a plan adopted for the abolition of it—but there is only one proper and effectual mode by which it can be accomplished, & that is by Legislative authority: and this, as far as my suffrage will go, shall never be wanting.

10. Gales, comp., *Debates and Proceedings*, 730–31.

But when slaves who are happy & content to remain with their present masters, are tampered with & seduced to leave them; when masters are taken at unawar[e]s by these practices; when a conduct of this sort begets discontent on one side and resentment on the other, & when it happens to fall on a man whose purse will not measure with that of the Society, & he looses his property for want of means to defend it—it is oppression in the latter case, & not humanity in any; because it introduces more evils than it can cure.

I will make no apology for writing to you on this subject; for if Mr Dalby has not misconceived the matter, an evil exists which requires a remedy; if he has, my intentions have been good though I may have been too precipitate in this address.[11]

Whether Morris took seriously President Washington's importunings on behalf of Philip Dalby and whether he tried to dissuade the Quakers from their energetic efforts directed against visiting slaveholders to Pennsylvania is not known. However, the Quakers and their abolitionist tactics were definitely a force to be reckoned with in 1790 when the national government relocated to Philadelphia from New York City. President Washington, forewarned by the experiences of Dalby in 1786, and aware that Pennsylvania law allowed that any adult slave brought into the state would automatically be set free after six months in residence,[12] carefully planned countermeasures to safeguard his slave property while temporarily residing in the state. He wrote to his secretary, Tobias Lear, from Richmond on April 12, 1791:

my residence is incidental as an Officer of Government only, but whether among people [the Quakers] who are in the practice of *enticing* slaves *even* when there is *no* colour of law for it, this distinction will avail, I know not, and therefore beg [that] you will take the best advise you can on the subject, and in case it shall be found that any of my Slaves may, or any of them shall attempt their freedom at the expiration of six months, it is my wish and desire that you would send the whole, or such part of them as Mrs. Washington may not chuse to keep, home, for although I do not think they would be benefitted by the change, yet the idea of freedom might be too great a temptation for them to resist. At any rate, it might, if they conceived they had a right to it, make them insolent in a State of Slavery. . . . If upon taking good advise it is found expedient to send them back to Virginia, I wish to have it accomplished under pretext that may deceive both them and the Public; and none I think would so effectually do this, as Mrs. Washington coming to Virginia next

11. *Papers: Confederation Series*, ed. Abbot and Twohig, 4:15–16.

12. "The act of 1780 permitted the resident of another state to bring his slave into Pennsylvania and keep him there for six months" (Edward R. Turner, *The Negro in Pennsylvania: Slavery—Servitude— Freedom, 1639–1861*, 86). "When Philadelphia became the national capital a bill was brought forward in the Pennsylvania Assembly to enable officers of the United States to hold slaves in the State, but the Pennsylvania Abolition Society vigorously opposed it, and it was finally suppressed" (Mary S. Locke, *Anti-Slavery in America: From the Introduction of African Slaves to the Prohibition of the Slave Trade, 1619–1808*, 133).

month (towards the middle or latter end of it, as she seemed to have a wish to do) if she can accomplish it by any convenient and agreeable means, with the assistance of the Stage Horses &c. This would naturally bring her maid and Austin, and Hercules under the idea of coming home to *Cook* whilst we remained there, might be sent on in the Stage. Whether there is occasion for this or not according to the result of your enquiries, or issue the thing as it may, I request that these Sentiments and this advise may be known to none but *yourself* and *Mrs. Washington.*[13]

Obviously, the president was prepared to circumvent the laws of Pennsylvania to make sure that he would retain possession of his slaves, who were prize targets of the abolitionists. Washington had become acutely aware of the growing pressures for emancipation, particularly in the large northern cities of Philadelphia, New York, and Boston. His directive to shield his intentions from the public eye had a double purpose. As president of the United States, not just a Virginia planter, he was especially anxious to hold on to the esteem and affection of all citizens. The act of deviously spiriting away his slaves in order to protect his property, though not illegal, would not, if it became known, reflect well on his character.

As an intelligent and thoughtful man, and as the political leader of the United States, President Washington could not help but be disturbed by the changing times: the changes signaled that the country was becoming polarized by the slavery issue; they were changes that the president, still steeped in the old Virginia plantation ways, had difficulty accepting and adjusting to. Yet slave restlessness was not limited to African Americans in the South. There were flames of rebellion and pent-up resentment breaking out in several different parts of the world. A violent and bloody slave insurrection against the colonial French on the Caribbean island of Santo Domingo (Hispaniola) in the summer of 1791 resulted in the wholesale slaughter of thousands of whites.[14] President Washington expressed his grave concern at this news in a letter dated December 27, 1791: "Lamentable! to see

---

13. Fitzpatrick, ed., *Writings*, 37:573–74.

14. "In Virginia the limited enthusiasm for emancipation roused by the Revolution was largely dissipated by 1797, and whatever lingered was destroyed by news of the massacres on Santo Domingo. An uprising of blacks seeking freedom under the Jamaican voodoo priest, Boukman, beginning in 1791, had started a race war, with whites murdering blacks, with blacks murdering whites, and the mulattoes—a distinct caste group—the victims of both. When the 6,000 French soldiers on the island dwindled almost to zero, the civilian whites, who had kept control of the cities and towns, invited in British soldiers for protection. But the charismatic black commander, Toussaint L'Ouverture, fired by the egalitarian idealism of the French Revolution, built up a formidable army of blacks and mulattoes and began to drive the British out of the island. Word of his phenomenal success filtered into Virginia in the summer of 1797, and a hysteria of terror concerning slave insurrection spread through the whole South" (Fawn M. Brodie, *Thomas Jefferson: An Intimate History*, 290).

such a spirit of revolt among the Blacks [in Santo Domingo]. Where it will stop, is difficult to say."[15]

On a presidential tour of the Southern states during the spring of 1791, Washington had occasion to issue orders to block fugitive slaves in Georgia from crossing the border and finding refuge in Spanish Florida. He instructed James Seagrove, the U.S. superintendent of the Creek Indians, to cooperate with the Spaniards in preventing Florida from becoming a haven for freedom-seeking slaves and to expedite the return of runaways: "Your first care will be to arrest the farther reception of fugitive slaves, your next to obtain restitution of those slaves who have fled to Florida . . . and your last object, which may demand the greatest address, will be to give a retrospective force to the orders of the Court of Spain, beyond the date of that letter, and to procure the Governor's order for a general relinquishment of all fugitive slaves, who were the property of citizens of the United States."[16]

While on the one hand vigorously deploring instances of slave unrest and zealously enforcing the laws that held African American men and women in bondage, on the other hand the president managed to sympathize with Gov. Charles Pinckney of South Carolina on the failure of that state's legislature to prohibit the slave trade. They commiserated on the bleak prospects for outlawing the slave traffic in South Carolina in this private exchange of correspondence, which Governor Pinckney initiated on January 8, 1792:

> Our legislature among other questions agitated the one respecting the future importation of slaves, as the prohibition expires in March, 1793. Great pains were used to effect a total prohibition; but upon the question being taken [up] in the Senate, it was lost by so decided a majority, that I think we may consider it as certain [that] this State will, after March 1793, import as largely as they ever did. It is a decision upon the policy of which I confess I have my doubts.[17]

President Washington replied from Philadelphia on March 17, 1792:

> I must say that I lament the decision of your legislature upon the question of importing Slaves after March 1793. I was in hopes that motives of policy, as well as other good reasons supported by the direful effects of Slavery which at this moment are presented, would have operated to produce a total prohibition

15. Washington to John Vaughn, Philadelphia, December 27, 1791 (Fitzpatrick, ed., *Writings,* 31:453).

16. Washington to Seagrove, May 20, 1791, Augusta, Ga. (ibid., 31:289–90).

17. Washington Papers, microfilm, ser. 4, reel 101, Manuscript Division, Library of Congress.

of the importation of Slaves whenever the question came to be agitated in any
State that might be interested in the measure.[18]

In his personal postwar correspondence, Washington consistently voiced his
belief that the gradual abolition of slavery in the United States was a foregone
conclusion. Typical of his strong feelings on the subject is this statement taken
from a letter that he wrote in Philadelphia to his friend and correspondent
Sir John Sinclair, in England, on December 11, 1796: "there are Laws here [in
Pennsylvania] for the gradual abolition of Slavery, which neither of the two States
above mentioned [Maryland and Virginia] have, at present, but which nothing
is more certain than that they must have, and at a period not remote."[19] But he
was just as consistent in his deliberate refusal to carry these positive sentiments
over into the public debate on slavery. During the entire eight years of his two
administrations, from 1789 to 1797, Washington stood aloof and officially silent
as the forces of confrontation continued to divide the nation. On the one side were
the Southerners, whose roots were firmly embedded in the slave system by virtue of
economic necessity and social convenience. Opposing them were the Northerners,
who by and large were not bound by these considerations but instead were strongly
influenced by the moral arguments against slavery, the foremost proponents of
these being the Quakers.

The Congress and the chief executive saw their respective roles in this developing
conflict as restricted by the mandate of the Constitution. Also, both the president
and many congressional legislators shared an underlying and pervasive fear that
the tenuous union of the states, so carefully crafted at the Federal Constitutional
Convention in Philadelphia in 1787 and painstakingly secured during the ratification process following, might be torn apart by the radical Southern dissidents
if they were sufficiently provoked on the subject of slavery. Even though the
Constitution authorized Congress to legislate on the slave trade—and serious
efforts were made to control the importation of Africans—once again a crosscur-
rent of economic, regional, and emotional pressures essentially immobilized the
House of Representatives. The federal government was never able to muster the
necessary votes during the two Washington administrations to cripple effectively
the commerce in human cargoes.

The only official action pertaining to slavery that Washington performed during
his entire presidency was to affix his signature to the Fugitive Slave Act. The act
was mandated by Congress on February 9, 1793: "Congress enacts a Fugitive
Slave Act, mandating the right of a slaveowner to recover a runaway slave. This

18. Fitzpatrick, ed., *Writings*, 32:6.
19. Ibid., 35:328.

bill implements the provisions of Article IV, Section 2 of the Constitution by establishing the mechanism for the recovery of fugitive slaves." *Journal of the Proceedings of the President, 1793–1797* simply notes, "The two Acts [which included the Fugitive Slave Act] laid before the President on the 9th. Inst. were signed this day [February 12, 1793]."[20] President Washington himself made no known comments on this piece of legislation. Yet he cannot escape his share of the blame for the pain and suffering inflicted on future generations of African Americans by these legislative actions.

Although President Washington, throughout his eight years in office, successfully managed to stand apart from the bitter and divisive partisan debates on slavery, he did become directly involved in the battle being waged behind the scenes between the abolitionists, who were ever alert to secure the release of slaves, and the slave owners, who were just as tenacious and determined in their resolve to retain their valuable property. There came a time, too, when he was even brazenly attacked for his ownership of slaves. A pamphlet—generally attributed to William Duane, the radical, muckraking publisher of the *Aurora,* a newspaper in Philadelphia—was privately printed in December 1796 and given wide circulation. Written in the first person in the form of a letter addressed directly to Washington by "Jasper Dwight of Vermont" (a fictitious name), it contains inflammatory passages on the theme of George Washington and the Mount Vernon slaves:

> Would to God! you had retired to a private station four years ago, while your public conduct threw a veil of sanctity round you, which you have yourself rashly broken down, Your fame would have been safe, your country without reproach, and I should not have the mortifying task of pointing out the blind temerity with which you come forward to defend the religion of Christ, who exist in the violation of its most sacred obligations, of the dearest ties of humanity, and in defiance of the sovereign calls of morality and liberty—by dealing in HUMAN SLAVES.
>
> . . . that the great champion of American Freedom, the rival of Timoleon and Cincinnatus, twenty years after the establishment of the republic, was possessed of FIVE HUNDRED of the HUMAN SPECIES IN SLAVERY, enjoying the fruits of their labour without remuneration, or even the consolations of religious instructions—
>
> . . . when your property, ample for the gratification of the most extravagant desires—would call loudly upon you to release your species from their unchristian bondage and ignorance, were it but to present an example of disinterestedness—of that virtue—that morality—of the sincerity of your love of liberty—of benevolence—of charity—of the love of God.[21]

20. Arthur M. Schlesinger Jr., gen. ed., *The Almanac of American History,* 163; *The Journal of the Proceedings of the President, 1793–1797,* ed. Dorothy Twohig, 51.

21. *A Letter to George Washington, President of the United States; Containing Strictures On His Address of the Seventeenth of September, 1796, Notifying His Relinquishment of the Presidential Office,* by Jasper

 Even the British, who had dominated the African slave trade for more than a century, were heard from in this new round of finger-pointing. An Englishman, Edward Rushton (with no known links to George Washington), apparently felt moved by great indignation to write a thirteen-page diatribe, dated February 20, 1797, entitled "Expostulatory Letter to George Washington of Mount Vernon, in Virginia, on his continuing to be a proprietor of Slaves." A brief extract will suffice to indicate the content and tone of the message: "Shame! Shame! That man should be deemed the property of man or that the name of Washington should be found among the lists of such proprietors."[22] With this kind of abuse in store for him, it was high time for the president to retire to the relative peace and quiet to be found along the banks of the Potomac.

Dwight, of Vermont, printed at Philadelphia, for the author, and sold by the booksellers, December 1796. A copy of this pamphlet is at the Library of the New-York Historical Society, New York City. Parts of the pamphlet are also quoted by Benson J. Lossing, *Washington and the American Republic,* 3:477, 477n. See also Kim Tousley Phillips, *William Duane, Radical Journalist in the Age of Jefferson,* 52.
 22. Signed autograph letter in the Washington Papers, Alderman Library, University of Virginia.

18

THE ABOLITIONISTS

O F THE many voices that were raised to denounce slavery in eighteenth-century America, none were more sustained, more sincere, and more effective than those of the Quakers, or the Society of Friends. This religious minority, comprising less than 2 percent of the total white population with perhaps two hundred meetinghouses and fifty to sixty thousand members in the United States at the end of the 1700s,[1] was a highly organized, well-disciplined group dedicated to the moral and ethical principles of humanity as defined by the Golden Rule. Alone among the early abolitionists, the Quakers achieved important and lasting results by their quiet, nonviolent, and determined perseverance. Thomas Carlyle, the Scottish essayist and historian, writing of George Fox (1624–1691), the founder of Quakerism, used this figure of speech in praise of the work of Fox and his followers: "Stitch away, thou noble Fox, every prick of that little instrument is pricking into the heart of slavery and world worship and the mammon god."[2]

The pinpricks of the Quakers were indeed felt by slave owners, including George Washington. On December 11, 1785, Robert Pleasants, the leading Quaker and antislavery advocate in Virginia, wrote to the general at length:

Curles 12th mo. 11th 1785

Honour'd General.

. . . Remember the cause for which thou wert call'd to the Command of the American Army, was the cause of liberty and the Rights of Mankind: How strange then must it appear to impartial thinking men, to be informed, that many who were warm advocates for that noble cause during the War,

---

1. Richard Hofstadter, *America at 1750: A Social Portrait,* 184.
2. Quoted in Stephen B. Weeks, *Southern Quakers and Slavery,* 198.

are now siting down in a state of ease, dissipation and extravigance on the labour of Slaves? And more especially that thou, who could forego all the Sweets of domestic felicity for a number of years, & expose thy Person to the greatest fatigue & dangers in that cause, should now withhold that enestimable blessing from any who are absolutely in thy power, & after the Right of freedom, is acknowledg'd to be the natural & unalienable Right of all Mankind.

I cannot suppose from the uncommon generosity of thy conduct in other respects, that this can proceed altogether from interested motives; but rather, that it is the effect of long custom, the prejudices of education towards a black skin, or that some other important concerns may have hitherto diverted thy attention from a Subject so Noble and interesting, as well to thy own Peace & reputation, as the general good of that People, and the community at large. But whatever may have been the Cause, I sincerely wish thou may not longer delay a matter of such importance. It is a Sacrifise which I fully believe the Lord is requiring of this Generation. . . . We Read, "where much is given, the more will be requird,["] and as thou hast acquired much fame, in being the Successful Champion of American Liberty; It seems highly probable to me, that thy example & influence at this time, towards a general emancipation, would be as productive of real happiness to mankind, as thy Sword may have been: I can but wish therefore, that thou may not loose the opertunity of Crowning the great Actions of thy Life, with the sattisfaction of, "doing to Others as thou would (in the like Situation) be done by," and finally transmit to future ages a Character, equally Famous for thy Christian Virtues, as thy worldly achievements. . . .

Perhaps General Washington may think it presumptuous in me, who cannot boast a particular acquaintance, to address him in this manner, but I hope when he considers the Nature of the Subject, and that I can have no selfish views in offering these hints to his serious consideration, than what may arise from the pleasure of hearing he had done those things—which belong to his present, & future happiness, and the good of those over whom Providence hath placed him, he will at least excuse the freedom; & believe that I am with great sincerity & Respect, his Real Friend,

Robert Pleasants

Pleasants added a postscript: "I herewith send thee a small Pamphlet on the Subject of Slavery, said to be wrote by John Dickinson, which if thou hast not before seen [it], *I* doubt not will afford pleasure in the perusal and am as above &c."[3]

In 1785, when Washington stood at the pinnacle of his popularity, very few friends—or strangers for that matter—would have dared to lecture him about slavery. With the exception of certain prominent foreigners, most Americans probably felt too intimidated to even bring up the subject of Washington's Mount Vernon slaves. If perchance they were presumptuous or impertinent enough to

3. *Papers: Confederation Series,* ed. Abbot and Twohig, 3:449–51.

raise the issue, and Robert Pleasants's letter is one of only a few known to historians, they were likely to be greeted by indifference. There is no record that Washington ever bothered to reply to, or even to acknowledge, this unwelcome and brash intrusion into his private affairs.

Indifference and hostility seldom deterred the Quakers from acting in accordance with their cherished principles and their belief in divine guidance. Washington learned early in his career that when it came to their basic convictions, the Quakers were intransigent to the point of fanaticism. When he was commander of the Virginia militia in 1756 during a particularly trying period of the French and Indian Wars following the disastrous defeat of Maj. Gen. Edward Braddock, the British commander in chief in North America during the beginning of the conflict, desperately needed recruits had been called into service to help defend the threatened frontier settlements. Six of the recruits were Quakers. They refused to cooperate, declaring that it was contrary to their faith to engage in warlike activities. Washington asked Gov. Robert Dinwiddie on June 25 for instructions on how to deal with the problem: "there remain now in confinement six Quakers; who will neither bear arms, work, receive provisions or pay, or do any thing that tends, in any respect, to self-defence. I should be glad of your Honours directions how to proceed with them." Ordinarily a tolerant and compassionate man, the governor angrily recommended in his reply that forceful measures be employed: "If the six Quakers will not fight You must compell them to work on the Forts, to carry Timber &ca if this will not do confine them with a short Allowance of Bread & Water till You bring them to reason or provide others in their room."[4]

Colonel Washington tried to carry out the governor's orders but without any noticeable success: "I could by no means bring the Quakers to any Terms— They chose rather to be whipped to death than bear arms, or lend us any assistance whatever upon the Fort, or any thing of self-defence. Some of their friends have been security for their appearance when they are called for; and I have released them from the Guard-House until I receive further orders from your Honour—which they have agreed to apply for." Humanity prevailed, and Governor Dinwiddie wrote to Washington on August 19, setting forth these conciliatory terms: "A great Body of Quakers waited on me in regard to their Friends with You, praying they may not be Whipped, u[se] them with lenity, but as they are at their own Expence I wou'd have them remain as long as the other Draughts." Washington did as he was instructed, writing to Dinwiddie that

4. Washington to Dinwiddie, Winchester, Va., June 25, 1756; Dinwiddie to Washington, Williamsburg, July 1, 1756 (*Papers: Colonial Series*, ed. Abbot and Twohig, 3:224, 232).

he had confined the six recalcitrant Quakers to camp until all the draftees were discharged.[5]

The lesson from this initial encounter with the stubborn Quakers was not lost on Washington. The Friends were men and women of deep-seated convictions who were not easily dissuaded from their chosen course of action. It may have been courtesy, or simple curiosity, that led Washington to attend a Quaker meeting in Philadelphia in 1774, while he was a delegate to the First Continental Congress.[6] He had no way of knowing then that the Quakers would turn out to be the proverbial thorn in his side for the rest of his life: first on the issue of war, and later on the issue of slavery.

The advent of the Revolutionary War put the Quaker belief in nonviolence to a stern test. The Friends refused to fight or bear arms, to help in any way in the common defense against the British, to serve in the local government, or even to handle the Continental paper money and bills of exchange. Patriotic Americans came to look upon them as traitors and Tory sympathizers. Neither stigma made life pleasant for the Quakers, and during those bitter and strife-torn years they suffered serious abuse for their professed pacifism. They found out, too, that General Washington, when angered, could be downright spiteful. In May 1777, there were strong suspicions that the Quakers were engaged in attempting to subvert recruiting activities in New Jersey. Washington lodged his complaint directly with Gov. William Livingston: "I have been informed by Colo. Forman, that the Quakers and disaffected are doing all in their Power to counteract your late Militia Law; but I hope, if your Officers are active and Spirited, that they will defeat their evil intentions and bring their Men into the Field."[7]

During the bleak, dark days at Valley Forge, when the success of the rebellion literally hung in the balance, the commander in chief vented his resentment at Quaker neutrality, or perhaps disloyalty, by issuing orders to Brig. Gen. John Lacey Jr. aimed at confiscating their goods and interfering with their freedom of movement:

> Head Quarters, Valley Forge, March 20, 1778.
> Sir:
> Sunday next, being the time on which the Quakers hold one of their general Meetings, a number of that Society will probably be attempting to go into Philadelphia. This is an intercourse that we should by all means endeavour

---

5. Washington to Dinwiddie, Winchester, August 4, 1756; Dinwiddie to Washington, Williamsburg, August 19, 1756; Washington to Dinwiddie, Winchester, September 8, 1756 (ibid., 3:315, 360, 397).

6. "Went to the Quaker meeting in the Forenoon" (September 25, 1774, *Diaries*, ed. Jackson and Twohig, 3:280).

7. Washington to Livingston, Morristown, N.J., May 11, 1777 (Fitzpatrick, ed., *Writings*, 8:44–45).

to interrupt, as the plans settled at these meetings are of the most pernicious tendency. I would therefore have you dispose of your parties in such a Manner, as will most probably fall in with these people, and if they should, and any of them should be mounted upon Horses fit for the draft or the Service of light Dragoons, I desire they may be taken from them and sent over to the Qr. Master General, any such are not to be considered as the property of the parties who may seize them as in other cases. Communicate the above orders to any of the officers of the Continental Army who may command scouting parties upon your side of the Schuylkill.[8]

A similar alert was relayed to Brig. Gen. Lachlan McIntosh on March 21, 1778. "As this is the time of one of the Quakers general Meetings, it is more than probable that many of that Society will be going into Philadelphia. If you fall in with any of them, I desire they may be stopped and turned back and their Horses taken from them." And to his foraging parties who were out scouring the countryside in search of clothing and other urgently needed supplies, General Washington had already distributed this blanket authorization dated November 1777: "By virtue of the powers vested in me by the Honorable Congress I hereby Authorize _____ to collect all such Blankets, Shoes, Stockings[s] and other Clothing suitable to the use of the Army, within the Counties of _____ in the State of Pennsylvania, as the Inhabitants can spare without greatly distressing their Families. In doing this you are to take care, that, the unfriendly Quakers and other notoriously disaffected to the cause of American Liberty do not escape your Vigilance." Col. John Siegfried also received orders on October 6, 1777, specifically directed against the Quakers: "Obtaining these things from the Quakers and disaffected inhabitants is recommended."[9]

Although General Washington tended to treat them as hostile, the Pennsylvania Quakers claimed only to be quietly praying and working for peace. A contemporary Quaker memoir gives this account of the Yearly Meeting that took place, coincidentally, on the same day, October 4, 1777, as the Battle of Germantown: "In the time of the battle, these friends of peace were engaged in prayer, that Divine protection might be granted to the city and the people; and in preparing to renew their testimony against the spirit of war. While James Thornton was writing their Testimony, the cannon shook the house, where they were assembled, and the air was darkened by the smoke of the guns."[10]

8. Washington to Lacey, Valley Forge, March 20, 1778 (ibid., 11:114).

9. Washington to McIntosh, Valley Forge, March 21, 1778; Washington, "Powers to Officers to Collect Clothing, Etc.," Valley Forge, November 1777; Washington to Siegfried, Philadelphia County, October 6, 1777 (ibid., 9:121, 124, 318).

10. Hilda Justice, comp., *Life and Ancestry of Warner Mifflin: Friend-Philanthropist-Patriot*, 74.

In due fairness to Washington, the general did behave humanely on more than one occasion in his face-to-face dealings with Quaker petitioners. One historian notes that

> during the siege of Boston, New England Quakers, assisted by donations from Quakers in Pennsylvania and New Jersey, organized a relief expedition to help the poor and needy in Boston and sent a committee of four to seek Washington's permission to enter the besieged city. . . . Washington told the committee: "Go to General Greene; he is a Quaker, and knows more about it than I do." The committee accordingly sought out Greene, wrote the letters with his assistance, and submitted them to Washington that evening. Washington approved the letters and sent the Quakers, under a flag of truce, on to the British lines, where they arranged with General Howe for distributing funds among the war-sufferers of Boston.[11]

When the wives of several of the Quaker leaders who had been interned because of their suspected pro-British leanings called on Washington for help in obtaining the release of their husbands, he wrote to Thomas L. Warton Jr., the president of Pennsylvania:

> Head Quarters, Valley Forge, April 6, 1778.
>
> Sir:
> Mrs. Jones, Mrs. Pleasants and two other Ladies, connected with the Quakers confined at Winchester in Virginia, waited upon me this day for permission to pass to York Town, to endeavour to obtain the release of their Friends. As they were admitted by the Officer at the advanced picket to come within the Camp, I thought it safer to suffer them to proceed than to oblige them to return immediately to the City. You will judge of the propriety of permitting them to proceed further than Lancaster; but from appearances, I imagine their request may be safely granted. As they seem much distressed, humanity pleads strongly in their behalf.[12]

It may seem incongruous but it is a fact that on two separate occasions in his communications to the Pennsylvania Council of Safety, Washington made it a point to ask them to respect the religious scruples of any conscientious objectors (presumably including Quakers) when drafting men for the Continental army:

> Head Quarters, Morris Town, January 19, 1777.
>
> Gentn.:
> . . . As there is not the least doubt at present, that the principle Object of the Enemy is to get Possession of the City of Philadelphia, it is absolutely necessary, that every Person able to bear Arms (except such as are Conscientiously scrupulous against it in every Case), should give their personal Service.

---

11. Paul F. Boller Jr., *George Washington and Religion,* 129–30.
12. Fitzpatrick, ed., *Writings,* 11:223–24.

Head Quarters, Morris Town, January 29, 1777.

Gentn.:

. . . But I would wish to see every Man (who is not really conscientiously scrupulous) obliged to turn out, when the good of his Country demands it.[13]

Warner Mifflin is the only Quaker leader known to have had direct personal interviews with Washington. The two men met for the first time when Mifflin was chosen to carry the Quaker testimony from the Philadelphia Yearly Meeting of October 1777, calling for a cease-fire to be followed by peace negotiations, to the opposing generals: "To perform this duty, he had to walk in blood, and among the dead bodies of those who had fallen in battle. He performed the service with great freedom and intrepidity. In the conversation with general Washington, he said expressly, 'I am opposed to the revolution, and to all changes of government which occasion war and blood-shed.'" A second meeting was the one that took place in New York City in March 1790, when Washington was president:

> After general Washington was elected president of the United States, Warner Mifflin went to visit him at New York, and was treated by the president with kindness and respect. In the course of the interview, the president recollected what Mifflin had said to him at Germantown, and thus addressed him: "Mr. Mifflin, will you please to inform me on what principles you were opposed to the revolution?" Mifflin answered, "Yes, friend Washington;— upon the same principles that I should be opposed to a change in this government. All that ever was gained by revolutions, are not adequate compensation to the poor mangled soldier, for the loss of life or limb." After some pause and reflection, the president replied, "Mr. Mifflin, I honour your sentiments;—there is more in *that*, than mankind have generally considered."[14]

The Quaker peace overtures to end the Revolution failed, and the war dragged on until the British were finally forced to concede defeat. While others returned to their farms and workshops to enjoy the fruits of the new order, Mifflin and his Quaker colleagues found themselves involved in another stirring crusade: a concerted effort to bring about the abolition of slavery from the North American continent. It was a crusade that was to become Mifflin's lifework and would again place him and the Quakers at loggerheads with George Washington.

Emancipation had been on the minds of the Quakers for many years. The earliest recorded public protest against slavery in the North American colonies was made by the Mennonites, a religious group affiliated with the Quakers who also rejected military service. At their Monthly Meeting in Germantown, Pennsylvania,

---

13. Ibid., 7:35, 79.
14. Justice, comp., *Mifflin*, 74–75.

on February 18, 1688, they expressed these sentiments: "There is a saying, that we should do to all men like as we will be done ourselves; making no difference of what generation, descent, or colour they are. And those who steal or rob men, and those who buy or purchase them, are they not all alike? Here [in America] is liberty of conscience, which is right and reasonable; here ought to be likewise liberty of the body. . . . But to bring men hither, or to rob and sell them against their will, we stand against."[15]

The antislavery literature is voluminous, reaching back to the earliest days of colonization and continuing until the end of the Civil War, a period of approximately two hundred years. Pioneer settlers of the American colonies, as diverse in philosophy and as geographically far apart as Roger Williams in Rhode Island, William Penn in Pennsylvania, and Gen. James Oglethorpe in Georgia, spoke out and acted to eliminate slavery and the slave trade. And religious groups, like the Mennonites and the Quakers in Pennsylvania, the Puritans in New England, and the Methodists in Maryland, worked intermittently to have the institution of slavery morally condemned and legally outlawed. But, as Mary Stoughton Locke wrote in her authoritative *Anti-Slavery in America,* "Combined action was found only among the Quakers, and they alone achieved important results." Why were the Quakers successful? Locke suggests an answer:

> Within a century of the Germantown Protest, the abolition of slavery among the Quakers had been practically accomplished. It was accomplished without great strife or schism or bitterness of feeling, by a policy of gentle but persistent pressure, in which the zeal of individuals was supplemented by organized efforts well directed and steadily applied. Individual Quakers, though lovers of peace, were tremendously in earnest and devoted their lives to the cause. The official organizations, though cautious in taking up the work and desirous of unanimity, never gave up a point they had once insisted on, and all worked together for their common end.
>
> Having freed their own consciences of slavery, the Friends next applied themselves to influencing those outside their own sect. After the Revolutionary War they joined in the political movements for the suppression of the slave-trade and for emancipation by law. They were also the founders and the leaders of many of the early abolition societies, and continued to hold a place in the literature by which public opinion was educated to anti-slavery views.[16]

---

15. Albert B. Hart, *American History Told by Contemporaries: Building of the Republic 1689–1783,* 2:291. The Mennonites, a Protestant religious denomination that originated in northern Europe in the sixteenth century, received their name from Menno Simons, a Dutch reformer and early organizer of the sect. Several thousand Swiss Mennonites, hoping to escape persecution and poverty in Europe, settled in eastern Pennsylvania before the Revolutionary War. Their first permanent settlement was at Germantown in 1683.

16. Locke, *Anti-Slavery in America,* 3, 39–40.

Realizing that the strained relations between them during the Revolutionary War were in neither side's long-term best interests, both General Washington and the Quakers took positive steps to try to bridge their differences and to resolve their misunderstandings. The active reconciliation began a few days after the Battle of Germantown, when Washington received six delegates from the Philadelphia Yearly Meeting, led by Mifflin. The visitors were especially eager to gain the release of a number of prominent Philadelphia Quakers who were being detained in protective custody as suspected subversives. At the same time, they welcomed the chance to clear the air and to refute the rumors and charges that the Friends were partial to the British and were secretly collaborating with them. The delegates "had a very full opportunity of clearing the Society from some aspersions which had been invidiously raised against them, and distributed a number of the testimonies amongst the officers, who received and read them and made no objections." Reporting subsequently to the Quaker Yearly Meeting, the emissaries seemed pleased with their reception: "we believe General Washington, and all the officers then present, being a pretty many, were fully satisfied as to Friends' clearness; and we hope and believe, through the Lord's blessing, the opportunity we had was useful [in] many ways; there having been great openness and many observations upon various subjects, to edification, and tending to remove and clear up some prejudices which had been imbibed."[17]

The thaw extended into the era of independence and nationhood. Jacques Pierre Brissot de Warville, the outspoken pro-Quaker French politician and journalist, following a three-day stay at Mount Vernon as Washington's houseguest, quoted him at length on the subject of Quakers:

> Nobody spoke to me with greater impartiality about the Quakers than that famous man, who is distinguished by his sense of justice. He admitted that during the war he had had a poor opinion of the Society. He had not known much about it, for there were then few Quakers in Virginia. He had attributed to their politics actions which were really expressions of their religious beliefs. When the army was encamped in Chester County [Pennsylvania], which is inhabited mainly by Quakers, he thought he was in enemy territory, because he could not persuade any Quakers to spy for him, although, on the other hand, neither did they spy on him for the English army. . . .
>
> When General Washington understood the Quaker spirit better he came to have a high regard for them. He told me that because of their simple way of life, their thrift, their fine moral standards, the excellent example they set, and their support of the Constitution, he considered them to be the strongest

17. Thomas Gilpin, *Exiles in Virginia: With Observations on the Conduct of the Society of Friends during the Revolutionary War*, 60–61.

pillars of the new government, which requires of its citizens both full loyalty and frugality.

The exuberant Frenchman then entered into a dialogue with Washington on the pros and cons of the abolitionist movement in Virginia:

> It would undoubtedly be fitting that such a lofty, pure, and disinterested soul be the one to make the first step in the abolition of slavery in Virginia. This great man, when I had the honor to talk with him, told me that he admired everything that was being done in the other states and that he desired the extension of the [abolitionist] movement in his own. But he did not conceal the fact that there are still many obstacles and that it would be dangerous to make a frontal attack on a prejudice which is beginning to decrease. "Time, patience, and education," he said, "and it will be overcome. Nearly all Virginians," he added, "are convinced that the general emancipation of Negroes cannot occur in the near future, and for this reason they do not wish to organize a society which might give their slaves dangerous ideas." Another obstacle which he pointed out is that most of this part of the country is made up of large plantations and people live far apart, so that it is difficult to hold meetings.

The conversation covered ground that Washington had heard before and would hear again with increasing frequency in the years ahead:

> "Virginians are wrong," I told him. "It is evident that sooner or later Negroes will win their freedom everywhere, and that this revolution will extend to Virginia. It is therefore to the interest of your fellow citizens to prepare for it and to try to reconcile the restitution of the Negroes' rights with their own right to property. The necessary steps can only be worked out by a society, and it would be fitting that the savior of America be its head and restore liberty to 300,000 unhappy inhabitants of his country." This great man told me that he was in favor of the formation of such a society and that he would support it, but that he did not believe the moment was favorable. No doubt there were greater problems which demanded his attention and preoccupied him at the time; America's destiny was about to be placed a second time in his hands.[18]

Following his election and inauguration as president of the United States in October 1789, congratulatory addresses were sent or read to Washington by representatives of various political, religious, fraternal, and other societies and organizations. The Pennsylvania Quakers, together with the New York Friends, eager to cement their reconciliation but also to publicly reaffirm their belief in nonviolence, took this opportunity to set the record straight: "and in a full Persuasion that the Divine Principle we profess, lead into Harmony and Concord, we can take no part in carrying on War on any Occasion, or under any Power, but are bound in Conscience to lead quiet and peaceable Lives in Godliness and

18. Warville, *New Travels*, 238, 329–30.

Honesty amongst Men." Washington replied to most of these laudations with innocuous phrases reflecting his appreciation of the good wishes, but for the Quakers he inserted an unusual admonition:

> To the Society of Quakers
> [October 1789]
>
> Gentlemen,
>
> I receive with pleasure your affectionate address, and thank you for the friendly Sentiments & good wishes which you express for the Success of my administration, and for my personal Happiness. . . .
>
> Your principles & conduct are well known to me—and it is doing the People called Quakers no more than Justice to say, that (except their declining to share with others the burthen of the common defence) there is no Denomination among us who are more exemplary and useful Citizens.[19]

As the Quakers won recognition for spearheading the abolitionist movement, they began to attract the attention of other religious activists. Among those who were beginning to search their consciences and to contemplate following in the path of the Quakers were the Methodists. Francis Asbury, a leading Methodist preacher who was destined to be named the first bishop of the Methodist Episcopal Church in America, noted as early as 1778: "I find the more pious part of the people called Quakers are exerting themselves for the liberation of the slaves. This is a very laudable design, and what the Methodists must come to, or, I fear, the Lord will depart from them." In 1780, at their conference in Baltimore, the Methodists openly avowed that slavery was "contrary to the laws of God, man, and nature, and hurtful to society."[20]

Then, in the spring of 1785, the Reverend Dr. Coke and his coadjutor, Francis Asbury, came calling at Mount Vernon. Washington gave the visit only passing notice in his diary: "Rid to Muddy hole and the Neck Plantations. . . . Upon my return found Mr. Magowan, and a Doctr. Coke & a Mr. Asbury here—the two last Methodest Preachers recommended by Genl. Roberdeau—the same who were expected yesterday. . . . After Dinner Mr. Coke & Mr. Asbury went away." Nor was Francis Asbury's record of the meeting any more informative: "We waited on General Washington, who received us very politely, and gave us his opinion against slavery."[21] It remained for Coke to elaborate on the purpose and the outcome of their private discussion with the general:

> He received us very politely, and was very open to access. He is quite the plain country gentleman and he is a *friend to mankind*. After dinner we desired

19. *Papers: Presidential Series*, ed. Abbot and Twohig, 4:265–66, 267n.
20. Ezra S. Tipple, ed., *The Heart of Asbury's Journal*, 130, 167.
21. *Diaries*, ed. Jackson and Twohig, 4:145; Tipple, ed., *Asbury's Journal*, 237.

a private interview, and opened to him the grand business on which we came, presenting to him our petition for the emancipation of the negroes, and intreating his signature, if the eminence of his station did not render it inexpedient for him to sign any petition. He informed us that he was of our sentiments, and had signified his thoughts on the subject to most of the great men of the State: that he did not see it proper to sign the petition, but if the [Virginia General] Assembly took it into consideration, would signify his sentiments to the Assembly by a letter. He asked us to spend the evening and lodge at his house, but our engagement at *Annapolis* the following day, would not admit of it. I was lo[a]th to leave him, for I greatly love and esteem him and if there was no pride in it, would say that we are *kindred Spirits,* formed in the same mould. O that God would give him the witness of his Spirit![22]

Irrespective of the polite lip service that Washington was inclined to offer his visitors, it was evident to the Methodist ministers that the abolitionist cause south of the Mason-Dixon Line had neither the solid endorsement of prominent leaders like Washington nor wide public support. Well aware of their vulnerable position with their flock, the Methodist clergymen carefully backed off. John Vickers, a recent biographer of Thomas Coke, explains their rationale:

> In his passionate advocacy of emancipation Coke had moved too far ahead of public opinion. Before the end of the tour [of America] he realized that, however just his sentiments may have been on this subject, it was ill-judged of him to deliver them from the pulpit. His public testimony had antagonized as many as it had converted to his cause. Nor was he able, as yet, to command the support of a majority among the Methodists. He had met with firm opposition at both the Carolina and the Virginia Conferences, and at the final Conference held in Baltimore on the eve of his sailing for home [England], prudence was allowed to prevail over principle. "We thought it prudent to suspend the minute concerning slavery for one year, on account of the great opposition that has been given [to] it, especially in the new circuits, our work being in too infantile a stage to push things to extremity."[23]

The Methodists dropped away, but the Quakers pressed on, apparently neither bothered nor daunted by any doubts, misgivings, or second thoughts. They were galvanized by the zeal of righteousness and united in their crusade; opposition only served to harden their resolve. The Friends were also remarkably versatile and ingenious in knowing exactly how to exploit every possible opening in pursuit of their objectives. They waged their campaign for African American civil rights on a number of different fronts at the same time: petitions and appeals to the federal, state, and local legislatures; articles and editorials in the press; personal pleas to men of influence; court actions to win freedom for slaves who were being

22. John Vickers, *Thomas Coke: Apostle of Methodism,* 98.
23. Ibid., 97–98.

held illegally or where the owner's title appeared defective and therefore subject to challenge; and programs for educating and employing freed blacks. Most of these undertakings were scrupulously carried out within the bounds of the law.

Although Washington tended to look with disfavor on the abolitionist initiatives of the Quakers, he had no valid basis for objecting to them. Whatever his private feelings may have been, the public Washington remained discreetly neutral. His relations with the Quaker community seemed to be cordial and outwardly unaffected. But then a new cloud formed on the horizon and raised all of the old bugaboos about the sinister motives, the duplicity, and the questionable methods of the Quakers: they were suspected of aiding and abetting in the escape of runaway slaves. Runaways, of course, were anathema to Washington. He hated the thought of losing a valuable slave, and he despised disloyalty to his Mount Vernon "family." As the record shows, he hounded relentlessly any African American fugitives from his estate.

Before the Revolution and prior to the appearance of an organized abolitionist movement, the chances of a fugitive slave successfully escaping to freedom and building a legitimate life for himself or herself were almost nil. Without money or friends, and with no safe place to live, the truant was a ready victim for bounty hunters. A strange black, wandering through any locality, was readily spotted, thrown in jail, and, if he or she was on the advertised list of runaways, promptly returned to his or her master. The owner generally paid for the expense of the slave's capture and imprisonment—in addition, of course, to the reward. In some cases the hapless African American was sold on the open market for a tidy sum. Once back on the plantation, the miscreant faced severe punishment, not only as personal chastisement, but as a warning to the other slaves of what lay in store for them if they dared try to follow the runaway's example.

The odds tilted dramatically in favor of the runaways, however, once the Quakers embraced the cause of emancipation. The news spread fast that African American fugitives making it across the borders of Virginia and Maryland and into Pennsylvania and Delaware, where Quakers were heavily concentrated, would find a welcome reception, protection against the designs of their former masters, freedom, and a chance to build a new life. The temptation for the slaves to escape increased enormously, and the discomfiture of the slaveholders mounted proportionately. It was one thing to debate slavery as an abstract philosophical concept, but it became a painfully acute pocketbook issue once the slaves started to take leave of the plantations in substantial numbers. Just how far the Quakers actually went in helping to entice the slaves from their owners cannot be stated with any degree of accuracy, for there are no statistics or reliable data available. Whether they operated an "underground railroad," as some claim, or whether they sent agitators among the plantation blacks urging them to abscond are questions that will probably never be satisfactorily or conclusively answered. Mifflin, as might be expected, vehemently denied any personal involvement or responsibility: "It has been reported that I have persuaded the blacks to run from their masters, and that I give them passes whenever they apply, without discriminating between those who are free, and others. But it is the reverse of my judgment of propriety, in preserving the peace of society, to persuade these people from their claimers' service; and beneath the uprightness of my profession, to recommend any as free people, who are not such."[24]

Such a disclaimer would hardly suffice to appease the skeptics. Washington was surely among those who assumed the worst-case scenario, and he was seemingly prepared to accept as fact that the Quakers and their followers were directly responsible for the unrest of his "people" and the loss of his slave property. His anger at their alleged intrigues and disregard of the laws of the land blinded him to their long-term goal of trying to create a truly free and equal multiracial society. In Washington's view, the ends did not justify the means. The Quakers had once again become the subversive enemy of the lawful established order. They had to be fought and their nefarious designs defeated. But by shutting the door on the Quakers and deliberately choosing to make them his adversaries, Washington cut himself off from the only abolitionist group that had developed workable programs for emancipating the slaves and integrating them as useful and productive citizens into the mainstream of American society and culture. The sad irony is that although Washington and the Quakers were in general agreement on the necessity for a gradual and orderly emancipation of the slaves, they would in actuality remain antagonists throughout Washington's life.

24. Justice, comp., *Mifflin*, 99.

V. FINALE

19

LAST WILL AND TESTAMENT

DURING THE summer of 1799, "in references that were casual and quite matter-of-fact," George Washington spoke often about his life drawing to a close, aware that "he was not far from the Biblical 'three score and ten.'"[1] In July he began the painstaking task of drawing up his last will and testament:

> For the finished document, he ordered elegant paper, approximately 8-1/8 by 6-1/4 inches, the watermark in the center of each sheet showing a goddess of agriculture seated upon a plough, holding in one hand a staff rising to a liberty cap, and in the other a flowering twig, the whole encircled with a broad band within which was written "GEORGE WASHINGTON." Using his most carefully elegant hand, spacing the lines evenly, breaking words without regard to syllabic structure so that the right-hand margin would be as straight as the left, Washington covered 28-1/3 pages.[2]

The document deserves scrutiny because it is the first and only tangible commitment that Washington made to the emancipation of the slaves. After providing for his debts, which were not consequential, and naming his wife the main beneficiary of his estate, Washington proceeded to set down detailed instructions for the disposal of his slave property:

> Item Upon the decease of my wife, it is my Will & desire that all the Slaves which I hold in *my own right,* shall receive their freedom,—To emancipate them during her life, would, tho' earnestly wished by me, be attended with such insuperable difficulties on account of their intermixture by Marriages with the

1. John Alexander Carroll and Mary Wells Ashworth, *George Washington: First in Peace,* 582.
2. Flexner, *Anguish and Farewell,* 453–54.

All his life George Washington treated his slaves as chattel property: to be bought, sold, or traded as he saw fit. They represented a considerable financial investment and were regarded as a major asset among his holdings. However, in his last will and testament, Washington turned his back on his commitment to slave property. In setting forth the terms of their emancipation after his and his wife's death (see the relevant pages in his will), he spoke of his African American slaves as human beings. Not only did he set them free but he arranged as well for their lifelong support, education (insofar as it was legally possible), and safety (from future enslavement). It was a remarkable about-face. (Courtesy of the Circuit Court of Fairfax County, Virginia, and the Library of Congress, Washington, D.C.)

In witness of all, and of
each of the things herein-
contained, I have set my
hand and seal, this ninth
day of July, in the year
One thousand seven hun=
dred and ninety and of
the Independence of the
United States the twenty
fourth. -

G: Washington

Dower Negroes, as to excite the most painful sensations, if not disagreeable consequences from the latter, while both descriptions are in the occupancy of the same Proprietor; it not being in my power, under the tenure by which the Dower Negroes are held, to manumit them.—And whereas among those who will receive freedom according to this devise, there may be some, who from old age or bodily infirmities, and others who on account of their infancy, that will be unable to support themselves; it is my Will and desire that all who come under the first & second description shall be comfortably cloathed & fed by my heirs while they live;—and that such of the latter description as have no parents living, or if living are unable, or unwilling to provide for them, shall be bound by the Court until they shall arrive at the age of twenty five years;—and in cases where no record can be produced, whereby their ages can be ascertained, the judgement of the Court upon its own view of the subject, shall be adequate and final.—The Negroes thus bound, are (by their Masters or Mistresses) to be taught to read & write; and to be brought up to some useful occupation, agreeably to the Laws of the Commonwealth of Virginia, providing for the support of Orphan and other poor Children.— And I do hereby expressly forbid the Sale, or transportation out of the said Commonwealth, of any Slave I may die possessed of, under any pretence whatsoever,—And I do moreover most pointedly, and most solemnly enjoin it upon my Executors hereafter named, or the Survivors of them, to see that *this* clause respecting Slaves, and every part thereof be religiously fulfilled at the Epoch at which it is directed to take place; without evasion, neglect or delay, after the Crops which may then be on the ground are harvested, particularly as it respects the aged and infirm,—Seeing that a regular and permanent fund be established for their Support so long as there are subjects requiring it; not trusting to the uncertain provision to be made by individuals.[3]

The exact number of slaves who were freed as a result of Washington's bequest were listed in the "Appraiser's Inventory of the Contents of Mount Vernon":

> The whole Number of Negroes left by Genl.
> Washington in his own right are as follows:
>
> | | |
> |---|---|
> | 40 | Men |
> | 37 | Women |
> | 4 | Working boys |
> | 3 | do (ditto) Girls |
> | 40 | children |
> | 124 | Total[4] |

The terms of his will with regard to the Mount Vernon slaves were generous and were obviously the culmination of pressures that had been building since Washington became a prominent public personality. During the winter of 1787–1788, while a houseguest at Mount Vernon, Col. David Humphreys, Washington's

---

3. Fitzpatrick, ed., *Last Will*, 2–4. Martha Washington's will appears on 56–62.
4. Appraiser's Inventory of the Contents of Mount Vernon—1810, 60, Mount Vernon Library.

longtime military aide and intimate friend, worked on, but did not complete, a biographical sketch of his former commander in chief. The original partial manuscript, in Humphreys's handwriting, bears marginal notes and corrections by Washington and contains this unusually frank insight: "The unfortunate condition of the persons, whose labour in part I employed, has been the only unavoidable subject of regret. To make the Adults among them as easy & as comfortable in their circumstances as their actual state of ignorance & improvidence would admit; & to lay a foundation to prepare the rising generation for a destiny different from that in which they were born; afforded some satisfaction to my mind, & could not I hoped be displeasing to the justice of the Creator."[5]

The outside world applauded Washington's emancipation decision. The Quakers reacted jubilantly to the news: "When it was learned that he [Washington] had granted manumission to his slaves in his Will, Friends felt they had won a most important point in the campaign for Freedom, convincement that one should grant freedom integrated into Truth." The *Spectator,* a New York City newspaper, reported, "A letter from Virginia, to a gentleman of the first respectability, in Baltimore, makes the following mention of the General's Will: ' . . . . Mrs. Washington has announced, that after this year all the negroes are to be emancipated. According to the General's wishes, the spirit of freedom has progressed, is progressing, and will progress.' "[6]

But for Martha Washington, left alone to run a large and extensive household and plantation, and saddened and depressed by the loss of her husband, it was not that simple or straightforward. The slaves at Mount Vernon were restless. Knowing that their freedom, in accordance with Washington's legacy, hung by the thin thread of her frail life, there were threatening rumors that she might be in danger, perhaps of being poisoned, at the hands of her own servants. The irony of Mrs. Washington's predicament, and the harsh prospects facing the freed slaves, were sympathetically portrayed in a letter that Abigail Adams, the wife of President John Adams, wrote to her elder sister Mary following a visit to Mount Vernon that coincided with the first anniversary of Washington's death:

5. The Humphreys manuscript is written in the first person, so it seems likely that the colonel was either taking down Washington's direct dictation or relying on his memory of Washington's exact words. It is highly improbable that Humphreys would dare to assume liberties with such an important statement attributed to Washington. See David Humphreys, "Manuscript Biography of George Washington," American Manuscript Collection, Rosenbach Museum and Library, Philadelphia. Also quoted in Rosemarie Zagarri, ed., *David Humphreys' "Life of General Washington" with George Washington's "Remarks,"* 78.

6. Robert M. Hazelton, *Let Freedom Ring! A Biography of Moses Brown,* 120–21; New York *Spectator,* February 1, 1800, Library of Congress, Serial and Government Publications Division, Newspaper and Current Periodical Room (#133), Washington, D.C.

Washington, D.C., December 21, 1800

My dear Sister:

On fryday the 19th I return'd from Mount Vernon where at the pressing invitation of Mrs. Washington I had been to pass a couple of day's. . . .

The House has an ancient appearance and is really so. . . . it is now going to decay: Mrs. Washington with all her fortune finds it difficult to support her family, which consists of three hundred slaves—one hundred and fifty of them are now to be liberated, men with wives & young children who have never seen an acre beyond the farm, are now about to quit it, and go adrift into the world without horse, Home, or Friend.

Mrs. Washington is distrest for them. At her own expence she has cloalkd them all and very many of them are already miserable at the thought of their Lot. The aged she retains at their request; but she is distrest for the fate of others. She feels a (responsibility as a) parent & a wife.

Many of those who are liberated have married with what are called the dower Negroes, so that they quit all their connections, yet what could she do? In the state in which they were left by the General, to be free at her death, she did not feel as tho her Life was safe in their Hands, many of whom would be told that it was [in] there interest to get rid of her—She therefore was advised to set them all free at the close of the year.—

If any person wishes to see the banefull affects of Slavery as it creates a torper and indolence and a Spirit of domination—let them come and take a view of the cultivation on this part of the United States.[7]

George Washington Parke Custis, who had lived at Mount Vernon both before and after the death of his legal guardian, George Washington, recorded similar impressions in his memoirs: "The slaves were left to be emancipated at the death of Mrs. Washington; but it was found necessary (for *prudential* reasons) to give them their freedom in one year after the general's decease. Although many of them, with a view to their liberation, had been instructed in mechanical trades, yet they succeeded very badly as freemen: so true is the axiom, 'that the hour which makes man a slave, takes half his worth away.' "[8] For her part, Martha Washington did not linger long to suffer further humiliations and indignities resulting from the slow disintegration of the estate that she and her husband had built over the years with so much love and care and pride. She died peacefully at Mount Vernon in May 1802 and was laid to rest next to her husband in their common tomb.[9]

So far as is known, the executors faithfully implemented the terms of Washington's will exactly as he had directed with respect to the Mount Vernon slaves. The African Americans were given their unconditional freedom; those who elected to

---

7. The original letter is in the possession of the Massachusetts Historical Society, Boston. A copy can be found in a notebook, "Earlier Descriptions: 1800–1841," at the Mount Vernon Library.

8. Custis, *Recollections,* 157–58.

9. The tomb is described in *Mount Vernon: A Handbook,* 118.

stay on were adequately sustained. There was one key provision of Washington's will that unfortunately could not be fulfilled, however. According to John C. Fitzpatrick: "All the provisions of the Will respecting the slaves were carried out in full, excepting the educational direction. This failed by reason of the Virginia 'black laws' then in force which prohibited schools for the education of negroes." This is confirmed by Eugene Prussing in *The Estate of George Washington, Deceased:* "The so-called 'black laws' of Virginia forbade the carrying out of Washington's beneficent provision that the freed Negroes should be taught to read and write and the growing fears and prejudices made the life of freedmen in the State well-nigh impossible."[10]

What actually happened to the emancipated Mount Vernon slaves? Prussing is the prime credible source for the scant information concerning this closing chapter of their lives:

> [M]ost of them were faithful and trusted to the wisdom and provision of "Old Marse Gin'l." They stayed at Mount Vernon and performed such duties as the easy-going Lawrence Lewis and Bushrod Washington [George Washington's nephew and the executor of his estate] assigned to them.
>
> Those that were able and wanted to go when Mrs. Washington died were properly outfitted and the estate paid the bills. Those that remained were fed, sheltered, clothed, nursed and in due course buried, at its expense; a considerable sum was kept invested in bank stocks for their benefit for nearly thirty-five years, until the last survivor was gathered to his rest.[11]

Frank E. Morse has compiled this information:

> Nor may one determine just where any of the negroes lived except one, Judy, who was in town for a time, and some who were domiciled at William Fitzhugh's for which the estate paid. It is possible that some who left returned and were supported though not entitled. Gabriel was one of the last three survivors of the pensioners though not entitled to support under Washington's will. In 1825, and again in 1829, two freed negroes were yet living at Mount Vernon. Bushrod Washington died this year and in 1832 John A. Washington collected from the estate $68.18 for care of free negroes. At least three seem to have lived out their lives at Dogue Run farm. Few are mentioned by name but Suky, Molly, and Gabriel were at Dogue Run at time of death in 1833. Myrtilla died there in 1832. As she and her husband lived at Dogue Run in General Washington's time she may have remained.

Morse adds: "The support included housing, food, clothes, fuel, medical attention, and funeral bills. Food seems to have included meal, fish, and pork. Clothes

---

10. Fitzpatrick, ed., *Last Will*, 31n; Eugene E. Prussing, *The Estate of George Washington, Deceased,* 158–59.

11. Prussing, *The Estate of Washington*, 158–59.

included summer clothes, winter clothes, shoes and stockings. Funeral expenses seem to have meant—$4. for a coffin."[12]

The financial burden on the Washington estate was substantial. Whatever his shortcomings may have been in life as a demanding slave master, Washington certainly tried to make up for them after his death.

> Mr. Lewis' first charge for the free Negroes was for the period prior to December 31, 1809, and is $1,645.05, while Bushrod Washington paid for pensioned Negroes from November, 1802, until May 31, 1811—$792.74½. William Fitzhugh was paid for rent of land for the free Negroes prior to 1817, $216.99, and in 1818, $55.33. The expense for food and clothing paid by Mr. Lewis from January, 1803, to January, 1820, was $5,305.09.
>
> Landon, Mary and Jane survived until late in the twenties and their support at Mount Vernon never failed. Six free men were then still living outside on rented land, but later they were brought back, as their age and infirmities required more care for them. On December 31, 1829, Bushrod Washington's last account tells that Judy died in October, 1828, and that the funeral expenses for three pensioned Negroes were $12. The last survivor was buried in 1833, a full generation after "Old Marse Gin'l" had planned and provided for his comfort and care. The total cost appears to have been $10,080.91½ in money, besides the food and shelter supplied on the plantations.[13]

Perhaps it had been hoped that Washington's example of benevolence toward his slaves would carry over to other members of his family. If it did, it was not apparent. Many of the relatives who lived in and around Mount Vernon in later years kept slaves and actively exercised their slaveholding prerogatives, which included hunting down runaways. The *Philadelphia Gazette* printed this informative fugitive slave advertisement in its edition of May 16, 1800:

> MARCUS
> *One of the House Servants at Mount Vernon*
> ABSCONDED on the second instant, and since has not been heard of. He is a young lad, about 16 years of age, a bright mulatto, dark blue eyes, long black hair, about 5 feet 4 or 5 inches high, and of a slender make. . . . originally his name was Billy, and possibly he may resume the same. It is very probable he may attempt to pass for one of those negroes that did belong to the late Gen. Washington, and whom Mrs. Washington intends in the fall of this year to liberate—the public are therefore warned against any such impressions, as he is one of those negroes which belong to the estate of Washington L. Custis, Esq. and held by right of dower by Mrs. Washington during her life.

12. Frank E. Morse, "About General Washington's Freed Negroes," 3.

13. Prussing, *Estate of Washington*, 159–60. Prussing points out, "Bushrod Washington became the president of the National Society whose purpose it was to encourage manumission and the settling of freedmen in Africa at Sierra Leone. Abolition societies found aid and comfort in Washington's example."

I will give Ten Dollars Reward to any person who shall apprehend the said negro and lodge him in some safe gaol; upon producing (for) me a certificate to that effect; and will also pay all reasonable charges over and above this reward, for the delivery of him to me at this place.

Ship Masters are hereby forewarned not to take on board Marcus; and those who are found to secret or harbour him, will be punished as the law directs.[14]

The institution of slavery remained alive and well at Mount Vernon, as it did in most of the rest of the plantation South. Washington's act of conscience, if that is what it really was, was widely hailed by antislavery ideologues, but the slaveholders themselves tended to ignore it. A more likely motive for the freeing of his slaves is the one that Colonel Humphreys ascribed to Washington in his remembrance: "To make . . . them as easy & as comfortable in their circumstances as their actual state of ignorance & improvidence would admit." That goal lay within his reach and was duly carried out. However, James T. Flexner has another interpretation:

Pity and guilt made Washington determined to free his slaves, but did not induce him to attempt radical alterations in their lot while they remained in bondage. This was in keeping with the eighteenth-century philosophical conception that freedom was so basic a human need that without it one can achieve nothing. As it would be useless to urge a chained man to run, the degradation inherent in slavery was only remediable by breaking the chains. Although Washington was to provide that his slaves should, after freedom, be taught to read and write, he made no effort to establish literacy in his slave quarters.[15]

Tradition has it that the Mount Vernon slaves were interred in unmarked graves in a separate burial ground not far from the grave of their former master and mistress. For over a hundred years the slave burying ground remained neglected and unnoticed, with trees, weeds, and underbrush covering the area. There were no signs or pathways to guide visitors, and no mention was made of the slave cemetery in the Mount Vernon literature or tourist pamphlets. Then, in 1929, a flat Georgian marble plaque was embedded in the earth less than fifty yards from the hillside crypt containing the remains of George and Martha Washington. It bears this laconic inscription: "In memory of the many faithful colored servants of the Washington family, buried at Mount Vernon from 1760 to 1860. Their unidentified graves surround this spot."

The stone was partially hidden in the summertime by heavy foliage and undergrowth. There was still no walkway to the site and still no mention of it in the

14. *Philadelphia Gazette and Universal Daily Advertiser,* May 16, 1800, Mount Vernon Library.
15. Flexner, *Washington and the New Nation,* 444.

Without any known documentary evidence, only an archaeological excavation could help determine how many slaves were actually buried here, provide clues to their identity, and indicate the nature of their interment. (Photograph by Nancy Emison; courtesy of the Mount Vernon Ladies' Association)

guidebooks. Possibly only a handful of people, of the million plus who visit Mount Vernon each year and make the pilgrimage to the tomb of the Washingtons, had ever seen the tablet. In 1983, with the growing awareness of African American contributions to the nation's history, including the contributions of slaves at Mount Vernon, a more distinctive and respectable monument was erected to mark the slave burial ground. A concrete column on a raised plot of ground covered with plantings, and complete with a viewing circle, carries this inscription: "In memory of the Afro Americans who served as slaves at Mount Vernon this monument marking their burial ground dedicated September 21, 1983. Mount Vernon Ladies' Association." Masters and servants share the same land on which they both worked and died, but the slaves, relatively obscure all of their lives, so remain today, anonymous in their unmarked graves.

And what of the dower slaves, who were not affected by George Washington's will? Nearly one year after his death, on September 22, 1800, Martha Washington completed the formalities pertaining to her will, which followed almost precisely the wording and format of her husband's. However, one notable difference is that her will makes no mention whatsoever of her substantial slave property: the so-called dower slaves. A last-minute codicil, dated March 4, 1802, gives "to my grandson George Washington Parke Custis my mulatto man Elish—that I bought of mr Butler Washington to him and his hair [heir] for ever."[16] But what of the others?

The Custis estate derived from the holdings of Martha Washington's first husband, Col. Daniel Parke Custis, who died suddenly and unexpectedly of an unspecified illness on July 8, 1757. He was forty-five years old at the time of his death; his widow was twenty-six. The estate that she and her two young children inherited made her one of the wealthiest women in Virginia:

> As finally apportioned, the estate was handsome and, for Virginia, notable in the amount of securities held. The real estate consisted of 17,438 acres. Without inclusion or appraisal of this, the sum credited to each of the three heirs was £7618, currency of the country, in slaves, live stock, notes and bonds and accounts receivable—an aggregate in personalty of almost £20,000 sterling. No less than £8958 of these personal assets in the currency of the country were represented by slaves. . . . One-third of the Negroes, two-thirds of the cattle, one-third of the hogs and one-third of the sheep were assigned Mrs. Washington.[17]

When the widow Custis married George Washington on January 6, 1759, in a ceremony at her home, called the White House, on the Pamunkey River in New Kent County, her estate automatically came under the control of her new husband. Washington was subsequently named by the courts, at his and his wife's request, to act as the legal guardian of her two small children, John (known as Jackie) and Martha (called Patsy), and as the official administrator of their combined estates. For the rest of his life Washington would manage the Custis estates with the same prudent care and diligence he exercised in his own business affairs. It has been estimated by Douglas Southall Freeman that the Custis estate owned about three hundred slaves; however, perhaps only a dozen of the household domestics moved with Mrs. Washington to Mount Vernon early in the summer of 1759. The majority of the dower slaves continued to work on the various Custis plantations along the York River and its tributaries. Later on, undoubtedly, Washington moved some of those dower slaves to Mount Vernon to supplement his slave population as he expanded his landholdings and thereby increased his need for field hands and other male and female laborers. By the summer of 1799, four decades after Washington and his wife had settled at Mount Vernon, his

16. Fitzpatrick, ed., *Last Will,* 61.
17. Douglas S. Freeman, *George Washington: A Biography,* vol. 3, *Planter and Patriot,* 20–22.

The 1983 monument marking the slave burying ground at Mount Vernon is a fitting memorial recognizing the contributions of Washington's African American slaves to the cultivation and operation of his estate. (Photographs by Nancy Emison; courtesy of the Mount Vernon Ladies' Association)

slave inventory showed a total of 153 dower slaves resident on the Mount Vernon plantations.[18]

The inventory of June 1799, entitled "NEGROES Belonging to George Washington in his own right and by Marriage," is the only authoritative source for what little information exists relating to the dower slaves at Mount Vernon at approximately the time of Washington's death. He meticulously listed in separate columns the names of the dower slaves, along with their ages and trades and usually their marital status. For example, under the column "Dower" there appears this entry: "Lucy . . . Cook . . . Husbd HO Frank . . . G.W.," which meant that Lucy, a cook, was a dower slave whose husband, Frank, worked in the mansion house and belonged to Washington. A confirming entry in the "G.W." column reads: "Frank . . . H. Servt. . . . Lucy . . . Cook." In all there were 29 men, 50 women, 37 working boys, and 37 working girls (although a number of these "workg Childn"

18. Fitzpatrick, ed., *Writings*, 37:268.

IN MEMORY OF
THE AFRO AMERICANS
WHO SERVED AS SLAVES
AT MOUNT VERNON
THIS MONUMENT MARKING THEIR
BURIAL GROUND
DEDICATED
SEPTEMBER 21, 1983
MOUNT VERNON
LADIES' ASSOCIATION

were clearly infants and toddlers). Of these 153 dower slaves, 19 male and female slaves have been identified and classified as married couples with children.[19]

Colonel Custis had died intestate, that is, without leaving a will. Under the existing Virginia statutes, this gave his widow a dower interest in the estate, allowing her lifetime use of a third of the Custis slaves and of their increase.

19. Washington's slave inventory (ibid., 37:256–68); Morse, "About Washington's Freed Negroes," 2.

But, as was specifically laid down by the law, the dower slaves would become the property of her heirs by her first husband upon her death. These legal technicalities and ramifications had no practical effect on the daily lives of the Mount Vernon slaves so long as Washington and his wife were alive. Over the years the dower slaves intermingled with Washington's slaves, developed bonds of one kind or another, and, of course, intermarried and procreated (the child of a dower slave mother always belonged to the dower estate). Washington, particularly as he grew older, did his best to protect the marital relationships of his Mount Vernon slave families; but as he wrote in his will, those family relationships would be placed in jeopardy once he and his wife were dead and the Custis estate was free to press its legal claims.

During her marriage to Colonel Custis, Martha Washington had given birth to four children over a period of eight years. Two of them died in infancy, and Patsy, an epileptic, died tragically in 1773 when she was just seventeen or eighteen years old.[20] Jack, the remaining son, lived to maturity, married, and fathered three daughters and a son before contracting a fever during the Yorktown campaign and dying suddenly in 1781. The four grandchildren of Martha Washington all married, raised large families, and outlived their grandparents. The dower slaves were thus divided between these members of the Custis clan and taken by them to their respective homes and plantations. The only one of the dower slaves who can be accurately accounted for is Elish, who Martha Washington designated be given to her grandson, George Washington Parke Custis. The rest of the dower slaves, whether numbering 145, as Prussing indicates, or 153, as Washington's 1799 inventory indicates,[21] disappeared into history. Nothing further is known of their lives or their whereabouts. It can be assumed that the "disagreeable consequences" Washington spoke of in his will actually came to pass: the Mount Vernon slave families probably were to a large extent broken up by the forced separation of the dower slaves from Washington's freed slaves. The Custis heirs were disinclined to follow in Washington's footsteps by embracing emancipation.

Washington was not the only Virginia slave owner who decided to emancipate his slaves in the post–Revolutionary War period: "A few blacks who had served the Revolutionary cause with particular distinction were able to gain freedom by special acts of the legislature. . . . A much larger number, more than 10,000, were emancipated by individual planters who had been influenced by the antislavery beliefs of the early evangelical movement. In 1782 the statutory law of the state

20. Freeman, *George Washington: A Biography,* 3:325n.
21. Prussing's information comes from the property schedule of Washington's estate, which was prepared shortly after his death in December 1799.

[of Virginia] legalized such voluntary manumissions."[22] But Washington's will—probably because of his eminence and because of the publicity given to his final legacy—may have had a greater impact on his peers than has been previously realized or than can be accurately measured.

22. Warren M. Billings, John E. Selby, and Thad W. Tate, *Colonial Virginia: A History,* 358–59.

20

In Retrospect

O N December 30, 1775, in Cambridge, when Gen. George Washington authorized the enlistment of African Americans in the Continental army,[1] he broke down a major barrier separating the slaves from the white community. That military decision, made reluctantly and under pressure, was nonetheless a bona fide legal loophole through which sizable numbers of slaves were able to obtain their freedom. In retrospect, it was a watershed in the transition of the African American slave from a nonperson held in lifelong and involuntary servitude to a citizen with at least limited political, social, and economic rights.

Several short- and long-term benefits flowed directly from Washington's historic decision. In addition to affording African American men a chance to throw off the yoke of slavery through their own choice and initiative,[2] it also provided them with the opportunity to prove their worth in terms of discipline and physical courage. The result was that the commonly held impression of blacks as ignorant, docile, servile creatures was publicly discounted. African American soldiers and seamen in the Continental army and navy and in the various state and local militias during the Revolutionary War carved out a military record of which all Americans,

---

1. According to Franklin and Moss, most states, either by specific legislation or by reversal of policy, also began to enlist both slaves and free blacks; by the end of the war this was being done with the understanding that the slaves would receive their freedom at the end of their service (*From Slavery to Freedom: A History of African Americans,* 76).

2. The slave's choice was obviously subject to the wishes of his owner, unless, of course, he chose to run away. Quarles notes, "Insofar as he [the slave] had freedom of choice, he was likely to join the side that made him the quickest and best offer in terms of those 'unalienable rights' of which Mr. Jefferson had spoken. Whoever invoked the image of liberty, be he American or British, could count on a ready response from the blacks" (*Negro in the American Revolution,* xvii). Whether the slaves served in the American or the British army, they enlisted and fought in the expectation of gaining their freedom.

black and white, can be justly proud. Furthermore, these African American soldiers established a legitimate claim to the honors, respect, and recognition that the nation has traditionally reserved for the original band of patriotic men who fought, suffered, and died for independence.[3]

The personal and institutional prejudices toward slaves that Washington had brought with him from Virginia were considerably revised—thanks in part to his wartime experiences with the black soldiers under his command.[4] Other military men were similarly impressed. And the record of patriotism and valor of the black soldiers who fought for freedom alongside their white comrades became a powerful argument for the abolitionists to use in lobbying for antislavery legislation following the Revolutionary War.[5]

By allowing African Americans to be recruited as fighting men into an integrated service (in the North but not in the South), and by officially allowing them the same privileges and prerogatives as those granted to white soldiers, Washington set a precedent that has been followed to a greater or lesser degree without exception in every subsequent conflict in which the United States has been engaged.[6] While the nature of the incentives has changed radically since Washington's enlistment policy was first promulgated more than two hundred years ago, the armed forces still continue to be a major vehicle for African Americans to better their economic and social status and to advance their careers.[7]

By outward appearances, Washington would seem to be an unlikely candidate to be cited for his contribution to the advancement of the African American dream of freedom. From the day he was born until the day he died, Washington relied almost

---

3. See Sidney Kaplan and Emma N. Kaplan, *The Black Presence in the Era of the American Revolution,* 35.

4. See, for example, Quarles, *Negro in the American Revolution,* xxviii–xxix.

5. Quarles writes: "In its total influence toward freedom the Revolutionary War extended beyond the manumission of Negroes who had served as soldiers. Since the war had been fought in the name of liberty, many Americans were led to reflect seriously upon the impropriety of holding men in bondage. The feeling that slavery was inconsistent with the ideals of the war cropped out in many quarters, becoming manifest in the attitude of prominent national figures, in the formation of abolitionist societies, in the concern for Negroes displayed by religious sects, and in the anti-slavery activities of state and federal governments" (ibid., 185).

6. Although it is true that blacks have fought in all of America's wars, it was not until after World War II that they were fully integrated into the armed services. "President Truman directed the armed forces to eliminate all segregation of troops by race. The Navy and the Air Force abolished their all-Negro units by June 1950, whereas the Army, with more Negro members than its sister services, would take some five years longer to desegregate" (Maurice Matloff, ed., *American Military History,* 533).

7. "With the coming of integration in 1948, black men widened their role in combat and support functions, often exhibiting a sense of pride in personal excellence and sometimes cultivating a framework of exclusivity. Today, both trends are in evidence: the constant policing by the military itself of placement and promotion opportunities, and the dynamic drive by young black men to express their manhood even before considering questions of involvement with whites" (Ploski and Williams, eds., *The Negro Almanac,* 5th ed., 829).

exclusively on slaves for his creature comforts. Slaves washed his linens, sewed his shirts, polished his boots, saddled his horse, chopped the wood for his fireplaces, powdered his wig, drove his carriage, cooked his meals, served his table, poured his wine, posted his letters, lit the lamps, swept the porch, looked after the guests, planted the flowers in the gardens, trimmed the hedges, dusted the furniture, cleaned the windows, made the beds, and performed the myriad domestic chores necessary to maintain an extensive household. Washington took all of this for granted, of course, for it was in the natural order of things for a gentleman of wealth and standing in the aristocratic plantation society of eighteenth-century Tidewater Virginia to be waited on by his slaves.

Washington also took in stride the obvious and essential condition that slaves were the workers who made possible the grandeur of his estate and his luxurious standard of living, for that, too, was part of the natural order. Although the Mount Vernon slaves are long since gone, as are most of the visible signs of their presence, it is instructive for the modern-day visitor to Mount Vernon to keep in mind that it was Washington's male and female slaves, adults and children, who plowed the fields, tended the crops, harvested the wheat and corn, dried the tobacco, cured the hams, picked the apples, built the barns, mended the fences, milked the cows, collected the eggs, operated the distillery, fished the Potomac, drained the swamps, herded the cattle, sheared the sheep, loaded the cargoes, and carried out the other menial tasks associated with the upkeep and operation of a large and mainly self-sufficient plantation—and that it was the profit from their toil that resulted in the creation of the luxury and great beauty, only the broad outlines of which can be seen and appreciated today, that made Washington's ancestral home a magnificent showplace during much of his lifetime. "There is a temptation to believe that life at Mount Vernon was idyllic. So it was, to a degree, for the Washingtons and their guests, but not for the blacks who waited upon them. Gazing upon the noble house perched high above the Potomac, one also saw rows of humble cabins that supplied shelter of a sort for the many scores of slaves who toiled for Washington."[8]

Washington was proud of Mount Vernon. A staunch supporter of the slave system that had enabled him to build and expand upon the relatively modest holdings he had inherited from his father, Augustine, and his half-brother Lawrence, he regarded the slaves at Mount Vernon as an integral part of his patrimony. Washington continually referred to them in his writings as "my family" and "my people," occasionally as "my blacks," and only rarely as "my slaves." He made it his business to know the background of many of his plantation slaves, and when he rode about the estate supervising their work, he often stopped to address them

8. John R. Alden, *George Washington: A Biography,* 212.

individually, being familiar with their capabilities, shortcomings, and personal idiosyncrasies. He had a long memory, and his voluminous instructions to his overseers are filled with specific and detailed references to this one's "laziness" and that one's "deceit," to such-and-such's inclination to "steal" and so-and-so's tendency to "feign illness." Under his discerning and watchful eye, loyalty and hard work were rewarded, generally by promotion to more desirable and responsible positions, while those guilty of malingering, slackness, and slovenly performance were dealt with summarily. Washington was known to listen patiently to the complaints of his slaves; when he felt that these were fair and justified, he would make an effort to correct the problems. He was concerned that his slaves, representing a substantial investment, were taken care of to the extent of being adequately fed, reasonably housed, and passably clothed. When sick or indisposed, the slaves were provided with medical attention. Holidays and festive occasions were celebrated with time off, amusements, and refreshments. Washington was, in principle, opposed to brutality and other forms of mistreatment, but he was not entirely against corporal punishment, including whipping, if the circumstances were serious enough to warrant it.

There is no indication that Washington, at least before the Revolutionary War, was dissatisfied with the institution of slavery—except for economic aspects of the African slave trade—or harbored any desire to see it changed. On the contrary, available evidence indicates that he was firmly wedded to the social and economic order from which he derived so many material benefits. The status quo meant continuing comfort, prosperity, and happiness for the ruling class. Always a pragmatist, Washington had little incentive to look beyond his balance sheet. The Mount Vernon estate, aside from providing its owner with a luxurious and prestigious residence, functioned as a serious business enterprise, designed to supply a variety of agricultural and animal commodities for home consumption and for sale or barter.

As a businessman, Washington saw his principal priority as making a profit, and he placed that concern far ahead of any interest in the welfare and personal fulfillment of his slaves. The African Americans were there to be exploited for their labor. They were paid no wages and were not entitled to any share of the proceeds;[9] to keep down the overhead, the expenditures for their upkeep were held to a bare minimum. The best that the slaves could look forward to, if they worked hard and diligently, from dawn to dusk, seven days a week, for most of the year, was

9. "When Washington had been, between the Revolution and the Presidency, a settled resident of Mount Vernon, he had brought forward so many of his promising blacks that in 1788 the overseers of all his five farms were slaves who, even if they were not paid salaries, lived in snug houses on an elevated scale" (Flexner, *Anguish and Farewell*, 436).

cradle-to-grave security. They were the sole property of their master, and he was the sole beneficiary of their labor. He could do with them arbitrarily as he saw fit, and they had no choice but to obey. There were few if any legal remedies open to them and certainly no independent body to hear their grievances. No matter the references to "my family" and "my people," the fact is that Mount Vernon was built on, and thrived on, the sweat and toil of its slave laborers.

Washington periodically sold slaves to maintain a sound ratio of productive to nonproductive workers and to attempt to control the size of the African American population on Mount Vernon. In addition, healthy and able-bodied slaves generally brought a good price on the marketplace and thus were a ready source of much-needed hard cash. Washington also sold off the troublemakers and the unruly and lazy blacks, and he used the fear of being sold as a powerful threat in helping to enforce discipline. "The sustained debate over punishments, rewards, and incentives since the publication of *Time on the Cross* has given new depth to our understanding of slave life and labor. Some general conclusions may be drawn from all the controversy. Clearly, the use of rewards and incentives, even if widespread, would not in itself prove that coercion was unimportant in making slaves work hard. It is surely in the nature of a slave system that force, or the threat of force, is fundamental and all other methods are secondary."[10] Slaves were purchased from time to time because that was usually the easiest way in the tight labor market that prevailed in Virginia in those days to obtain plantation workers with certain skills. However, when Washington returned to Mount Vernon following the Revolutionary War and resolved not to buy or sell any more slaves, he undoubtedly regarded this act of forbearance as a significant and humane concession that would be conducive to easing the anxiety of his enslaved workers.

Like his fellow Virginians, Washington had few illusions about the exploitation of African slaves or the depravities inherent in the slave trade. He knew that the blacks who were being imported to American shores from Africa had been forcibly uprooted from their native villages, brutalized, transported on slave ships under circumstances that were dehumanizing beyond description, and then auctioned off in public slave markets like animals.[11] The arriving Africans owned nothing other than the rags on their backs; they could communicate in no language except their regional tribal dialects; and their identities had been lost in transit. They were nameless beings in a strange culture, at the mercy of the whites who bought and sold them. Little wonder that Washington himself frequently employed in his

10. Parish, *Slavery*, 34.
11. Washington uses the phrase "cattle in the market" in a letter to Alexander Spotswood, Philadelphia, November 23, 1794 (Fitzpatrick, ed., *Writings*, 34:47).

writings the adjectives *miserable* and *wretched* to describe these victimized black Africans.

Many blacks committed suicide or succumbed to disease or otherwise died in passage. For those who, in spite of their many disabilities and disadvantages, maintained the will to live, the basic instinct was for survival—which meant adapting as quickly as possible to the ways of the white society. The African slaves soon learned that the only interest the Virginia planters had in them was in using their bodies: the males primarily for hard work in the fields and the females mainly for household duties, although the girls and women were also often subjected to the predatory sexual advances of white men and had no choice but to comply with the wishes of the dominant class.

The consequence of this one-sided exploitation was a large body of submissive menial laborers, doomed to a lifetime of drudgery, and a rapidly increasing population of mulattoes. As the blacks gradually began to acclimate and establish their own communal networks, a significant number of them showed an uncanny ability to learn to perform skilled functions, and they often became highly proficient artisans, craftsmen, and mechanics.[12] Some, like Phillis Wheatley, claimed intellectual accomplishments. However, most of them could never hope to rise above the level of manual workers and servants unless they were given the same chance as the whites to develop, and capitalize on, their innate talents. And that could only be brought about by emancipation, an adequate education, and equal employment opportunities. In eighteenth-century America these were utopian goals. Yet the voice of abolition had been heard in the country since the earliest days of colonization—from pioneer settlers as diverse as Roger Williams in Rhode Island, William Penn in Pennsylvania, and Gen. James Oglethorpe in Georgia—and grew louder and more persistent with the passing years. Until after the Revolutionary War, however, the voice of abolition was never able to compete with the tune sung by those with a vested economic interest in slavery.

There was hardly a person or an institution in all thirteen of the original colonies that was not, at one time or another, directly or indirectly, tainted by the African slave trade and its corollary, the exploitation of cheap black slave labor. Nor was slavery by any means the exclusive province of the southern plantation proprietors. "Up until the War for Independence the slave trade was vital to the economic life of New England,"[13] and many of the oldest and most respected families in Boston

---

12. "While the effects of conditioning imposed by white society from the cradle to the grave were clearly important and often damaging, slaves did not necessarily learn from their masters only the lessons they were intended to learn. . . . [there] grew a distinctive Afro-American culture, synthesizing elements both from the African heritage (personified in slaves recently arrived from Africa) and from the pervasive white influence, which dominated so much of slave life" (Parish, *Slavery,* 17).

13. Franklin and Moss, *From Slavery to Freedom,* 66.

helped build their fortunes on the traffic in black bodies.[14] No less a proud New Englander than John Adams, one of the founding fathers, who was completely free of any association with the slave business, nonetheless conceded that "the best men in my vicinity thought it [slavery] was not inconsistent with their character."[15] The residents of Newport, Rhode Island, for example, grew immensely wealthy by importing molasses from the West Indies, distilling it into rum, trading the rum in Africa for black slaves, and selling the latter in the Caribbean for more molasses.[16] Judge Samuel Sewall, who is credited with writing one of the first antislavery tracts, owned a slave.[17] Slaves could be found serving as domestics in the households of such prominent clergymen as Cotton Mather and Ezra Stiles.[18] Even the pious Quakers had a long and arduous road to travel before they were finally able to place principle ahead of profit.[19] For almost two decades, Benjamin Franklin's Philadelphia newspaper, the *Pennsylvania Gazette*, carried regular notices of slave sales and advertisements for slave runaways.[20] On the fertile lands of the Hudson River Valley of New Netherland, the patrician Dutch, who lived in baronial splendor, were among the earliest recorded colonists to import large gangs of African slaves to work on their expansive estates.[21] "By the second quarter of the eighteenth century one out of every five families in Boston owned at least one slave. At mid-century, black slaves made up nearly 12 percent of the population of Rhode Island. By 1746 more than a quarter of New York City's working-age males were black slaves; perhaps one-half of the households in the city held at least one slave."[22]

---

14. See, for example, William B. Weeden, *Economic and Social History of New England, 1620–1789*, 2:456, 466–68.

15. Frederick M. Binder, *The Color Problem in Early National America as Viewed by John Adams, Jefferson and Jackson*, 20. John Adams's wife, Abigail, "was one of four children in the Smith family, a clan that lived comfortably, supported by the revenue from two farms, the Reverend Smith's clerical salary, and the labor of four slaves" (John Ferling, *John Adams: A Life*, 31).

16. See John R. Spears, *The African Slave Trade: An Account of Its Origin, Growth and Suppression*, 82, and Thomas E. Drake, *Quakers and Slavery in America*, 1–2.

17. Locke, *Anti-Slavery in America*, 19.

18. Weeden, *New England*, 2:450; *Dictionary of American Biography*, 18:19. Ezra Stiles (1727–1795) was the pastor of the Second Congregational Church of Newport, Rhode Island, from 1755 to 1776. In 1778, he was elected president of Yale College.

19. According to Thomas Drake, "In Barbados especially, where Quakerism flourished in the early days of the sugar industry, Quaker slaveholding reached great heights" (*Quakers*, 4, 32–33).

20. On the back page of the *Pennsylvania Gazette*, June 5, 1740, "Printed by B. Franklin, Postmaster," the following two advertisements appear: "A likely young Negroe Fellow to be disposed of, fit for either town or country, Enquire of the printer" and "A likely Mollatto Girl, aged about 16 years, has had the small pox, is fit for either town or country, to be disposed of very reasonably, enquire of the printer hereof."

21. Franklin and Moss, *From Slavery to Freedom*, 63.

22. Gordon S. Wood, *The Radicalism of the American Revolution*, 51.

When Sam Adams and his coconspirators in Boston began inciting their countrymen to rebel against the tyrannies of the British crown, they made no mention of freeing the slaves. When Patrick Henry delivered his stirring "liberty or death" peroration before his revolutionary compatriots in Richmond, he was speaking to white men about white men. When Thomas Jefferson, writing the Declaration of Independence in Philadelphia, penned the immortal words, "all Men are created equal," he may have embraced blacks and whites in his rhetoric, but his colleagues made certain that those arresting passages applied exclusively to a white society.[23] And when George Washington was appointed commander in chief of the Continental army in the summer of 1775, he interpreted his mandate to be the leadership of an army of white soldiers. In other words, until the actual armed revolt was well underway, there was barely a clue that the power struggle between Great Britain and its thirteen breakaway colonies would have any effect whatsoever on the lives of roughly half a million black African Americans.[24]

Washington brought with him to Cambridge the lifelong prejudices of the Southern plantation class to which he belonged. This was patently obvious by his prompt public actions in dismantling the preliminary efforts that had been made by the Massachusetts authorities in recruiting a limited number of African Americans for service in the local militias. In his determination to keep the army white, Washington had the full backing of both his military staff and key members of the Continental Congress. Thus, racism was to be given no reprieve, even in the midst of an uphill struggle for national independence and survival. Once open conflict broke out, however, events took on a momentum of their own. Due to the actions of Lord Dunmore in Virginia, the slave population was suddenly and unexpectedly drawn into an active role in the contest. Lord Dunmore opened the bidding for black soldiers and military laborers, and the Americans were quick to respond to his gambit. Soon, the opposing field commanders, primarily interested in jockeying for immediate tactical advantage and desperate for manpower, had inadvertently taken steps to inaugurate a profound new chapter in race relations in America.

Confronted with the practical choice of accepting blacks as soldiers or allowing them to go by default to the enemy, Washington showed himself at his best. Having overcome his initial inhibitions about blacks in the army, he acted without further equivocation to bring them into the Continental ranks. He ignored the protests of

23. Franklin and Moss, *From Slavery to Freedom*, 71–72.

24. "During the Revolutionary war, for example, blacks seized new opportunities for freedom. Thousands of slaves escaped amid the confusion and upheavals caused by rampaging armies . . . the periodic collapse of local authority encouraged slaves to flee their masters" (Randall M. Miller and John D. Smith, eds., *Dictionary of Afro-American Slavery*, 48–49).

the diehard racists from South Carolina and Georgia, who under no circumstances wanted any part of a plan to arm and train slaves as fighting men. He did not object to the promises of freedom that were being made to the slaves to induce them to volunteer. He gave his subordinates a liberal hand in pursuing their often far-reaching and ambitious schemes for African American recruitment. He even permitted programs to move forward for integrating blacks into white regiments and showed no signs of bias or discrimination in dealing with the African American soldiers under his command. Most impressively, he demonstrated by his words and deeds that he could rise above his personal feelings and parochial prejudices whenever he believed that the public interest was at stake.

As the victorious hero of the American Revolution and the universally acclaimed and respected military leader and premier statesman of the new nation, Washington felt a strong responsibility for the future of the country that he had helped to create. As a public-spirited citizen, his uppermost concern was the establishment of a secure and permanent union of the thirteen former colonies. "The Federal Convention was not interested in the redistribution of property, nor did it meet for such a purpose. . . . That a large part of America rested upon slavery was again no part of the Convention's immediate problem; they were met not to reform society but to create a government for society as it existed."[25] This concern led him to play a prominent role in the drafting of the Constitution at the convention in Philadelphia in the summer of 1787. There followed his unanimous election in 1789 as the first president of the United States. But these successive political triumphs were marred by nagging reminders that the controversial issue of slavery remained unresolved—an open, festering sore that was increasingly dividing and alienating the North from the South. "The word 'slavery,' Abraham Lincoln would someday note, was 'hid away in the Constitution, just as an afflicted man hides away a wen or cancer, which he dares not cut out at once, lest he bleed to death.'"[26] The battle lines had been drawn at the federal convention; as the presiding officer, Washington had listened closely to the often acrimonious and heated debates between the pro- and antislavery advocates.

In 1774, Washington had publicly announced his opposition to the African slave trade when he signed his name to the Fairfax Resolves. He had agreed to admit African Americans into the Continental army and had given his direct or tacit approval to a variety of schemes for emancipating the slaves through the medium of military service. Therefore, it seemed logical and consistent to many observers that in peacetime an enlightened Washington would continue to champion the

25. Bowen, *Miracle at Philadelphia*, 72.
26. Richard B. Morris, *Witnesses at the Creation: Hamilton, Madison, Jay, and the Constitution*, 216.

growing movement to free the slaves. The emotional appeals to Washington's sense of justice, humanity, and compassion boiled down to two specific requests: that he immediately set free his Mount Vernon slaves and that he publicly declare himself in favor of the abolition of slavery. Washington politely but firmly rejected both suggestions, probably because he regarded them as unrealistic and visionary.

There is no documentation to prove that anyone ever proposed to Washington a workable and comprehensive program of emancipation that took into account such practical and hardheaded considerations as: How were the slave owners to be compensated for their liberated property? What long-range measures were to be undertaken to help the mostly illiterate and unskilled slaves become economically productive and self-sufficient? How were the freed slaves to be clothed and fed and housed in the interim period? How were those sectors of the economy that were heavily dependent on slaves to be supplied with an alternative and adequate labor pool? It looked as though no one, except maybe the Quakers, had given serious thought to a pragmatic blueprint for effectively integrating some three-quarters of a million blacks (according to the 1790 federal census) into a white social and economic structure. Even Washington's two most trusted and talented advisers during the presidential years, Thomas Jefferson and Alexander Hamilton, who were otherwise so prolific, versatile, and creative in solving problems ranging from finances to foreign affairs, were strangely silent on this increasingly divisive and potentially explosive domestic issue.

Lacking a viable scenario for the emancipation of the slaves, and not willing to risk the nation's fragile and hard-won political unity for nebulous and perhaps unattainable ends, Washington evidently concluded that he would do nothing to rock the ship of state. That convenient posture suited both his conservative nature and his Southern bias. In private, Washington graciously gave lip service to the abolitionists and to their professed goals. But in public, where it really counted, he remained neutral. "For some time before taking office Washington had spoken privately about the evils of slavery, yet he made no such public statements during his early presidential years, and he remained silent on the matter both in his valedictory and his final address to Congress."[27] However, as a consequence of having opted out of the antislavery movement, Washington lost any ability he may have had to control or influence the progression of events. He could grumble, criticize, complain, and philosophize in conversations with friends, colleagues, and visitors, and in confidential letters to his correspondents, but such irrelevancies were of little or no import in the ongoing slavery debate.

27. Ferling, *The First of Men*, 474.

This impotence carried over into his personal affairs at Mount Vernon. Washington's act of benevolence in stating that he would no longer buy or sell slaves backfired. The African Americans continued to multiply and to add to the overhead, but their productivity did not increase in proportion because of the growing number of young, old, sick, and infirm who were unable to work yet had to be supported. The slave problem was a major contributing factor, together with worn-out lands and falling commodity prices, in Washington's being forced to consider for the first time in his life the specter of bankruptcy. He tried hard to accommodate to the changing times, but whichever way he turned he found himself stymied. For instance, his relaxed and progressive attitude as a plantation proprietor only served to make the slaves more unruly and difficult to discipline. The antislavery propaganda of the Quakers made them even more restless. Washington was left to vent his anger and frustrations in fruitless pursuit of runaways, several of whom apparently found shelter with the Quakers and their allies. More than once he wrote that he devoutedly wished he could be rid of the burden of slavery.

Only the Quakers were ready and willing to step into the leadership vacuum and come to grips with the slavery dilemma. To their lasting credit, they were able to evolve and put into action sound, practical programs to help blacks move into the mainstream of American society. Their three-pronged approach is as valid today as it was two centuries ago: emancipation (which, of course, is no longer an issue) education, and employment.[28] Since the Quakers were generally well schooled and were often individuals of substance and high standing within their communities, and united in their aims, they became the single most potent force in the country for promoting the cause of abolition. Blocked in their attempt to introduce antislavery legislation into the U.S. House of Representatives by the opposition of the Southerners and the indifference of many of the Northern legislators, and rebuffed by President Washington in their efforts to enlist him in their crusade, the Quakers concentrated on state and local governments. They were remarkably successful in mobilizing public opinion through newspaper articles and by using the courts to test the validity of slave laws and of specific slave titles. Thus, they were gradually able to eliminate many of the restrictive slave statutes.[29] Soon the

28. "To the Quakers is therefore due the earliest formulation of a definite remedy for the evils of slavery. Nowhere is the duty of emancipation more clearly pointed out than by Benjamin Lay. His plan is entirely typical of the Quaker attitude. Friends, he says, should 'bring up their Negroes to some Learning, Reading and Writing, and endeavour to the utmost of their power in the sweet Love of Truth to instruct and teach 'em the principles of truth and righteousness, and learn them some Honest Trade or Imployment, and then set them free; and all the time Friends are teaching of them let them know that they intend to let them go free in a very reasonable time: and that our Religious Principle will not allow of such Severity, as to keep them in everlasting Bondage and Slavery'" (Locke, *Anti-Slavery in America*, 31).

29. Slavery was banned in Pennsylvania in 1789, in Massachusetts in 1783, in Connecticut and Rhode Island in 1784, in New York in 1785, and in New Jersey in 1786. In 1783, Thomas Jefferson

Northern states from New England to Pennsylvania had quietly but effectually removed most of the onerous and repressive slave laws, and free blacks were beginning to emerge to take their places alongside whites in agriculture, commerce, and industry. "Nevertheless, by 1790 there were still 3,763 slaves in New England and 36,323 in the Middle Atlantic states. Emancipation in the North was a slow and difficult process; political leaders were intent on gradual and minimally disruptive change. Usually, they enacted laws freeing only the children of slaves who were born after specific dates—1 March 1784 in Connecticut, for example, 4 July 1799 in New York, and 4 July 1804 in New Jersey. Moreover, freeborn children were to serve as unpaid apprentices until their mid or late twenties."[30] Not satisfied with their political achievements, the Quakers went on to establish the first schools in America to expose black children to the rudiments of a formal education.[31] Quaker leaders such as Warner Mifflin and Robert Pleasants gave their former slaves land and tools, showed them how to till and plant their acreage, and offered them moral support and encouragement in becoming independent yeomen farmers.

The Quakers went out of their way to try to gain Washington's public endorsement for their civil rights campaign on behalf of the slaves. But Washington had a blind side when it came to the Quakers. Despite his official disclaimers that he bore them no grudge, it is nonetheless clear from his snide and offhand remarks about the Society of Friends that he had neither forgotten nor forgiven them for their refusal to take an active part in the Revolutionary War. Their pacifist faith may have been unimpeachable and their peace motives laudable, but the fact of the matter was that the Quakers had sat on their hands during the most critical and difficult hours of the fight for Independence. Stated in purely emotional terms, while General Washington and his loyal band of soldiers had endured the privations of hunger and cold at Valley Forge in that long and bitter winter of 1777–1778, the Pennsylvania Quakers had stayed quietly on the sidelines, well fed and comfortable in their warm homes, tending to their own affairs. Furthermore, although it has never been conclusively proved, there were strong suspicions that the Quakers may have aided the British by selling them needed supplies for hard cash while withholding their provisions from the starving patriots, who had little or no

---

convinced the Virginia legislature to make it legal for slave owners to free their slaves. By 1790 there were 59,000 free blacks in the United States (Harry A. Ploski and James Williams, eds., *The Negro Almanac: A Reference Work on the Afro-American*, 4th ed., 1437).

30. Miller and Smith, eds., *Afro-American Slavery*, 2.

31. Quarles notes that Anthony Benezet "sought to prepare Negroes for freedom by giving them an education under Christian auspices. He was the leading figure in the operation of the racially mixed Quaker school founded in Philadelphia in 1770. Five years later this school had six whites and forty Negroes in attendance. . . . Concerned about the emancipated Negro, they had become pioneers in establishing schools, like that of Benezet, for colored girls and boys" (*Negro in the American Revolution*, 35–36, 192).

sound currency with which to pay for these necessities. Profiteering was rampant throughout the Revolution, and some of the Quakers, having the reputation of being shrewd and calculating businessmen, may well have been involved in black market transactions with the enemy. Whatever the truth of these allegations, Washington was among those who were inclined to believe the worst.[32]

The struggle for black equality was one revolution that George Washington would not lead or even join. Whether he had no real stomach for the fight and its certain divisive repercussions; whether he was convinced that the majority of Americans were not yet ready to accept African Americans as equals; whether he was truly in favor of seeing slavery abolished in the plantation South; whether he instinctively placed the preservation of his own property and welfare ahead of any other consideration; or whether he did not wish to be linked with the Quakers—all are possibilities. His neutrality, however, was a serious setback for the abolitionist movement, for without his backing the Quakers could not hope to penetrate the Southern bastion of slavery in Maryland, Virginia, the Carolinas, and Georgia; nor could they rally sufficient public pressure to push through antislavery legislation at the federal level. Their successes, while notable in virtually sweeping slavery out of the Northern states, stopped short at the Mason-Dixon Line.[33] "The Revolution in effect set in motion ideological and social forces that doomed the institution of slavery in the North and led inexorably to the Civil War."[34]

The question remains: If he truly believed in the ideals and principles of freedom and democracy, the bedrock on which the new nation had been founded, how could Washington—and so many other Americans—countenance the presence within the nation of an institutionalized system of slavery? In the last quarter century of his life, Washington found himself more and more absorbed in trying to come to terms, both as a public servant and as a private citizen, with the rapid polarization of the country, a nation half free and half slave. He was torn between his official duties and responsibilities as a national leader and a prominent world

32. "What he [Washington] could not understand, however, was the insistence of Pennsylvania Quakers (who seem to have been more uncompromising than Quakers elsewhere) upon total abstention from the independence movement to which he was so passionately dedicated. They would not bear arms, of course, and Washington respected their religious scruples. But neither would they hold office under the Revolutionary government of Pennsylvania, affirm allegiance to it, pay its taxes, or even handle its paper money, and this Washington could not understand. Like most patriots, he wrongly concluded from the intransigence of Pennsylvania Friends that the Quakers wanted the British to win the war and perhaps were even secretly aiding them. Although, unlike many of the patriots, he strove to treat them with fairness and decency, he could never quite convince himself that they were not guilty of 'evil intentions' toward the American cause" (Boller, George Washington and Religion, 136).

33. Quarles, Negro in the American Revolution, 194–95.

34. Wood, Radicalism, 186–87.

figure and his emotional ties and personal obligations. It was, in a sense, like the unraveling of a classic Greek tragedy: the hero, at the very pinnacle of his success, was already condemned by his past. Washington surely recognized that his commitment to freedom and democracy must lead, in the final analysis, to the severing of his ties with slavery. But he somehow could not bring himself to turn his back on the culture and heritage from which he sprang—that is, not until the very end, when it was too late to do any public good. And so, in his old age, he was destined to watch helplessly while the country he loved drifted slowly but steadily toward the inevitable showdown between two antagonistic ideologies.

There is substance for the argument that Washington's lifelong commitment to slavery diminishes his character. Some modern historians even refer to him as a racist. Few of Washington's contemporaries would agree with that harsh characterization. They tended to regard him as a highly successful plantation proprietor in the best tradition of Virginia's slaveholding aristocracy, that is, as a benevolent slave master. We have practically no firsthand knowledge of what the Mount Vernon slaves thought of their master except for the fact that when given the opportunity some of them gladly walked away from the estate. For most Americans, Washington's act of emancipating his slaves in his will was sufficient proof that he stood on the "side of the angels." That single act apparently expunged his behavior and record as a slave owner. Whether this conclusion is also the final judgment of history remains to be seen.

It would have been impossible for Washington to have imagined that the descendants of the same black men and women he had known as pitiful slaves, and whom he had emancipated with remorse and trepidation, would one day be proud and independent citizens in a multiracial society of free Americans— among them scientists and social workers, doctors and lawyers, professors and engineers, judges and politicians, bankers and entrepreneurs, mayors and police chiefs, teachers and publishers, bishops and generals, athletes and astronauts. Yet Washington, the lifelong slave owner, actually spoke of the day when slavery would finally be forever banished, "it being among my first wishes to see some plan adopted, by the legislature by which slavery in this Country may be abolished."[35] But he did not live to see the day, and there would be no cheers or applause or public monuments for his contributions to the emancipation process. The best that he could hope for was that his well-intentioned motives and positive actions would not, in the end, "be displeasing to the justice of the Creator."

35. Washington to John Francis Mercer, Mount Vernon, September 9, 1786 (*Papers: Confederation Series,* ed. Abbot and Twohig, 4:243).

BIBLIOGRAPHY

PRIMARY SOURCES

T HERE ARE three major repositories for the papers of George Washington. The Library of Congress acquired the bulk of Washington's original documents and papers from his heirs (Bushrod and George Corbin Washington) in 1834 and since then has continued to build on those holdings. The Washington Papers at the Library of Congress are available in the Manuscript Division and on 124 reels of microfilm published as the *George Washington Papers: Presidential Papers on Microfilm* (Washington, D.C.: Government Printing Office, 1961). The Government Printing Office has also published an *Index* listing all of the above Washington Papers.

The second major repository is at Mount Vernon, the home of George and Martha Washington during their lifetimes. The remains of the original estate— including, of course, the Mansion House—were acquired in the 1850s by the Mount Vernon Ladies' Association of the Union, an organization founded in 1853 by Ann Pamela Cunningham and officially chartered in 1858 by the Commonwealth of Virginia. Over the years, the library at Mount Vernon has expanded to house many original Washington documents, memorabilia, and ancillary materials as well as an extensive collection of secondary literature relating to Washington.

The third major repository is located in the Alderman Library at the University of Virginia (UVA) in Charlottesville. UVA gained its status as a major repository of Washington papers when the trustees of the Mount Vernon Ladies' Association decided in the 1970s to sponsor a comprehensive publication of all the writings of George Washington, including not only his diaries, his letters, and papers that he personally wrote and/or signed but also those that originated with him but do not necessarily bear his signature. In addition, the published works are intended to incorporate all the correspondence and documents addressed and sent to Washington during his lifetime—both as a private citizen and as a public servant. In a search that took approximately ten years, the editors of the Washington Papers project at the Alderman Library have drawn on the existing resources at the Library of Congress and the Mount Vernon Library in establishing their own independent repository of photographic copies of all known Washington documents and papers. They, of course, have also cooperated with other sources and depositories around the world in assembling their collection.

Therefore, it is reasonably safe to assume that at these three institutions (the Library of Congress, the Mount Vernon Library, and the Alderman Library) there can be found—either in the original or as copies—the known documents in existence relating to Washington. Missing only is the personal correspondence between himself and Martha that she deliberately burned following his death, and whatever Washington papers may remain hidden in currently undiscovered caches.

The latest and undoubtedly the final authoritative collection of Washington's writings is presently in preparation at the Alderman Library. To date, the following volumes have been published:

The Diaries of George Washington. Edited by Donald Jackson and Dorothy Twohig. 6 vols. Charlottesville: University Press of Virginia, 1976–1979.

The Papers of George Washington: Colonial Series. Edited by W. W. Abbot and Dorothy Twohig. 10 vols. Charlottesville: University Press of Virginia, 1983–1995.

The Papers of George Washington: Confederation Series. Edited by W. W. Abbot and Dorothy Twohig. 6 vols. Charlottesville: University Press of Virginia, 1992–1994.

The Papers of George Washington: The Journal of the Proceedings of the President, 1783–1793. Edited by Dorothy Twohig. Charlottesville: University Press of Virginia, 1981.

The Papers of George Washington: Presidential Series. Edited by W. W. Abbot and Dorothy Twohig. 6 vols. to date. Charlottesville: University Press of Virginia, 1987–1996. (The remainder of this series covering the period from December 1790 to March 1797 is still in preparation.)

The Papers of George Washington: Retirement Series. Edited by W. W. Abbot and Dorothy Twohig. Charlottesville: University Press of Virginia, in preparation. (This series will cover the period from March 1797 to December 1799.)

The Papers of George Washington: Revolutionary War Series. Edited by W. W. Abbot and Dorothy Twohig. 7 vols. to date. Charlottesville: University Press of

Virginia, 1985–1991. (The remainder of this series covering the period from January 1777 to December 1783 is still in preparation.)

These volumes are the main sources for the Washington quotations used in the text. Where gaps exist, the author has fallen back on the next best collection of Washington's writings, the 39 volumes of *The Writings of Washington from the Original Manuscript Sources, 1745–1799,* ed. John C. Fitzpatrick (Washington, D.C.: Government Printing Office, 1931–1944). The limitations of the Fitzpatrick edition lie in the fact that it is based almost exclusively on the Washington Papers held at the Library of Congress and thus does not include most of Washington's incoming correspondence and papers.

OTHER SOURCES

Acomb, Evelyn M., ed. *The Revolutionary Journal of Baron Ludwig von Closen, 1780–1783.* Chapel Hill: University of North Carolina Press, 1958.

Alden, John R. *George Washington: A Biography.* Baton Rouge: Louisiana State University Press, 1984.

Arnold, Samuel G. *History of the State of Rhode Island and Providence Plantations.* 2 vols. New York: D. Appleton and Co., 1860.

Bell, Malcolm, Jr. *Major Butler's Legacy: Five Generations of a Slaveholding Family.* Athens: University of Georgia Press, 1987.

Bennett, Lerone, Jr. *Before the Mayflower: A History of Black America.* 6th ed. Chicago: Johnson Publishing Co., 1987.

Bernard, John. *Retrospections of America, 1797–1811.* New York: Benjamin Blom, 1969.

Bernstein, Richard B., with Kym S. Rice. *Are We to Be a Nation? The Making of the Constitution.* Cambridge: Harvard University Press, 1987.

Billings, Warren M., John E. Selby, and Thad W. Tate. *Colonial Virginia: A History.* White Plains, N.Y.: KTO Press, 1986.

Binder, Frederick M. *The Color Problem in Early National America as Viewed by John Adams, Jefferson and Jackson.* The Hague: Mouton and Co., 1968.

Boller, Paul F., Jr. *George Washington and Religion.* Dallas: Southern Methodist University Press, 1963.

Bolton, Charles K. *The Private Soldier under Washington.* New York: Charles Scribner's Sons, 1902.

Bowen, Catherine D. *Miracle at Philadelphia: The Story of the Constitutional Convention, May to September 1787.* Boston: Little, Brown and Co., 1966.

Bowling, Kenneth R., and Helen E. Veit, eds. *The Diary of William MacLay and Other Notes on Senate Debates.* 10 vols. Baltimore: Johns Hopkins University Press, 1988.

Brodie, Fawn M. *Thomas Jefferson: An Intimate History.* New York: W. W. Norton and Co., 1974.

Bryan, William A. *George Washington in American Literature, 1775–1865.* New York: Columbia University Press, 1952.

Carroll, John A., and Mary W. Ashworth. *George Washington: First in Peace.* Vol. 7 of Douglas S. Freeman's *George Washington: A Biography.* New York: Charles Scribner's Sons, 1957.

Chastellux, Marquis de. *Travels in North America in the Years 1780, 1781 and 1782.* A Revised Translation with Introduction and Notes by Howard C. Rice Jr. 2 vols. Chapel Hill: University of North Carolina Press, 1963.

Custis, George W. P. *Recollections and Private Memoirs of Washington.* New York: Derby and Jackson, 1860.

Dearden, Paul F. *The Rhode Island Campaign of 1798: Inauspicious Dawn of Alliance.* Providence: Rhode Island Publications Society, 1980.

Debates and Proceedings in the Congress of the United States, Second Congress. Washington, D.C., 1851.

Decatur, Stephen, Jr. *Private Affairs of George Washington: From the Records and Accounts of Tobias Lear, Esquire, His Secretary.* Boston: Riverside Press, Houghton Mifflin Co., 1933.

Detweiler, Susan G. *George Washington's Chinaware.* New York: Harry N. Abrams, 1982.

Doren, Carl van. *Benjamin Franklin.* New York: Viking Press, 1938.

Drake, Thomas E. *Quakers and Slavery in America.* New Haven: Yale University Press, 1950.

Dumbauld, Edward. *The Constitution of the United States.* Norman: University of Oklahoma Press, 1964.

Farrand, Max. *The Fathers of the Constitution: A Chronicle of the Establishment of the Union.* New Haven: Yale University Press, 1921.

Farrand, Max, ed. *The Records of the Federal Convention of 1787.* 4 vols. New Haven: Yale University Press, 1911.

Ferling, John. *The First of Men: A Life of George Washington.* Knoxville: University of Tennessee Press, 1988.

———. *John Adams: A Life.* Knoxville: University of Tennessee Press, 1992.

Fields, Joseph E., comp. *"Worthy Partner": The Papers of Martha Washington.* Westport, Conn.: Greenwood Press, 1994.

Fitzpatrick, John C., ed. *The Last Will and Testament of George Washington and Schedule of His Property.* Mount Vernon, Va.: Mount Vernon Ladies' Association of the Union, 1992.

Flexner, James T. *George Washington: Anguish and Farewell, 1793–1799*. Boston: Little, Brown and Co., 1969.

———. *George Washington and the New Nation, 1783–1793*. Boston: Little, Brown and Co., 1969.

Foner, Philip S. *History of Black Americans: From Africa to the Emergence of the Cotton Kingdom*. Westport, Conn.: Greenwood Press, 1975.

———. *History of Black Americans: From the Emergence of the Cotton Kingdom to the Event of the Compromise of 1850*. Westport, Conn.: Greenwood Press, 1983.

Force, Peter, ed. *American Archives: Fourth Series*. 9 vols. Washington, D.C., M. St. Clair Clarke and Peter Force, 1840.

Ford, Worthington C., ed. *The Spurious Letters Attributed to Washington*. Brooklyn, N.Y.: Privately Printed, 1889.

———. *The Writings of George Washington, 1782–1785*. 14 vols. New York: G. P. Putnam's Sons, Knickerbocker Press, 1891.

Franklin, Benjamin. *The Papers of Benjamin Franklin*. Edited by William B. Willcox. 32 vols. New Haven: Yale University Press, 1976.

———. *The Writings of Benjamin Franklin*. Edited by Albert H. Smith. New York: Macmillan, 1907.

Franklin, John Hope, and Alfred A. Moss Jr. *From Slavery to Freedom: A History of African Americans*. 7th ed. New York: McGraw-Hill, 1994.

Freeman, Douglas S. *George Washington: A Biography*. Vol. 3. *Planter and Patriot*. New York: Charles Scribner's Sons, 1951.

———. *George Washington: A Biography*. Vol. 6. *Patriot and President*. New York: Charles Scribner's Sons, 1954.

Frey, Sylvia R. *The British Soldiers in America: A Social History of Military Life in the Revolutionary Period*. Austin: University of Texas Press, 1981.

———. *Water from the Rock: Black Resistance in a Revolutionary Age*. Princeton: Princeton University Press, 1991.

Gales, Joseph, Sr., comp. *The Debates and Proceedings in the Congress of the United States*. 42 vols. Washington, D.C.: Gales and Seaton, 1834.

"George Washington and Mount Vernon." In *Memoirs of the Long Island Historical Society*, vol. 4. Brooklyn, N.Y.: Published by the Society, 1889.

Gilpin, Thomas. *Exiles in Virginia: With Observations on the Conduct of the Society of Friends during the Revolutionary War*. Philadelphia: Published for the Subscribers, 1848.

Gottschalk, Louis, *Lafayette between the American and the French Revolution, 1783–1789*. Chicago: University of Chicago Press, 1950.

————. *Lafayette Joins the American Army.* Chicago: University of Chicago Press, 1937.

Gottschalk, Louis, ed. *The Letters of Lafayette to Washington, 1777–1799.* New York: Privately Printed by Helen Fahnestock Hubbard, 1944.

Hart, Albert B. *American History Told by Contemporaries: Building of the Republic, 1689–1783.* 4 vols. New York: MacMillan Co., 1901.

Haworth, Paul L. *George Washington: Country Gentleman.* Indianapolis: Bobbs-Merrill Co., 1925.

Hazelton, Robert M. *Let Freedom Ring! A Biography of Moses Brown.* New York: New Voices Publishing Co., 1957.

Hirschfeld, Fritz, ed. " 'Burnt All Their Houses': The Log of HMS *Savage* during a Raid up the Potomac River, Spring 1781." *Virginia Magazine of History and Biography* 99:4 (October 1991): 513–30.

Hofstadter, Richard. *America at 1750: A Social Portrait.* New York: Alfred A. Knopf, 1971.

Humphreys, David. *The Miscellaneous Works of David Humphreys.* New York: T. and J. Swords, 1804.

Humphreys, Frank Landon. *Life and Times of David Humphreys.* 2 vols. New York: G. P. Putnam's Sons, 1917.

Idzerda, Stanley J., ed. *Lafayette in the Age of the American Revolution.* 5 vols. Ithaca: Cornell University Press, 1977.

Innes, Stephen, ed. *Work and Labor in Early America.* Chapel Hill: University of North Carolina Press, 1988.

James, Edward T., Janet W. James, and Paul S. Boyer, eds. *Notable American Women, 1607–1950: A Biographical Dictionary.* 3 vols. Cambridge: Belknap Press of Harvard University Press, 1971.

Journal of the House of Delegates of the Commonwealth of Virginia; Begun and Held in the City of Richmond . . . Richmond, 1828.

"A Journal of the Proceedings of His Majesty's Sloop *Savage*, Thomas Graves Esqr. Commander Between the 15th March 1779 and the 20th May 1781. By Captn. Tho. Graves (signature)." Public Records Office, Kew, Richmond, Surrey, England.

Justice, Hilda, comp. *Life and Ancestry of Warner Mifflin: Friend-Philanthropist-Patriot.* Philadelphia: Ferris and Leach, 1905.

Kaplan, Sidney, and Emma N. Kaplan. *The Black Presence in the Era of the American Revolution.* Amherst: University of Massachusetts Press, 1989.

Kennedy, Melvin D. *Lafayette and Slavery.* Easton, Pa.: American Friends of Lafayette, 1950.

Kimball, Marie. *The Martha Washington Cook Book.* New York: Coward-McCann, 1940.

Latzko, Andreas. *Lafayette: A Life.* Garden City, N.Y.: Doubleday, Doran and Co., 1936.

Laurens, John. *The Army Correspondence of Colonel John Laurens in the Years 1777–8.* New York, 1867.

Lee, Jean B. "Laboring Hands and the Transformation of Mount Vernon Plantation, 1783–1799." Paper presented at a Conference on Re-Creating the World of the Virginia Plantation, 1750–1820, Charlottesville, Va., May 31, 1990.

Lemay, J. A. Leo, ed. *Reappraising Benjamin Franklin: A Bicentennial Perspective.* Newark: University of Delaware Press, 1993.

Livermore, George. *On Negroes as Slaves, as Citizens, and as Soldiers.* New York: Burt Franklin, 1969.

Locke, Mary S. *Anti-Slavery in America: From the Introduction of African Slaves to the Prohibition of the Slave Trade, 1619–1808.* Gloucester, Mass.: Peter Smith, 1965.

Logan, Rayford W., and Michael R. Winston, eds. *Dictionary of American Negro Biography.* New York: W. W. Norton and Co., 1982.

Lossing, Benson J. *Life of Washington: A Biography, Personal, Military, and Political.* 3 vols. New York: Virtue and Co., 1860.

———. *Mary and Martha: The Mother and the Wife of George Washington.* New York: Harper and Brothers, 1886.

———. *The Pictorial Field-Book of the American Revolution.* 2 vols. New York: Harper and Brothers, 1850.

———. *Washington and the American Republic.* 3 vols. New York: Virtue and Yorston, 1870.

Louis-Philippe. *Diary of My Travels in America, Louis-Philippe, King of France, 1830–1848.* Translated by Stephen Becker. New York: Delacorte Press, 1977.

Marraro, Howard R. "Count Luigi Castiglione: An Early Italian Traveller in Virginia, 1785–1786." *Virginia Magazine of History and Biography* 58:4 (October 1950): 484–91.

Matloff, Maurice, ed. *American Military History.* Washington, D.C.: United States Army, 1969.

McColley, Robert. *Slavery and Jeffersonian Virginia.* 2d ed. Urbana: University of Illinois Press, 1973.

McCrady, Edward. *The History of South Carolina in the Revolution, 1780–1785.* New York: MacMillan Co., 1902.

Miller, Helen H. *George Mason: Gentleman Revolutionary.* Chapel Hill: University of North Carolina Press, 1975.

Miller, Randall M., and John D. Smith, eds. *Dictionary of Afro-American Slavery.* Westport, Conn.: Greenwood Press, 1988.

Morris, Richard B. *Witnesses at the Creation: Hamilton, Madison, Jay, and the Constitution.* New York: Holt, Rinehart and Winston, 1985.

Morse, Frank E. "About General Washington's Freed Negroes." Paper in the Mount Vernon Library, Mount Vernon, Va., 1968.

Mount Vernon: A Handbook. Mount Vernon, Va.: Mount Vernon Ladies' Association of the Union, 1985.

Mount Vernon Ladies' Association of the Union. *Annual Report.* Mount Vernon, Va., 1945.

The Naval Chronicle. Vol. 8. London: J. Gold, 1802.

Nell, William C. *The Colored Patriots of the American Revolution.* Boston: Robert F. Wallcot, 1855.

Niemcewicz, Julian Ursyn. *Under Their Vine and Fig Tree: Travels through America in 1797–1799, 1805 with Some Further Account of Life in New Jersey.* Translated and edited by Metchie J. E. Budka. Elizabeth, N.J.: Grassman Publishing Co., 1965.

Nolan, J. Bennett. *Lafayette in America Day by Day.* Baltimore: Johns Hopkins Press, 1934.

Padover, Saul K. *To Secure These Blessings: The Great Debates of the Constitutional Convention of 1787.* New York: Ridge Press, Kraus Reprint Co., 1970.

Parkinson, Richard. *A Tour in America in 1798, 1799, and 1800.* 2 vols. London: Printed for J. Harding, St. James's Street; and J. Murray, Fleet Street, 1805.

Parish, Peter J. *Slavery: History and Historians.* New York: Harper and Row, 1989.

Phillips, Kim Tousley. *William Duane, Radical Journalist in the Age of Jefferson.* New York: Garland, 1989.

Ploski, Harry A., and James Williams, eds. *The Negro Almanac: A Reference Work on the Afro-American.* 4th ed. New York: John Wiley and Sons, 1983.

————. *The Negro Almanac: A Reference Work on the African-American.* 5th ed. Detroit: Gale, 1989.

Prussing, Eugene E. *The Estate of George Washington, Deceased.* Boston: Little, Brown and Co., 1927.

Quarles, Benjamin. *Black Mosaic: Essays in Afro-American History and Historiography.* Amherst: University of Massachusetts Press, 1988.

————. *The Negro in the American Revolution.* Chapel Hill: University of North Carolina Press, 1996.

Renfro, G. Herbert. *Life and Works of Phillis Wheatley.* Washington, D.C.: Robert L. Pendleton, 1916.

Rice, Howard C., Jr., and Anne S. K. Brown, eds. *The American Campaigns* of Rochambeau's Army 1780, 1781, 1782, 1783. Princeton, N.J.: Princeton University Press; Providence, R.I.: Brown University Press, 1972.

Roche, John F. *Joseph Reed: A Moderate in the American Revolution.* New York: Columbia University Press, 1957.

Schlesinger, Arthur M., Jr., gen. ed. *The Almanac of American History.* New York: G. P. Putnam's Sons, 1983.

Sellers, Charles C. *Charles Willson Peale.* New York: Charles Scribner's Sons, 1969.

Sparks, Jared, ed. *Correspondence of the American Revolution: Being Letters of Eminent Men to George Washington.* 4 vols. Boston: Little, Brown and Co., 1853.

————. *The Writings of George Washington.* 12 vols. Boston: John B. Russell, 1857.

Spears, John R. *The American Slave Trade: An Account of Its Origin, Growth and Suppression.* New York: Ballantine Books, 1960.

Syrett, Harold C., ed. *The Papers of Alexander Hamilton.* 27 vols. New York: Columbia University Press, 1961.

Thane, Elswyth. *Potomac Squire.* New York: Duell, Sloan and Pearce, 1963.

Tipple, Ezra S., ed. *The Heart of Asbury's Journal.* New York: Eaton and Mains, 1904.

Tower, Charlemagne, Jr. *The Marquis de La Fayette in the American Revolution.* 2 vols. Philadelphia: J. B. Lippincott Co., 1895.

Townsend, Sara B. *An American Soldier: The Life of John Laurens.* Raleigh, N.C.: Edwards and Broughton Co., 1958.

Turner, Edward R. *The Negro in Pennsylvania: Slavery—Servitude—Freedom, 1639–1861.* New York: Negro Universities Press, 1969.

Vickers, John. *Thomas Coke: Apostle of Methodism.* London: Epworth Press, 1969.

Wallace, David D. *The Life of Henry Laurens.* New York: G. P. Putnam's Sons, 1915.

Warville, Jacques Pierre Brissot de. *New Travels in the United States of America, 1788.* Translated by Mara Soceano Vamos and Durand Echevarria. Edited by Durand Echevarria. Cambridge: Belknap Press of Harvard University Press, 1964.

Watson, Winslow C. *Men and Times of the Revolution; or Memoirs of Elkanah Watson.* New York: D. Appleton and Co., 1861.

Weeden, William B. *Economic and Social History of New England, 1620–1789.* 2 vols. Boston: Houghton, Mifflin and Co., 1891.

Weeks, Stephen B. *Southern Quakers and Slavery.* Baltimore: Johns Hopkins University Press, 1896.

Wheatley, Phillis. *The Collected Works of Phillis Wheatley.* Edited by John C. Shields. New York: Oxford University Press, 1988.

————. *The Poems of Phillis Wheatley.* Edited by Julian D. Mason Jr. Chapel Hill: University of North Carolina Press, 1989.

————. *Poems on Various Subjects, Religious and Moral.* Philadelphia: Joseph Crukshank, 1786.

White, David O. *Connecticut's Black Soldiers, 1775–1783.* A Publication of the American Revolution Bicentennial Commission of Connecticut. Chester, Conn.: Pequot Press, 1973.

Whitlock, Brand. *La Fayette.* 2 vols. New York: D. Appleton and Co., 1929.

Wick, Wendy C. *George Washington, an American Icon: The Eighteenth-Century Graphic Portraits.* Washington, D.C.: Smithsonian Institution Traveling Exhibition Service, 1982.

Wills, Garry. *Cincinnatus: George Washington and the Enlightenment.* Garden City: Doubleday and Co., 1984.

Wilstach, Paul. *Mount Vernon: Washington's Home and the Nation's Shrine.* Garden City: Doubleday, Page and Co., 1925.

Wood, Gordon S. *The Radicalism of the American Revolution.* New York: Alfred A. Knopf, 1992.

Zagarri, Rosemarie, ed., *David Humphreys' "Life of George Washington" with George Washington's "Remarks."* Athens: University of Georgia Press, 1991.

INDEX